CW00393348

A-level Psychology
Revision Guide
For The 2015
Edexcel Specification

Year 1 and 2

Faye Carlisle

Text Copyright @ 2016 Faye C Carlisle
All Right Reserved

Contents

Chapter 2-Cognitive Psychology

Chapter 4-Learning Theories 106

Chapter 5-Clinical Psychology

Chapter 8-Issues and debates...254

Chapter 9-Research Methods 261

Introduction

About this guide

This revision guide covers the following topics: social psychology, cognitive psychology, biological psychology, learning theories, clinical psychology, criminological psychology, child psychology, research methods and issues and debates. The guide includes descriptions of key studies, theories, treatments and example practicals. It uses a clear system of evaluation throughout, which makes it easier to evaluate in the exam.

Edexcel Examination Structure

Paper 1 examines your knowledge of social psychology, cognitive psychology, biological psychology and learning theories. It includes questions on issues and debates related to these topics. Paper 1 is worth 35% of the marks for the whole A-level and is assessed in a 2 hour exam.

Paper 2 examines your knowledge clinical psychology and one of the following optional topic areas: Criminological psychology, child psychology or health psychology. This revision guide covers only two options: Criminological psychology and child psychology. Paper 2 is worth 35% of the marks for the whole A-level and is assessed in a 2 hour exam.

Paper 3 examines psychological skills. Section A has 24 marks and covers the topic area of research methods. Section B has 24 marks asks questions on psychological studies from social psychology, cognitive psychology, biological psychology and learning theories. Section C has 32 marks and covers the topic area of issues and debates in psychology. Paper 3 is worth 30% of the marks for the whole A-level and is assessed in a 2 hour exam.

Note: Both paper 1 and paper 2 have 90 marks available so you have 1 minute 20 seconds for each mark. A 12 mark question should take you 16 minutes and a 16 mark question should take you 21 minutes so make sure you leave enough time to do the extended response questions.
Paper 3 has 80 marks available so you have 1 minute 30 seconds for each mark. A 20 mark extended response question should take you 30 minutes so it is important to plan for this.

Revision strategies

Complete sample or past exam papers and look at the mark schemes and examiners reports to see what the examiner wants.

Focus on what you find difficult to understand and get to grips with it.

Revise in 25 minutes chunks, with 5 minute breaks in the middle to keep your mind alert.

Do not just read this revision guide. Active revision is more effective: Make notes, draw mind maps, record audio clips and write revision cards.

Remember to revise methodology i.e. research methods, types of design, levels of data, inferential tests and any practicals you carried out. You will be able to gain lots of marks for understanding scientific procedures and techniques.

Assessment objectives (taken from Edexcel specification)

AO1-Demonstrate a knowledge and understanding of scientific ideas, processes, techniques and procedures
AO2-Apply knowledge and understanding of scientific ideas, processes, techniques and procedures
AO3-Analyse, interpret and evaluate scientific information, ideas and evidence

Evaluating Studies, Theories and Treatments

Studies

You can use GRAVE to help you evaluate a study.

Generalisability-How generalisable is the study? Are the participants in the sample representative of the wider population?

Reliability-How easy is the study to replicate and get similar results? If a study have a standardised procedure and was done under controlled conditions, then it is easy to replicate. A study is reliable if it has been replicated and similar results have been found.

Application to real life-Can the study explain real life events or be applied to real life situations.

Validity-Does the study have internal validity? Internal validity reflects on the experimenter's competence-The person who is doing the experiment's ability to carry out the study well. Was the experiment well-designed? Did any factors interfere with the experiment?

A study has **internal validity** when the material or procedures used in the research measured what they were supposed to measure. For example, in Milgram's experiment on obedience, participants had to giving increasing levels of electric shock to another person on the orders of an authority figure. The number of shocks the participants were prepared to give was a good indicator of their obedience level and so the study has construct validity (an indicator of internal validity).

Avoiding **demand characteristics** is important to ensure internal validity. Demand characteristics refer to when participants guess what a study is about and then change their behaviour. For example, a participant might guess that a study is on obedience and deliberately change their behaviour to show how easily people obey or to show how difficult it is to get people to obey.

A study has **experimental validity** if participants believe in the experimental situation. For example, in Milgram's study, if the participants believed they really were giving real electric shocks and thought that Mr. Wallace was another participant rather than a confederate, then the study has experimental validity (an indicator of internal validity).

If a study has predictive validity, then this is another indicator of internal validity. A study has **predictive validity** if it accurately predicts a result in the future. For example, if a person gains a high score on a test measuring racial prejudice and then engages in acts of discrimination, then the test has predictive validity.

Does the study have **external validity**? A study has external validity if the findings can be generalised to other situations and populations. If a study is done in participants' natural environment and involves a natural task that might be experienced in everyday life then it has **ecological validity**, which is an indicator of external validity.

Population validity relates to whether the sample can be generalised to the population it is meant to represent. For example, if you are looking at sixth form students' views on university tuition fees but only use a sample of private school students, then the sample lacks population validity. If a study has population validity then this is an indicator of external validity.

Ethics-Does the study have any ethical issues? Were participants protected from physical and psychological harm? Were participants given the right to withdraw? Did the participants give fully informed consent or were they deceived about any aspect of the study? Were the participants debriefed? Was the anonymity of the participants protected? Was the researcher competent to carry out the research?

You do not have to discuss all these points in your evaluation. For example, if there are no ethical issues then you don't need to discuss them. GRAVE is just a trigger to jog your memory and to help you evaluate.

You should also consider the objectivity and credibility of the research.

Objectivity- This refers to whether the study has collected data that is unbiased. Quantitative (numerical) data is likely to be impartial.

Credibility-This refers to whether the study is trustworthy. Research is more trustworthy if it is scientific, reliable, valid and unbiased.

Theories

You can use SEA to evaluate a theory.

Studies that support/contradict the theory. You can also make one evaluative point per study you use in your evaluation. Do not spend too long evaluating any studies as you have been asked to focus on evaluating the theory. Remember that a theory is someone's idea about how something works.

Explanation-What are the problems/limitations of the theory? Are there alternative explanations?

Application to real life-How can the study be applied to real life situations or events?

Treatments

You can use DESERT to help you evaluate a treatment.

<u>D</u>irective- Is the patient reliant on the therapist for all the answers? Is there a power imbalance? If the therapist has too much power then the treatment is directive.

<u>E</u>ffectiveness-How effective is the therapy at treating the behaviour?

<u>S</u>ide effects-Are there any side effects to the therapy?

<u>E</u>xpense-How expensive is the therapy in terms of time and money?

<u>R</u>easons-Does the therapy looks at the underlying causes/reasons for the behaviour?

<u>T</u>ypes of people-Does the therapy only work on certain types of people?

What level of detail should you give in an evaluation?

For a short-answer evaluation question, your answer should only contain evaluative points i.e. assume the examiner knows the material already.

However, when you have 8 or more marks for evaluating, then you are expected to give some description to set up your argument. For example, for an 8 mark question on evaluating a study, 4 marks are for describing those things that you are then going to evaluate i.e. if you are going to discuss generalisability, then you should talk about the sample and the population used. The other 4 marks are for evaluation.

For a 12 mark question, 6 marks are for showing knowledge and understanding and 6 marks are for evaluation.

Compare the following two answers:

Evaluate Milgram's basic study (4 marks)

Milgram used a volunteer sample, which is not representative of the wider population. The volunteers may have been more obedient than other participants as they had agreed to take part in the study and may have felt more obliged to continue (1 AO3 mark).
Milgram's study was reliable because it had a standardised procedure, which makes it easy to repeat and get the same results. All participants were given the role of teacher in a rigged draw and asked to give increasing levels of electric shock in 15V increments and they all heard the same recorded protests from Mr. Wallace (1 AO3 mark).
The study has experimental validity, as the participants believed the shocks were real. The fact that participants showed signs of distress such as nervous laughter shows that they believed in the experimental situation (1 AO3 mark).
Milgram's study lacks ecological validity as it involved an artificial situation and mundane realism as people are not normally asked to give electric shocks to another person for wrong answers on a word pair task (1 AO3 mark).

Evaluate Milgram's basic study (8 marks)

Milgram was investigating obedience (1 AO1 mark). He recruited 40 male participants via an advert in a local newspaper (1 AO1 mark). This makes it difficult to generalise as it was an all-male, volunteer sample from the USA. The volunteers may have been more obedient than other participants as they had agreed to take part in the study and may have felt obliged to continue. Furthermore, males are not representative of how females would behave (1 AO3 mark).

Participants were asked to give electric shocks to Mr. Wallace. They thought the shocks were real when they were fake and they believed that Mr. Wallace was another participant when he was in fact a confederate of the experimenter (1 AO1 mark). Therefore, the participants were deceived, which is an ethical issue (1 AO3 mark). The participants were given verbal prods to continue throughout the experiment (1 AO1 mark). Many experienced distress during the experiment but felt compelled to continue giving the electric shocks. Therefore, participants were not protected from psychological harm, which is another ethical issue (1 AO3 mark).

The experiment took place in a laboratory at Yale university and followed a standardised procedure (1 AO1 mark). The artificial situation means the study lacks ecological validity but the control over extraneous variables means the study has good internal validity (1 AO3 mark).

Note: AO1 marks are for knowledge and understanding and AO3 marks are for evaluating.

Chapter 1-Social Psychology

You need to be able to describe what the social psychology is about

Social psychology is about how our behaviour is affected by other people. At AS level, topics such as group behaviour, prejudice and obedience are covered. However, social psychology also covers topics such as why people help or do not help others, why people are attracted to certain people and crowd behaviour.

You need to be able to describe obedience

Obedience is when you follow orders given by a person with authority over you. Social psychologists have studied obedience to understand what makes people obey and the circumstances under which people are more obedient.

You need to be able to describe and evaluate Milgram's (1963) study of obedience

Description of basic study:

Aim-To investigate what level of obedience would be shown when participants were told by an authority figure to administer electric shocks to another person.

Procedure-A volunteer sample of 40 males aged between 20 and 50 years of age, were recruited from a newspaper advertisement. Participants were told that the study was about the effects of punishment on learning and that they would be paid $4.50 for taking part. When participants arrived at Yale University, they were asked to draw lots for who would have the role of teacher or learner in the experiment. The draw was set up so that the participant was always the teacher and Mr. Wallace (the confederate) was always the learner. Participants were then shown an electric shock generator, which had 30 switches from 15V to 450V. They were then asked to give increasing levels of electric shocks to the learner if he got any words incorrect on a word pair task. Unbeknown to the participants the electric shocks were fake. At certain voltages, Mr. Wallace pretended to show signs of pain. At 315V, Mr. Wallace became silent. Whenever the participants said they wanted to stop giving the electric shocks, they were given verbal prods to continue.

Results-100% (40/40) of the participants obeyed up to 300 volts and 65% (26/40) of the participants were fully obedient and gave all the shocks to 450V. During the study many participants showed distress at having to give the electric shocks.

Conclusion-People will obey authority figures even when it means causing harm to an innocent person. Milgram suggested the high levels of obedience in the study may have been due to the fact that the experiment took place at the prestigious Yale University. The participants may also have felt they should continue with the study because they had volunteered and were offered payment for their participation.

Evaluation:

Generalisability- All of Milgram's participants were volunteers who are likely to be more obedient than other participants so the sample is not generalisable in this respect.
It could also be argued that Milgram's study is not generalisable as it was only carried out on American males who are not representative of the wider population. However, when

Milgram tested females in exactly the same way, he found identical levels of obedience. Studies testing obedience across the world have found similar levels of obedience.

Reliability-Milgram's study was reliable because it had a standardised procedure, which makes it easy to repeat and get the same results. A script was followed and all participants heard the same recordings from Mr. Wallace. They were also give the same verbal prods such as 'You must continue' when they said they wanted to stop. This makes the study easily replicable.

Application to real life-The study can be applied to real life as it shows how under pressure people will obey an authority figure. The study has been used to explain why the Nazis were so obedient to Hitler even when it harmed innocent people. It can also explain why people are so obedient to their bosses at work even when it might cause harm to others such as firing colleagues.

Internal validity- The number of shocks participants were prepared to give was a good indicator of their obedience level and so the study has construct validity (an indicator of internal validity). The study has experimental validity, another indicator of internal validity, as the participants believed the shocks were real. The fact that participants showed signs of distress such as nervous laughter shows that their belief in the experimental situation was genuine. In fact, Milgram took great care to make sure his study had experimental validity so that the participants believed the situation was real. He rigged a draw with the participant and Mr. Wallace so that participants thought they had randomly been allocated the role of teacher. He also gave a sample 45V shock so that participants believed the shocks they were giving were real.

External validity-Some psychologists have suggested that Milgram's study lacks ecological validity as it involved an artificial situation. People do not usually attend a university to take part in a psychology experiment in everyday life. The study also lacks mundane realism as people are not normally asked to give electric shocks to another person for wrong answers on a word pair task. However, Milgram argued that the study does reflect how people behave in the real world as people do recognise authority figures and follow orders in the real world.

Ethics-One of the main criticisms of Milgram's study was the effects it had on participants. Participants did not give informed consent and were deceived. They were told that the aim of the study was to investigate the effects of punishment on learning when it was actually about obedience. They also thought they were giving real electric shocks when they were fake. Furthermore, participants were not protected from psychological harm as many experienced distress and may have felt bad about themselves after the experiment for being so obedient. They were also given verbal prods to continue throughout the experiment. However, Milgram did give participants the right to withdraw at the beginning of the experiment. He also thoroughly debriefed his participants and they were followed up a year later by psychiatrists. 84% of participants said they were glad or very glad to have taken part in the experiment.

Objectivity-Obedience was measured in terms of the level of shocks given on the shock generator. This is a quantitative and scientific way of measuring obedience and so the study is objective.

Credibility-The study was reliable, objective and scientific so it was credible in many ways. However, Milgram's study has been criticised for over-stating the obedience rate.

You need to be able to describe and evaluate the 'Telephonic instructions' (experiment 7) variation of Milgram's obedience studies

Description

Aim-To see if it is easier to resist the orders from an authority figure if they are not close by.

Procedure-The experimenter gave orders to participants over the telephone from another room. All other aspects of the study were the same.

Results-Obedience fell to 22.5% and many participants cheated and missed out shocks or gave less voltage than ordered to.

Conclusion-This shows that people are more obedient to authority figures who are close by.

Specific evaluative points for this variation: It can be applied to real life in that it shows that authority figures need to be present in order for levels of obedience to remain high. For example, students are more likely to be obedient if their teacher is close by.

You need to be able to describe and evaluate the 'Rundown office block' (Experiment 10) variation of Milgram's obedience studies

Description:

Aim-To see whether environment can influence levels of obedience.

Procedure-The experiment was conducted in an office suite in Bridgeport away from Yale university. Participants were told that a private research company was carrying out the study. All other aspects such as recruitment and payment were the same as in the original study.

Results-48% of the participants obeyed up to the maximum 450V.

Conclusion-Environment can influence levels of obedience.

Specific evaluative point for this variation: As this variation took place in the natural environment of an office block, it has higher ecological validity than the other variations, which took place in a laboratory.

You need to be able to describe and evaluate the 'Ordinary man give orders' (experiment 13) variation of Milgram's obedience studies

Description:

Aim-To see whether the status of the person giving orders affects obedience levels.

Procedure-This experiment involved two confederates. As in the original study, the draw was rigged so that Mr. Wallace received the fake electric shocks. The second confederate was then assigned the task of recording the time taken to give the shocks. A telephone call took the experimenter away from the laboratory and the experimenter told the participants to go on with the experiment until all the word pairs were learned perfectly (without mentioning which shock levels are to be used). The second confederate suggests a system for administering the shocks, specifically, to increase the shock level one step each time the learner makes a mistake.

Results-Only 20% of participants obeyed the ordinary man's orders.

Conclusion-People are less likely to obey orders from a person who is not perceived to be an authority figure.

Specific evaluative points for this variation: The study lacks credibility for the following reasons: The withdrawal of the experimenter from the laboratory was awkward. Even though the experimenter was absent, he had said to carry on with the experiment so the 'ordinary man' was only giving orders about the exact shock levels. He had not decided to administer the shocks himself.

Note: For the variations, you can make many of the same evaluative points as you would for the basic study.
For example, the study was reliable because it had a standardised procedure, which makes it easy to repeat and get the same results. A script was followed and all participants heard the same comments from Mr. Wallace. They were also give the same verbal prods such as 'You must continue' when they said they wanted to stop. This makes the study easily replicable.

Tip: Remember don't just say a study is reliable because it is easy to repeat and has a standardised procedure as you can say this about most laboratory experiments. Explain why this particular study is easy to repeat and give details.
Don't just say a study lacks ecological validity because it was done in an artificial environment. Explain what aspects of this particular study were artificial.

You need to be able to describe and evaluate agency theory as a theory of obedience

Description:

This theory says that we obey others in order to create a stable society. Milgram identifies two different states of being: The autonomous state, when our behaviour is controlled by our own free will and the agentic state, when we put aside our personal beliefs and wishes to obey authority figures. Milgram suggested that we acquire the agentic state in childhood as we become socialised at home and at school. The agentic shift refers to when people shift from an autonomous state when they are taking responsibility for their own actions to an agentic state when they pass this responsibility to the authority figure. If people believe the authority figure is legitimate such as a police officer or doctor, they are more likely to obey. They are also more likely to follow orders if they believe the authority figure will accept responsibility for what happens. Whilst in the agentic state we may experience moral strain. This is the sense that we are acting against our own beliefs. We might use a strategy called denial in order to cope.

Evaluation:

Studies-Milgram's study supports agency theory as it found that participants would obey an authority figure and give electric shocks to another person. Blass showed students an edited film of Milgram's study and questioned them about whether Milgram or his participants were more responsible for the shocks. Participants said Milgram was more responsible. This supports agency theory. Meeus and Raaijmaker's study found that participants would obey an authority figure and give negative remarks to someone they thought was a job applicant. This study supports the notion that people can be agents of authority and act against their own conscience.

Explanation-The idea that obedience helps to maintain as stable society makes sense. Agency theory explains a range of real-life situations in which people obey orders. However, Agency theory does not explain individual differences in obedience, for example why some people did not obey Milgram. 35% of participants did not give all the electric shocks. Furthermore, Agency theory does not explain why some people, who are not in a position of authority, can still be highly skilled in commanding obedience from other people. The theory of charismatic leadership is better at explaining why some people are particularly good at obtaining obedience from others. Some argue that agency theory is more a description of obedience rather than a detailed explanation. Social power offers another explanation of obedience. It explains how we are more likely to obey those with legitimate power over us or who have expert power. The concept of the agentic shift is hard to test experimentally, which reduces the credibility of the theory.

Application to real life-Agency theory can help to explain why the Nazis were so obedient to Hitler during the Holocaust. Eichmann said in his testimony that he was only following orders. It could also be used to explain why US soldiers tortured Iraqi prisoners in Abu Ghraib. Agency theory can also explain why people are willing to fire or reprimand their colleagues on the orders of their boss. The implications of agency theory are that training should be given to professionals such as nurses, police officers and the armed forces so that they don't obey authority figures without question.

You need to be able to describe and evaluate social impact theory as a theory of obedience

Description:

Social impact theory describes how people are influenced by others in social situations. The person or people doing the influencing are called the source(s) and the person or people being influenced are called the target(s). The greater the strength, immediacy and number of sources the greater the impact. The number of sources relates to the idea that the more people trying to influence you the greater their impact. For example, you may be persuaded to go to university if a large number of your friends and teachers argue that you should go. The strength of the sources relates to the status, expertise and power of the sources. For example, a message will be strengthened if the person doing the convincing is an expert in the field. A careers advisor who points out that it will increase your job prospects if you go to university is more likely to be listened to than a person with no expertise in the area. Immediacy relates to the physical and psychological distance of the source to the target. For example, a message will have more impact if it comes from friends rather than strangers due to their psychological immediacy. Your friend trying to convince you to go to university is going to have more impact than a person you've just met at a party. Social impact theory can be applied to obedience not just social influence.

For example, students might change their behaviour if the headmaster enters their classroom due to his status and physical immediacy to them.

The theory can be represented as a mathematical formula:

i = f (SIN)

Impact = function of (strength of the sources x immediacy of sources x number of sources)

Evaluation:

Studies-Sedikides and Jackson (1990) found that high strength sources (people with power and social status) and high immediacy sources (people who were psychologically or physically close) had more influence on the participants' opinions and behaviour than low-strength and low-immediacy sources. This supports social impact theory.
Milgram, Bickman, and Berkowitz (1969) investigated the influence of the number of confederates looking up at a building on the behaviour of people walking past. They found that more passers-by stopped as the size of the crowd looking up increased. This supports the idea that the more people persuading us to do something the more likely we will be influenced.

When Milgram moved his experiment from Yale university to a rundown office block in Bridgeport, obedience dropped as the experimenter/source's status or strength reduced. In the variation 'Ordinary man gives orders', in which the experimenter is called out of the room and asks an ordinary man to play his role and give orders. The number of teachers/targets who were prepared to give the full 450V fell from 65% to 20% and so the intensity of impact fell as the strength of the source reduced. This supports Latane's theory that the strength of the source affects their impact.
In the variation, 'Telephonic Instructions', the experimenter gave orders over the telephone to administer the electric shocks. The immediacy of the experimenter was reduced and obedience dropped from 65% to 22.5%. This is in line with Latane's theory that the impact of the source is affected by their proximity (closeness) to the target.

Explanation-As the theory has a mathematical formula, it can be used to predict how obedient someone might be in a particular situation assuming we can measure the strength of the sources (e.g. their expertise or status), the immediacy of the sources (how close they are) and the number of sources. However, reducing obedience down to a mathematical formula may be too simplistic a way of understanding obedience as there are so many different factors that can affect it. The theory also ignores individual differences in obedience. Furthermore, it cannot predict what will happen if two equal groups impact on each other.

Application to real life-Social impact theory can explain a number of everyday situations where people are influenced by others. For example, we are more likely to be convinced that capital punishment is wrong if all of our friends are in agreement. Students are also more likely to obey a teacher if they are in the same room as them and if they have higher status in the school.

You need to be able to compare agency theory and social impact theory

Social impact theory explains the different factors involved in obedience better than agency theory. Social impact theory says that an individual's obedience is affected by the number of people trying to influence them, the sources' status, expertise and power and their immediacy to the individual in terms of physical and psychological distance. In contrast, agency theory is more a description of obedience than an explanation. It says that we obey authority figures when we are in the agentic state but it does not really explain how the agentic shift occurs.

Agency theory was designed to explain obedience whereas social impact theory is more a theory of social influence. Therefore, agency theory can better explain the different levels of obedience found in Milgram's variation studies as it is more focused on obedience.

Agency theory suggests that we have evolved to obey authority figures in order to maintain a stable society. Understanding obedience as an evolutionary mechanism helps us to understand why people may commit atrocities such as those during the Holocaust under the orders of an authority figure.

You need to be able to describe and evaluate one contemporary study. For example, Burger (2009) 'Would people still obey today?'

Description:

Aim-To replicate Milgram's finding and to see whether people would still obey today but under more ethical conditions.

Procedure-To ensure that all the participants were psychologically stable, Burger used a two-step screening process. Questionnaires filled out in step 1 were given to a clinical psychologist, who conducted an interview with the participants. Of the 123 people who participated in this second screening process, 47 (38.2%) were excluded from the study by the clinical psychologist.
In Burger's base condition, the experimental setup was the same as Milgram. There was a rigged draw to determine who would be the learner and who would be the teacher, with the confederate always made the learner. The confederate was strapped into a chair with electrodes attached. The teacher sat down in front of a shock machine asked to give increasing electric shocks to the learner when they got answers wrong on a word pair task. At 150V the confederate said 'Ugh. That's all. Get me out of here. I told you I had heart trouble. My heart's starting to bother me now. Get me out of here please. My heart's starting to bother me. I refuse to go on. Let me out.' The experimenter gave same prods as in Milgram's study, for example, 'The experiment requires that you continue' and, 'You have no other choice you must continue.' The experiment ended when either the teacher refused to continue or the teacher read the next item on the list of word pairs after having pressed the 150V switch. Burger argued that as the majority of participants in Milgram's study who went past 150V continued to 450V, then this was an indication of full obedience. Participants were then debriefed by being told the experiment was on obedience and that the electric shocks were fake. The confederate then entered the room to show the participants that he was fine.

Results-70% of participants had to be stopped after administering the 150V shock. It was predicted that they would have gone on to 450V.

Conclusion-People are just as likely to obey an authority figure and harm an innocent person today as when Milgram conducted his study. The same situational factors that led to obedience in Milgram's study affect obedience in the present day.

Evaluation:

Generalisability- All of Burger's participants were volunteers who are likely to be more obedient than other participants so the sample is not representative of the wider population. Furthermore, Burger's participants went through a double screening process to make sure they were psychologically stable. The participants who were allowed to take part may have been more obedient than average. However, Burger did use male and female participants from a very wide age range (20 to 81 years old), which make the sample more generalisable.

Reliability-Burger's study was reliable because it had a standardised procedure, which makes it easy to repeat and get the same results. A script was followed and all participants heard the same recordings from the confederate. They were also given the same verbal prods such as, 'The experiment requires that you continue,' when they said they wanted to stop. This makes the study easily replicable.

Application to real life-The study can be applied to real life as it shows how people under pressure will obey an authority figure. It can explain why people even in the present day are so obedient to authority figures. For example, people may obey their bosses at work to fire their colleagues even when it goes against their own wishes.

Internal validity- The number of shocks participants were prepared to give was a good indicator of their obedience level and so the study has construct validity (an indicator of internal validity). The study has experimental validity, another indicator of internal validity, as the participants believed the shocks were real. Like Milgram, Burger took care to make sure his study had experimental validity so that the participants believed the situation was real. He rigged a draw with the participant and confederate so that participants thought they had randomly been allocated the role of teacher. However, Burger gave his participants only a 15 volt sample shock instead of Milgram's 45 volts. This 'may have led them to assume that the shock generator was not really that shocking,' and may have made them more likely to obey.
External validity-Burger's study lacks ecological validity as it involved an artificial situation. People do not usually attend a university to take part in a psychology experiment in everyday life. The study also lacks mundane realism as people are not normally asked to give electric shocks to another person for wrong answers on a word pair task.

Ethics-Burger made great efforts to ensure his study was ethical. He stopped the study at 150 volts to ensure that the participants did not experience the intense stress that they did in the subsequent parts of Milgram's study. Burger also implemented a two-step screening processing to exclude anyone who might have a negative reaction to his study. Participants were told at least three times (twice in writing) that they could withdraw from the study at any time and still receive their $50 for participation. Participants were only given a mild 15 volt sample shock rather than the 45 volt shock in Milgram's study. As soon as the study ended, participants were informed that the learner had received no shocks and within a few seconds the learner entered the room to reassure the participant that he was fine. The experimenter who ran the study was also a clinical psychologist who knew he needed to stop the study if he saw signs of excessive stress.

Objectivity-Obedience was measured in terms of the level of shocks given on the shock generator. This is a quantitative and scientific way of measuring obedience and so the study is objective.

Credibility-The study was reliable, objective and scientific so it was credible in many ways. However, there is no certainty that participants who went to 150V would have continued to 450V as in Milgram's study.

You need to be able to describe individual differences in obedience and dissent/resistance to obedience

Individual differences in personality can affect obedience. Adorno (1950) suggested that an authoritarian personality type is more likely to obey an authority. These are people who tend to look up to those of higher status and look down on those of inferior status, they have more rigid opinions and beliefs and they are more suspicious and hostile. Milgram and Elms (1966) found that obedient participants were likely to have more authoritarian personalities (measured using the F-scale) than disobedient participants.
People who have an internal locus of control and believe that they are responsible for their own behaviour are less likely to obey. Dambrum & Vatine (2010) found that those who took more responsibility for their own behaviour rather than blaming others such as the experimenter, generally gave lower shocks in the Milgram experiment.
People with a higher level of education are also less likely to obey without question.
There does not appear to be any real difference between men and women in their ability to resist obeying an authority figure. Milgram (1963) found that men and women were equally obedient. Blass (1999) analysed the results of ten obedience studies using male and female participants and found that only one study reported a significant difference between men and women in levels of obedience. Kilham & Mann (1974) found that 40% of men and 16% of women were obedient in the Australian study.
Non-conformists are not aware of social norms or not bothered by them and so are less likely to feel the pressure to obey an authority figure. Anti-conformists, in contrast to non-conformists, deliberately go out of their way to not conform. This could be due to deeply held personal beliefs or perhaps just wanting to be seen as different. Anti-conformists are less likely to be obedient.

You need to be able to describe situational factors in obedience and dissent/resistance to obedience

Milgram demonstrated in his variation studies that situational factors have an effect on obedience. Milgram found that having a disobedient ally (a confederate) who refused to give the shocks led to only 10% of participants giving the full 450V. Running the experiment in a rundown office block rather than the prestigious Yale university or having an ordinary man give orders also reduced obedience. This suggests that the status of the authority figure affects obedience levels. The proximity of the authority figure was another factor in obedience. Participants were less likely to obey when the authority figure was not in the room.

You need to be able to describe cultural factors in obedience and dissent/resistance to obedience

Culture may have an impact on obedience. Individualistic cultures emphasize the importance of personal freedom and independence. Children are brought up to respect authority but they are also encouraged to be assertive. This can lead to lower levels of obedience in contrast to collectivist cultures, which place more emphasis on the wider group. In contrast, in collectivistic cultures, children are taught to conform to the majority and this is viewed positively as a way of connecting with others and becoming responsible for one's own actions. This suggests that people from collectivistic cultures should be more obedient. However, research into obedience in other cultures suggests that variations in obedience may be to do with how the studies were carried out rather than cultural differences. For example, Ancona and Paryeson (1968) found a higher obedience rate in Italy but they only used 330V as their maximum shock level.

You need to be able to describe what is meant by prejudice and discrimination

Prejudice: To form a judgement about a person before finding out anything about them as individuals. Prejudice is usually based on negative stereotypes about certain groups of people.

Discrimination: A behaviour towards another person based on prejudice.

You need to be able to describe and evaluate social identity theory

Description:

Social identity theory says that prejudice can arise from the mere existence of another group. Prejudice can be explained by our tendency to identify ourselves as part of a group and to classify other people as either within or outside that group. There are three stages to social identity theory: 1)Social Categorisation-This is when we categorise ourselves as being in a particular group often based on stereotypes. The group that we belong to is the in-group and any comparison group is the out-group. For example, when someone classifies themselves as a football supporter of a certain team, all other football teams are then viewed as the out-group.
2)Social Identification-This refers to when we identify with a particular group and adopt the behaviours of that group. We may also take on the group's values and norms. The way we view ourselves is affected by how well the group is doing relative to other groups. For example, a football supporter may adopting the behaviours of their club such as certain football chants and they may wear clothes that identify them as being part o the group such as wearing the club's scarf.
3)Social Comparison-Comparing our own group (the in-group) more favourably against other groups (out-groups) to boost our self-esteem. For example, football supporters viewing their team as the best. This can lead to discrimination and sometimes even dehumanisation of the out-group. Football supporters of one football team may even end up fighting supporters of a different football team.

Evaluation:

Studies- Tajfel et al.'s (1971) minimal groups study found that boys overwhelmingly chose to allocate points to boys who had been identified as in the same group as themselves, which supports social identity theory. Poppe and Linssen found that Eastern Europeans favour their own country over other Eastern Europeans, which supports the idea that people show in-group favouritism. Sherifs' Robbers Cave study provides further evidence for social identity theory in that the two groups of boys showed prejudice to the boys not in their group even before competition was introduced. Crocker and Luhtanen's (1990) study also supports social identity theory as it found that people tend to have high self-esteem if they think well of the group to which they belong. On the other hand, Dobbs and Crano's (2001) study contradicts social identity theory as it found that mere categorisation of people into groups is not always sufficient to create in group favouritism.

Explanation- However, social identity theory does not explain individual differences in prejudice. Some people are much more prejudiced than others to people in the out-group. Realistic conflict theory may be a better explanation of prejudice. It says that people become prejudiced when there is 'competition over scarce resources'. This may explain prejudice in competitive situations better.

Application to real life- Social identity theory has face validity as it can explain behaviour real life prejudice such as racism, snobbery and football violence.

You need to be able to describe and evaluate realistic conflict theory as a theory of prejudice

Description:

Realistic conflict theory says that prejudice occurs between different groups of people when there is competition over limited resources. So if two groups want the same thing but only one group can have it, conflict can arise. The group to which you belong is called the in-group. The others are thought of as the out-group. People tend to favour members of their own in-group and be hostile towards the out-group. People may also over-estimate their in-group's achievements and abilities. Prejudice can be reduced when groups have to work together to solve a problem. A superordinate goal is a something that can only be achieved by the groups working together cooperatively. Superordinate goals help to reduce prejudice.

Evaluation:

Studies- Sherif's Robber's Cave study supports realistic conflict theory as the boys became particularly hostile to each other during the tournament.
Explanation- The theory has face validity as groups do seem to become hostile towards each other in real life when there is competition over a scarce resource e.g. land, a football cup.
Realistic conflict theory can better explain widespread prejudice compared to the authoritarian personality approach. The boys in the Robber's Cave study could not all have had authoritarian personalities but they all became prejudiced to the out-group.

Application to real life-Realistic conflict theory can explain why groups in competition with each other can become very hostile towards each other such as the supporters of rival football teams.

You need to be able to describe and evaluate the classic study by Sherif (1954/1961) 'Intergroup conflict and cooperation: The Robbers Cave Experiment'

Aim-To see whether it is possible to create prejudice between two similar groups when they are put in competition with each other and to see if prejudice can be reduced through getting the groups to work together to achieve a superordinate goal (a goal that can only be achieved through cooperative working).

Procedure-Twenty-two eleven year-old boys were chosen to take part because they were well-adjusted. They were all from a similar background. Before the start of the experiment, the boys were randomly divided into two groups with eleven boys each.
The two groups of boys were taken to a summer camp in Robbers Cave State Park in Oklahoma. Initially, each group did not know the existence of the other group. In the first

week the groups spent time bonding with each other while hiking in the park or swimming. Each group was asked to decide on a group name. One group chose the name Eagles and the other group chose the name Rattlers. The names were stencilled on to their flags and shirts to help build a sense of in-group identity.

During the second phase of the experiment, the two groups found out about each other's existence. A tournament with prizes was set up to create in-group favouritism. There was so much conflict between the two groups, phase two was cut short.

In phase three, the experimenters attempted to bring about cooperation between the two groups by getting them to work towards superordinate goals (task that can only be achieved by working together). The two groups were told that they had to work together to restore the drinking water supply as it had been damaged by vandals.

Results-The boys developed a strong in-group preference and even before the tournament started, the groups were fighting each other and calling each other names. The competition increased the antagonism between the two groups. The group that lost the tournament even stole the prizes of the winning group.

After the groups had to cooperate with the each other in phase three, tension between the groups diminished.

Conclusion-Competition increased prejudice and led to conflict between the two groups. Cooperation reduced conflict between the two groups.

Evaluation:

Generalisability-The study lacks generalisability as it only consisted of young boys who are not representative of the wider population. If the study was done with girls they may not have acted the same, as girls are often thought to be less competitive than boys.

Reliability-The study would be hard to replicate as it was a field study. Extraneous variables in the natural environment of the summer camp could have affected results. For example, if there was storm during the tournament that might have affected the boy's behaviour. However, Sherif et al. some elements of the study are easy to replicate, for example, they carefully controlled how long the boys had to bond and when they introduced the competition element of the study.

Application to real life-The study can be applied to real life by helping reduce prejudice between groups in society through use of superordinate goals.

Validity-This field study has high ecological validity as the boys were in a natural setting of a summer camp. The study also has experimental validity as the boys were unaware they were being observed and so would not have shown demand characteristics.

Note: Demand characteristics occur when participants guess the aim of the study and change their behaviour to please the researchers.

Ethics-There are ethical issues with Sherif's study. The researcher's deliberately created prejudice between the two groups of boys and this led to name-calling and even fighting between the boys. Therefore, the boys were not protected from psychological and physical harm. The boys did not know they were in the study and were not offered the right to withdraw. Although parents gave consent for the study, they did not know the full details of the study and probably would not have been happy at the idea of their boys being placed in situation where conflict was likely to occur.

You need to be able to describe one key question in social psychology. For example, 'How can social psychology be used to explain heroism?'

Zimbardo defines heroism as having four key elements: It is performed to help others in need; it is done voluntarily; it is performed even when the person knows they are at risk of psychological or physical harm and it is done without expectation of a reward. Understanding heroism and encouraging people to be heroic can have a positive impact on society.

Zimbardo founded the Heroic Imagination Project to research heroism and to learn how to train people to develop the characteristics of heroes. He also wanted to understand how to prevent the negative aspects of social influence such as the bystander effect, where people don't take responsibility for helping someone in need. His research has shown that 20% of people qualify as heroes. The most common acts of heroism are helping another person in an emergency and whistle-blowing on an injustice. Research has also found that volunteers, more educated people and those who have survived a disaster or trauma are more likely to be heroes. There are also factors that might stop us helping others such feeling powerless to change the world around us, anxiety about being rejected by other people for speaking out and relying on other people to take responsibility in difficult situations.

Linking the key questions to theories, concepts and studies:

Milgram's study shows how obedient people are to authority figures. As a result, they may feel unable to speak out against a destructive authority figure.

Sherif's study shows how we tend to favour our own in-group, which can prevent us helping those outside our group.

Social impact theory suggests that we are more likely to obey if the authority figures are nearby, great in number and legitimate. It may be hard to speak out against destructive authority in such situations.

The bystander effect refers to when people choose not to help someone in need because they rely on other people to take responsibility. Latane and Darley (1970) found that people are less likely to help a person in trouble if there are other people around. They said this was due to a 'diffusion of responsibility'.

Note: You may have to apply concepts, theories and/or research to a completely new issue/scenario in the exam that you have not studied.

You need to able to describe a practical you conducted in social psychology: A questionnaire collecting both quantitative data and qualitative data on in-group/out-group attitudes based age

Aim: To investigate in-group behaviour and whether participants show an in-group bias towards those of the same age as them.

Alternative directional hypothesis: Participants will have more positive attitudes towards people of the same age as them. People in a young age group (25 and under) will have more positive attitudes towards people in their own age group compared to people in an older age group (60+)

Null hypothesis: There will be no significant difference in the participants' attitudes towards people in a different age group to them. Participants who are 25 and under will not show an in-group preference for their own age group compared to the older age group (60+).

Sampling: An opportunity sample was used drawing on students from the sixth form. The sample size was 20 and they were all students between 16-17 years old. 9 males and 11 females were used.

Ethics: The participants were briefed before the questionnaire was administered and fully informed consent was obtained. They were given the right to withdraw during and after the questionnaire. They were also debriefed at the end of the questionnaire. Participants were assured that their responses would be kept anonymous and confidential as they were answering questions about their personal beliefs and attitudes.

Procedure: A questionnaire was designed to test participants' in-group attitudes towards people of the same age as them and out-group attitudes towards people of a different age to them. The questionnaire used a Likert scale to collect quantitative data about participants in-group/out-group attitudes and it also had four open questions to collect qualitative data. A pilot study was undertaken on three people to make sure the questions on the questionnaire were clear and unambiguous and to establish the reliability and validity of the questionnaire. 20 participants completed the questionnaire with the researcher present in small groups. Participants were briefed before the questionnaire and they completed it in silence so that they could not discuss answers. Participants were given the right to withdraw and debriefed at the end of the questionnaire. The quantitative part of the questionnaire was scored to measure attitudes to the in-group and attitudes to the out-group. The qualitative responses were analysed to look for dominant themes.

Results:

Quantitative research:

Attitude Score	Positive attitude to in-group	Positive attitude to out-group
Mean	3.4	2.4
Median	3.2	2.2
Mode	3.8	2.6
Range	1.4	1.2

Participants had a more positive attitude towards people of the same age as them. The mean score for positive attitude to the in-group was 3.4 compared to 2.4 for the out-group.

Qualitative research:

One theme was that younger people dress better.

Another theme was that younger people are more adaptable to change. For example, younger people are better with new technology.

Conclusion: The results suggest that younger people do favour those of the same age as them and have more negative attitudes towards people of a different age to them. Social identity theory suggests we prefer our in-group and devalue the out-group. Ageism is an example of this in-group preference.

Evaluation:

Participants may have given socially desirable answers on the questionnaire so that they did not appear too prejudiced to the out-group even though they might have been privately. Participants may have been influenced by the age of the researcher carrying out the questionnaire. There can be problems with the Likert scale in collecting data on attitudes as participants can be inclined to give answers towards the middle of the scale rather than at the extremes, which could have affected overall scores. As an opportunity sample was used the sample may be unrepresentative of the wider population. There may also have been subjective interpretation of the qualitative data. Personal views and experience may have affected how the qualitative data was interpreted leading to a biased report being made.

You need to be able to describe and evaluate surveys

Surveys are used to find out about people's opinions and attitudes. Questionnaires and interviews are types of surveys and are used to gather self-report data.

Questionnaires

Description:

Questionnaires involve written questions to find out about people's views and opinions. They are able to collect data from lots of people as everyone is asked the same questions and can answer them in their own time. Questionnaires can be sent by post, filled in on the internet, given face-to-face or left in a public place for people to pick up. The questions can either be closed or open. Closed questions may involve a Likert type scale or yes/no questions. Open questions ask people to explain what they think about a certain topic in their own words. If closed questions are used then quantitative data can be obtained. If open questions are used then qualitative data can be obtained.

Evaluation:

Questionnaires allow data to be gathered from large samples without too much cost. If closed questions are used, the quantitative data can be statistically analysed. It is also easy to compare the data from closed questionnaires as everyone answers the same questions. Furthermore, questionnaires with closed questions can be easy to replicate. A test-retest method can be used to establish the external reliability of a questionnaire. This is when the same people are given a questionnaire on different days to see if they give the same responses. If they give the same responses this shows that the questionnaire has external reliability.

Questionnaires with open questions can collect rich, qualitative data but they are harder to replicate. People are unlikely to give exactly the same responses to questions such as 'What do you think about your school?' on different days. Therefore, questionnaires with open questions tend to have less external reliability.

If a questionnaire has internal reliability then all the questions should be measuring the same concept. For example, if a questionnaire is looking at empathy, then all the questions should relate to this personality characteristic. The internal reliability of a questionnaire can be assessed using a split-half method. This involves splitting the questionnaire up into two halves and seeing whether participants' scores on both halves of the questionnaire are the same. If the participants have a similar score for empathy on both halves of the questionnaire, then it has internal reliability.

A key problem with questionnaires is that people may give socially desirable answers because they want the researchers to think well of them. Participants may also misunderstand the questions and interpret the questions differently. Questions asked beforehand could affect later answers. Questionnaires with closed questions can limit participants' responses, which affects validity. Questionnaires with open questions are open to interpretation.

Sometimes the questions may not be measuring what they were intended to measure. A questionnaire has face validity if the questions make sense in terms of what they are trying to measure. For example, if a questionnaire is looking at aggression and participants are asked how often they swear as a measure of aggression, the questionnaire may lack validity. This is because some people may swear as a means of expression rather than out of aggression. A questionnaire has predictive validity if it can predict future behaviour. For example, a questionnaire looking at helpfulness should be able to predict future helping behaviour. A questionnaire has concurrent validity if a different questionnaire is used and it finds similar results. For example, if two different questionnaires are used to measure competitiveness and they both suggest that the person is competitive then they have concurrent validity.

Unstructured, structured and semi-structured interviews

Description:

An interview involves asking participants questions verbally. This could be face-to face or on the phone.

Structured interviews involve closed questions and produce quantitative data. Questions are decided upon in advance and all participants answer the same questions in the same order. Unstructured interviews involve open questions and produce qualitative data. A couple of questions are decided on in advance but the researcher adapts their questions based on participants' responses. An unstructured interview often involves an in-depth discussion on a certain topic. Semi-structured interviews have prepared questions but allow participants to expand on some of their answers.

Evaluation:

Structured interviews allow quantitative data to be obtained, which can be statistically analysed. Unlike questionnaires, interviews allow the researcher to explain any questions that have been misunderstood. Unstructured interviews allow rich, detailed information to be obtained about people's opinions and views. Participants can expand on their answers and the researcher can follow up on any issues raised.

A disadvantage of interviews is that participants may give socially desirable answers to appear in a good light. Structured interviews can also limit participants' responses. Unstructured interviews are open to interpretation and bias. Furthermore, interviews can be time-consuming and expensive as they need to be delivered face-to-face.

You need to be able to describe and evaluate quantitative and qualitative data

Studies that focus on producing numerical results or data that can in some way be 'counted' (quantified) are described as quantitative research. Such studies tend to use large samples of people or animals so that results can be generalised to the wider population. Experiments, questionnaires and structured interviews are good sources of quantitative data. Quantitative data are measurable and firm conclusions can be drawn from the data. Statistical tests can be done to see how far the results are likely to be due to chance. In experiments, the independent variable is manipulated and the dependent variable is measured. Variables are also carefully operationalised and there are good controls. This makes the research more scientific. If a quantitative research is repeated, often the same data will be found. This shows that quantitative data is reliable. However, the careful operationalising of variables in quantitative research means that real life events and interactions are not being measured (lack of validity).

In comparison, qualitative data can be gathered in more natural situations and reflects real life behaviour more. So where quantitative data can have a lack of validity, qualitative data can be more valid. Qualitative data can be gathered from case studies, unstructured interviews and observations in participants' natural environments. However, qualitative data is harder to replicate and can lack reliability.

You need to be able to explain how different research methods produce qualitative and quantitative data

Structured interviews and questionnaires give quantitative data because they involve set closed questions. The questions have yes/no answers or are rated on a scale such as the Likert scale (where participants can give answers from strongly agree to strongly disagree and these answers can be scored). This gives numerical data, which is quantitative. Unstructured interviews and questionnaires use open questions and are good sources of qualitative data. For example, unstructured interviews may begin with a particular topic but then proceed like a conversation. They do not have set questions. The interviewer can explore areas that come up. No numerical data is obtained so the data is qualitative. An unstructured questionnaire would have open questions and then researchers would look for themes emerging from the participants' answers.

You need to be able to calculate measures of central tendency: mean, median and mode

The mean

The mean is often referred to as the average of a set of numbers. You calculate the mean by adding up all the numbers and then dividing by the number of numbers.

Consider the following data set: 12, 17, 23, 27

Add the numbers together: 12+17+23+27=79
Divide 79 by 4: 79/4 =19.75

The 'Mean' (Average) is 19.75

The median

The median is the 'middle value' in a list of numbers. To find the median, your numbers have to be listed in numerical order. If you have an odd number of numbers, the median is the middle entry in the list. If you have an even number of numbers, the median is equal to the sum of the two middle numbers divided by two.

Consider the following data set: 13, 17, 21, 8

Sort the numbers into numerical order: 8, 13, 17, 21

There is not a single middle number in this data set as there is an even number of numbers. Therefore, add the two middle numbers, 13 and 17, and divide by two:

13+17=30
30/2=15

The median is 15

The mode

The mode is the number that occurs most frequently in a set of data. If no number is repeated, then there is no mode for the set of data.

You need to be able to calculate measures of dispersion: range and standard deviation

The range

Note: The range is a measure of dispersion. It refers to how the data is spread out or 'dispersed'.

The range is the difference between the largest and smallest numbers.

Consider the following data set: 11, 15, 16, 21

Subtract the smallest number from the largest number: 21-11=10

The range is 10

Standard deviation

The standard deviation is a way of telling how far apart or how close together the data is.

Why are we interested in standard deviation?

Consider the following two data sets:
Data set 1: 28, 29, 30, 31, 32   Mean = (28+29+30+31+32)/5=30
Data set 2: 10, 20, 30, 40, 50   Mean = (10+20+30+40+50)/5=30

Both data sets have a mean of 30 but the data is spread much further apart in data set 2. Therefore, data set 2 has a larger standard deviation.

Standard deviation is a measure of dispersion, which means it's useful in determining how spread out the data is. For example, if one school has students who end up with a high mean number of UCAS points and a very small standard deviation, that means that the all the students at this school got good A-levels. If a second school has students that have an equally high mean number of UCAS points with a very high standard deviation as well, that means that the students had a much wider range of A-level grades with some getting high grades and some getting much worse grades. UCAS points with a very high standard deviation as well, that means that the students had a much wider range of A-level grades with some getting high grades and some getting much worse grades.

Calculating standard deviation

$$s = \sqrt{\frac{\sum(x - \bar{x})^2}{n - 1}}$$

X= each value
$\bar{X}$= mean of the data set
n = the number of values
$\sum$=sum of
For example, for the data set 46, 42, 44, 45 ,43:
1) Calculate the mean: $\bar{X}$ = (46+42+44+45+43)/5=44
2) Take away the mean from each value (x - $\bar{X}$) and then square it.
3) Add up all the (x - $\bar{X}$)^2 values 4+4+0+1+1=10
4) Divide the sum of all the (x - $\bar{X}$)^2 values by n-1: 10/(5-1)=10/4=2.5
5) Square root it all for the standard deviation, s. $\sqrt{}$ 2.5= 1.6

Note: Using a table can help you get your calculation right.

X	$\bar{X}$	(X - $\bar{X}$)	(X - $\bar{X}$)2
46	44	2	4
42	44	-2	4
44	44	0	0
45	44	1	1
43	44	-1	1

$\bar{X}$ = 44 $\sum$ = 10

$$S = \sqrt{\frac{\sum(X - \bar{X})2}{n - 1}} = 1.6$$

How can you interpret standard deviation?

For datasets that have a normal distribution the standard deviation can be used to determine the proportion of values that lie within a particular range of the mean value. For such distributions, 68% of values are less than one standard deviation (1SD) away from the mean value, 95% of values are less than two standard deviations (2SD) away from the mean and 99% of values are less than three standard deviations (3SD) away from the mean.

The mean of our data set was 44 and the standard deviation (SD) is 1.6. Therefore, 68% of values in the data set lie between mean-1SD (44-1.6 =42.4) and mean +1SD (44+1.6=45.6). 99% of the values will lie between mean-3SD (44-4.8=39.2) and mean +3SD (44+4.8=48.8).

If the data set had the same mean of 44 but a larger standard deviation e.g. 2.4, it would suggest that the values were more dispersed.

You need to be able to understand normal distributions and skewed distributions

Data can be spread out in different ways. For example, it can be spread to the left or spread to the right. Normal distributions have data, which is symmetric around the mean and the mean, median and mode are equal. IQ follows a normal distribution. Most people have an IQ between 70 and 130 with a mean, median and mode of 100. Only a small percentage of people have an IQ under 70 or over 130.

If a distribution is skewed, then the mean is usually not in the middle.

For example, ten participants take part in a memory test and are asked to remember a list of 20 words. The mean of their scores was 9 but the median was 12. A distribution that is skewed to the left has mean that is smaller than the median i.e. it has a 'tail' on the left hand side.

A distribution that is skewed to the right has a mean that is larger than the median. This is common for a distribution that is skewed to the right i.e. it has a 'tail' stretching on the right hand side.

You need to be able to analyse qualitative data using thematic analysis

Qualitative data can be analysed using thematic analysis. A thematic analysis involves looking for 'themes' in descriptive text. For example, if an interview has been carried out, a researcher would look for themes in the interview transcript. The researcher would then identify, analyse and report patterns within the data.

An inductive thematic analysis would involve the researcher reading and re-reading the transcript until certain themes emerged.

In contrast, in a deductive thematic analysis, the researcher would decide what themes they were going to look for before they started analysing the transcript.

There are a number of stages in carrying out a thematic analysis: 1) The researcher familiarises themself with the data by reading it several times; 2) Initial codes are generated based on prominent features of the data; 3) The researcher looks for themes by examining the codes and collated data to identify broader patterns of meaning (potential themes); 4) The themes are reviewed by checking them against what people have said. At this stage, themes may be refined or discarded; 5) Themes are named and a detailed analysis of each theme is carried out; 6) Finally, the themes are written up with quotes from the data collected. The analysis is linked to existing theories.

Evaluation:

A thematic analysis can be used for a wide range of research questions. Rich, detailed data can be obtained, which can lead to a deeper insight into people's experiences, opinions and representations. However, thematic analyses are open to interpretation and hence subjective. They can be hard to replicate and so they have problems with reliability.

You need to be able to describe and evaluate sampling techniques

Description:

Random Sample-Each member of the population has an equal chance of being selected. For a small sample, you might draw names out of a hat/container. For a large sample, you might use birth records or the electoral role, allocate everyone a number and then get a random number generator to select certain people.

Systematic Sampling-This is when a clear system is used to select participants. For example you might choose every fifth or tenth person who walks down the street or from a register.

Opportunity Sample-This is when you select people based on who is available at a given time, often friends and family.

Stratified Sample-To ensure a cross-section of the target population is picked. For example, if you wanted to investigate the general population's attitude to childcare, you would select the right number of young females, young males, older males etc. that represents the proportion of them in the general population. Other criteria might include geographical locations and racial origins.

Volunteer Sample-This is when your sample consists of a group of participants who have chosen to take part.

Self-Selected Sampling-You advertise for participants with specific characteristics e.g women over forty and they participants self-select themselves if they have those characteristics to take part in the study.

Evaluation:

Random sample-Everyone in the chosen population has a chance of being in the sample. This is the best way of getting fair representation. However, if not everyone is in the sample, so there is still a chance that it will be biased (e.g. regarding age).

Systematic Sample-This is a manageable way of sampling. For example, if you choose every fifth person who comes along, this is a practical solution and reasonably fair as you will not be biased by personal preferences. This often involves people in one situation at a particular time e.g. walking down the High Street on Saturday morning, and this can cause bias.

Opportunity Sample-It is manageable and quick, as you can choose whoever is available. This often means friends and acquaintances. However, family and friends might be too cooperative and this might give bias to the findings as the participants are more likely to say what they think is wanted.

Stratified Sample-The required types of people are selected and there will be a spread of different types (using the desired criteria), whereas other types of sampling may not ensure this. However, choosing certain criteria and then finding people that fit those criteria does not necessarily mean that the people selected are representative of those criteria-they may have individual differences that give bias.

Volunteer Sample and Self-Selected Sample-This can be more ethical as the participants are interested in the study and can feel they are part of what is happening. However, volunteers are likely to be particular types of people, if only because they have time to take part in the study. They are not likely to be representative of the whole population.

You need to be able to describe the British Psychology Society code of ethics and conduct (2009) including risk management when carrying out research in psychology

Informed consent: Participants should be told about what the procedure entails and the aims of the study.

Debriefing: At the end of a study, participants should be told about any aspects of the study they were not informed about at the start. Participants should also be told about expected results and given the right to withdraw their data. The researchers should also check that the participants have not experienced any psychological harm.

Right to withdraw: Participants must be given the right to withdraw from the study at any time and given the option to withdraw their data at the end.

Deception: Participants should not be deceived about the aims of the study, what the procedure entails, the role of other participants or how their results will be used. Sometimes, it may be necessary to deceive participants about the aim of the study in order to investigate certain topics such as obedience. However, participants should only be deceived if they are not likely to come to any harm.

Protection from harm: Participants should be protected from physical and psychological harm. Psychological harm included distress and damage to self-image. The risk of harm should be no more than participants might expect in everyday life.

Confidentiality: All data should be confidential and anonymous. When data is collected, participants' names should not be recorded and numbers or pseudonyms used instead to ensure anonymity.

Competence: Researchers should be qualified and have the experience necessary to carry out the research.

Risk management: Researchers need to consider whether the study they wish to conduct exposes the participants to any greater risk than they would be exposed to in their normal lifestyle. They should also think about whether the research could cause the participants distress or self-doubt. A risk assessment should be carried out before conducting any research and the researcher should show an awareness of the power imbalance between themselves and their participants.

You need to be able to discuss ethics when researching obedience and prejudice in social psychology

Milgram's studies on obedience can be considered unethical as they did not protect participants from psychological harm. Contemporary studies on obedience such as Burger (2009) have aimed to investigate obedience whilst protecting participants from harm. The problem with obedience research is that it is difficult to study obedience without deceiving participants. When participants are ordered to harm another person as in much obedience research, the participants are going to be at risk of psychological harm.

Studies on prejudice can also cause psychological harm to participants especially when groups are put in competition with each other. For example, Sherif's study caused conflict between two groups of boys at a summer camp. In this study, the boys were also deceived.

It is questionable whether the findings from obedience and prejudice research are important enough to justify the deception and psychological harm caused.

You need to be able to discuss practical issues in the design and implementation of research in social psychology

One practical issue with obedience research is demand characteristics. Participants may guess the aim of an experiment and change their behaviour. Milgram told participants that he was looking at the effects of punishment on learning rather than obedience to prevent demand characteristics. He also used a confederate and a fake electric shock machine to deceive participants and avoid demand characteristics.

A practical issue with prejudice research is that people are unlikely to admit to being prejudiced in questionnaires and interviews as this is not socially desirable. Questionnaires need to be designed carefully in order to assess prejudiced attitudes. One way to see whether a questionnaire is valid is to assess whether participants respond in the same way to questions that are worded differently but are asking the same thing.

You need to be able to discuss reductionism in social psychology

Reductionism refers to explaining complex human behaviour in terms of simpler elements. Social psychology aims to understand human behaviour in social situations without being reductionist. However, there are some theories within the social approach that are reductionist. For example, social impact theory describes how people are influenced by others in social situations and reduces it to a formula: impact = function of (strength of the sources x immediacy of sources x number of sources). Reducing social impact down to a mathematical formula may be too simplistic a way of understanding how people are influenced by others as there are so many different factors involved. The theory also ignores individual differences in obedience such as having a non-conformist personality.

You need to be able to make comparisons between ways of explaining behaviour using different themes

Realistic conflict theory and social identity theory both refer to in-groups and out-groups when describing prejudice. However, realistic conflict theory focuses on how competition over resources can lead to prejudice whereas social identity theory says that the mere existence of another group can lead to prejudice.

Agency theory and social impact theory explain obedience differently. Agency theory says we have evolved to be obedient as this helps maintain a stable society. It also says that we are socialised in childhood to be obedient. In contrast, social impact theory focuses on the social conditions required for obedience such as how close the authority figures are to us.

You need to be able to discuss social psychology as a science

Experimental social psychology is scientific. For example, Milgram carried out his studies on obedience in a laboratory setting and Tajfel et al. (1971) investigated prejudice under controlled conditions. However, some aspects of social psychology are less scientific. For example, when unstructured interviews are used find out about people's opinions, feelings and experiences they can be subject to interpretation.

You need to be able to discuss cultural issues in social psychology

Culture may have an impact on obedience. For example, collectivist cultures may value obedience more than individualistic cultures. However, research into obedience in other cultures suggests that variations in obedience may be to do with how the studies were carried out rather than cultural differences. For example, Ancona and Paryeson (1968) found a higher obedience rate in Italy but they only used 330V as their maximum shock level.

You need to be able to discuss gender issues in social psychology

Gender stereotypes might suggest that females would be more obedient than males to authority figures. However, research by Milgram and others have found no significant differences in obedience levels between males and females.

You need to be able to discuss the nature-nurture debate in social psychology

Research into prejudice has looked at whether it is cause by dispositional factors (nature) or situational factors (nurture). Adorno et al. suggest that prejudice is related to having an authoritarian personality type. People who are status orientated, conventional and right-wing are more likely to be prejudiced. Therefore, the theory emphasises the nature side of the debate. However, authoritarian personality theory also suggests that parenting style (an environmental factor) affects personality. Social identity theory and realistic conflict theory focus on situational factors in prejudice. Both theories argue that prejudice is related to stereotypes in society and group membership so they support the nurture side of the debate.

You need to be able to show an understanding of how psychological knowledge had developed over time in social psychology

Research in social psychology is influenced by changes in society and important events. For example, the Holocaust led to research on obedience. Riots have led to research into crowd behaviour. More recently, research has been carried out looking at people's experiences on social networking sites.

You need to be able to discuss issues of social control in social psychology

Research on obedience can be used to control people. For example, the military could use such psychological knowledge to train soldiers to be unquestioningly obedient. However, social control can be positive as well. Research into obedience can be used to train people to avoid blind obedience. For example, nurses can be trained to question doctor's orders if they think it may cause the patient harm.

You need to be able to discuss the use of social psychological knowledge in society

Sherif et al.'s study showed how prejudice could be reduced by getting groups to work towards a superordinate goal (a goal that can only be achieved by working together). Other research has shown how education and equal status contact can reduce prejudice. Gaertner et al. found that combining intergroup contact with cooperative interaction is particularly effective at reducing prejudice. They interviewed 1,300 pupils at a multicultural American high school and found that pupils who had engaged in the most cooperative interaction were the least prejudiced.

You need to be able to discuss issues related to socially sensitive research in social psychology

Sieber and Stanley define socially sensitive research as: 'Studies in which there are potential consequences or implications, either directly for the participants in the research or for the class of individuals represented by the research'. Research looking at group behaviour has the potential to be socially sensitive. For example, a study looking at prejudiced attitudes to immigration might perpetuate prejudiced views. Psychologists also need to consider where the funding for their research is coming from and how their research will be used. For example, funding for the Zimbardo prison simulation experiment came from the military. Research could be used by the military as a form of social control. Psychologists need to consider whether their research can be used to restrict individual choice.

Exemplar exam questions:

Apply concepts, theories and research in the social approach to the problem of terrorism. (6 marks)

Student answer:

Terrorists may believe they are the in-group based on religion, race or political beliefs. Other people are in the out-group.

Social identity theory can be used to explain terrorism. Terrorists may categorise themselves as belonging to an in group based on religion, race or political beliefs and categorise people of other religions, race or political beliefs as being the out-group. They identify strongly with their in-group by taking on their values, beliefs and appearance. The terrorists may the compare themselves more favourably the out-group in order to boost their self-esteem. Terrorists may focus on the fact people from other religions are more immoral or greedy and this feeling of superiority might lead them to dehumanise the out-group so much that they are willing to kill them in an act of terrorism.

Realistic conflict theory explains how competition over resources can lead to conflict between groups. This theory explains terrorism as being related to competition over resources such as land. For example, the IRA wanted Northern Ireland to be governed by an Irish government not a British government. The IRA became so hostile towards the British government that they classed all British citizens as the out-group and bombed certain places in England.

Sherif's study showed how prejudice can occur between rival groups. Two groups of boys at a summer camp were put in competition with each other and prejudice quickly led to fighting and name-calling. This relates to how groups in competition with each other might commit terrorist acts against each other.

5/6 marks

Commentary:

This student applies their knowledge of social identity theory, realistic conflict theory and the Sherif study to terrorism well. One extra mark could have been gained by referring to agency theory. Agency theory might explain terrorism in terms of obedience to authority figures. People may commit acts of terrorism on the orders of their leader who they view as an authority figure. They may feel moral strain at committing the acts of terrorism.

Explain one key question for society in terms of concepts, theories or studies from the social approach (6 marks)

Student answer:

One key question is whether social psychology can be used to explain heroism. This is an important question as understanding heroism and encouraging people to be heroic can have a positive impact on society. One study that helps us understand why it is difficult to be a hero is Milgram's (1963) study on obedience. Milgram found that people would obey an authority figure even when they believed they were causing harm to an innocent person. Such studies can be used to teach people when it is important to disobey. Whistleblowers who are willing to speak out against corruption in public services or in companies are society's heroes because they go against authority. Agency theory says that we are socialised to obey from childhood as this helps to create a stable society. In the agentic state, we put aside our personal beliefs and wishes to obey authority figures. If people believe the authority figure is legitimate such as a police officer or doctor, they are more likely to obey. They are also more likely to follow orders if they believe the authority figure will accept responsibility for what happens. Encouraging people to take responsibility for their own actions can help people to behave like heroes. The bystander effect refers to when people choose not to help someone in need because they rely on other people to take responsibility. Latane and Darley (1970) found that people are less likely to help a person in trouble if there are other people around. When people stop expecting others to take responsibility, then they are more likely to help people in need. Social identity theory says that we favour our own in-group over comparable out-groups. This means that we are less likely to help those who we perceive to be in a different group to us. Overcoming these negative influences on our behaviour can enable us to act heroically towards those who we perceive to be different.

6/6 marks

Commentary:

This student applies both studies and theories to the key question. They also justify why these concepts relate to the key question in their answer, which is important as the exam question requires the student to 'explain'. There are other studies and theories that could have been referred to but there is enough here for 6 marks.

Chapter 2-Cognitive Psychology

You need to be able to describe what the cognitive approach is about

The cognitive approach studies how we process information. One of the assumptions of the cognitive approach is that the human mind can be seen as a system for handling information. Information from the environment is interpreted to make sense of it. Thinking, perceiving, using language and memorising are all ways of processing information.

Information processing occurs when information is taken in by the senses (input) and processed by the brain. Once the brain has processed the information, there is an output in some form.

Psychologists use a computer metaphor to describe how the brain processes information. Like a computer, the mind has an input in the form of senses, a store in the form of memory and an output in the form of behaviour. Cognitive processes are like computer software.

You need to be able to describe and evaluate the working memory model (Baddeley and Hitch, 1974)

Description:

The working memory model (Baddeley and Hitch, 1974) suggests that we have an active memory store that holds and manipulate information that is currently being thought about. The term 'working memory' reflects the concept that stored information is being worked on. The original model consisted of three separate components: the central executive, phonological loop and visuo-spatial sketchpad. The central executive is responsible for the control and coordination of mental operations including reasoning, comprehension, learning and memory. It can process information in different forms, for example, by sound, touch, sight etc. so it is modality free. It has a limited capacity, which means that it can only attend to a certain number of things at a time. Originally, the central executive was seen as only monitoring and coordinating the phonological loop and visuo-spatial sketch pad (slave stores) it is now believed to control our attention, allowing us to switch our attention from one thing to another.

The phonological loop deals with verbal material. It consists of two parts: a phonological store (inner ear), which is used to store speech-based sounds for a few seconds and an articulatory rehearsal system (inner voice), which is used to rehearse verbal information in our heads rather than out loud.

The visuo-spatial sketchpad (inner eye) stores and processes visual and spatial information.

The phonological loop and visuo-spatial sketchpad process information independently. Therefore, processing visual information should not interfere with processing verbal information.

Note: The phonological similarity effect refers to difficulty with remembering words that sound similar. This supports the view that the phonological store processes information by sound (acoustically).

The word length effect refers to being able to remember short monosyllabic words better than longer polysyllabic words. This supports the view that the articulatory rehearsal system has limited capacity.

People with a specific language impairment (SLI) have problems dealing with language. They do worse on language-based tasks than their IQ would suggest. Research has shown that children with SLI find it difficult to learn non-words such as blit because they have a deficit in their phonological loop, which stops them being able to learn and understand new words.

Evaluation:

Studies-Baddeley and Hitch carried out a number of experiments to see whether people could perform an irrelevant short-term memory task at the same time as cognitive task that involved learning new information, reasoning or understanding language. These experiments were called dual task experiments because they required participants to perform two tasks at the the same time. For example, in one experiment participants had to remember a sequence of random numbers while completing a verbal reasoning task. They found that participants found it difficult to carry out the verbal reasoning task when the number sequences were longer. From this, Baddeley and Hitch concluded that we have a limited capacity working memory system, which is able to both carry out mental operations and hold information temporarily. Baddeley and Hitch also found that when participants were asked to perform tasks that involved different types of processing, for example verbal and visual, their ability to carry out the tasks was not affected. This supports the idea that we have different visual and verbal systems within working memory for different types of task.

Case studies of brain-damaged patients (neurophysiological evidence) have been used to support the idea that working memory consists of different sub-systems. After a motorbike accident, KF had a digit span of one, suggesting that his phonological store was damaged. However, his visual memory was fine. In contrast, after a brain operation that was supposed to help his epilepsy, HM had problems with his visual memory but not verbal memory. These case studies provide evidence for separate visual and verbal systems within working memory.

Brain scans (neuroimaging) have also been used to support the idea of different sub-components within working memory. Paulesu et al. (1993) used PET scans to measure blood flow in different regions of the brain. He found that different parts of the brain are activated when participants are asked to carry out verbal (phonological) and non-verbal memory tasks. He identified the Broca's area and the supramarginal gyrus areas of the brain as being involved in phonological memory tasks. He then wanted to see whether he could identify which areas of the brain are used by the articulatory rehearsal system and the phonological store (sub-components of the phonological loop). In order to find this out, he asked participants to carry out a rhyme judgement task involving the articulatory rehearsal loop but not the phonological store. The Broca's area of the brain was activated when participants carried out the task. He concluded that the Broca's area can be identified with the articulatory rehearsal system. By using a subtraction method, he deduced that the supramarginal gyrus is related to the phonological store.

Explanation-A problem with the original model of working memory is that it could not explain how the working memory system could keep track of all the information across the different sub-systems and sub-components. In order to address this issue, Baddeley (2000), proposed that the working memory system has a limited capacity episodic buffer, which can bind information across the different sub-systems and integrate it with information from long-term memory.

Application to real life- Baddeley (1991) found that Alzheimer's patients had problems carrying out visual and verbal tasks at the same time. This is in contrast to 'normally functioning' people who can usually carry out different types of task at the same time easily. Baddeley suggested that the Alzheimer's patients had decreased central executive function and so they couldn't coordinate information from the different sub-systems within their working memory. Understanding why Alzheimer's patients struggle with memory and thinking, could lead to possible treatments for them in the future.

You need to be able to describe and evaluate the multi-store model of memory (Atkinson and Shiffrin, 1968), including short- and long-term memory, and ideas about information processing, encoding, storage and retrieval, capacity and duration.

Description:

Atkinson and Shiffrin (1968, 1971) described memory as having separate stores. These are referred to as sensory memory, short-term memory (STM) and long-term memory (LTM). For information to go from your sensory memory to your STM, attention is needed. Information in the STM that is sufficiently rehearsed is coded into LTM. Information that is stored in the sensory memory is only stored for a fraction of a second. The STM holds plus or minus seven items or chunks of information and can last between 18 and 30 seconds. The capacity of LTM is unlimited and information can last a lifetime. LTM is a single store which means that everything is stored together and items are stored in the order in which they have been learnt. In STM, information is held in acoustic form while in LTM it is held in semantic form.

Evaluation:

Studies-Glanzer and Cunitz (1966) presented participants with a list of words and found that people remembered more words from the beginning (primacy effect) and the end of the list (recency effect) and the fewest words from the middle. This primacy and recency effect support the idea of a separate STM and LTM. Participants remember more words from the beginning of the word list because they have had time to rehearse them and put them into LTM and they remember more words from the end of the word list because they are still in STM. The words in the middle of the list are forgotten because they have not been rehearsed and they are no longer in STM.

Other evidence for the existence of a separate STM and LTM comes from case studies of brain damaged patients. One example is the case of HM who had difficulty forming new long term memories but his short term memory was relatively normal.

Explanation-The multi-store model of memory is too simplistic. It is now widely believed that both STM and LTM have several separate storage systems. Seitz and Schumann-Hengsteler found that a visual-spatial task would not interfere with someone's ability to do sums. This suggests that there are separate short-term memory systems to handle visual and verbal information. HM could remember new motor skills and past information, suggesting that there are separate stores for LTM (facts, events, skills stores).

Application to real life-The concept of a separate STM and LTM is useful in helping psychologists think about memory. The multi-store model of memory helps to explain some of the memory problems with anterograde amnesia as people with this type of amnesia cannot form new long-term memories although they still have old memories and their STM is intact e.g. Clive Wearing.

You need to be able to describe and evaluate Tulving's (1972) explanation of long-term memory: Episodic and semantic memory

Description:

Episodic memory is a record of the episodes/experiences in our lives. As the events that have happened in our lives are linked to the time when they occurred, they are time-referenced. Retrieval of episodic memories is also dependent on recalling the context of the situation. Semantic memory is our general knowledge store and holds factual information. The time when we learnt the information is not important so semantic memories are not time-referenced. However, fragments of information in semantic memory can be pieced together so that they are in a temporal form. For example, we might learn about Roman times separately from the Middle Ages but we can then understand that the Middle Ages occurred at a later time. Retrieval of semantic memories is not dependent on context as we do not need to recall the context of when we learnt factual information to remember it. Semantic memory is unlikely to change when we recall facts because it is independent of context. In contrast, when we recall experiences from our lives and reflect on them within context, they are likely to be transformed.

Evaluation:

Studies-Case studies of amnesic patients have been used to support the distinction between episodic and semantic memory. Tulving argued that people with amnesia suffer from problems with episodic memory combined with an intact semantic memory. The case study of KC (1951-2014), who could not recall many personal events in his life but could learn new facts supports the idea of separate memory systems. Ostergaard (1987) described the case of a 10-year-old boy who had problems with his episodic memory but who was still able to learn new things. It was concluded that he was able to store information in his semantic memory. This study supports the idea that there are separate episodic and semantic memory systems. However, this boy did have some deficits in his semantic memory too. Cermak and O'Connor (1983) reported the case of an amnesic patient who could read a factual article on laser technology and discuss it at the time but who could not remember anything about it later. This suggests that he had deficits in both semantic and episodic memory. Therefore, some case studies of amnesic patients do not support a distinction between episodic and semantic memory as deficits are observed across both types of memory.

Case studies of brain-damaged patients suggest that long-term memory consists of more than episodic memory and semantic memory. Clive Wearing, a musician, could not remember episodes in his life but could remember how to play the piano. This case study suggests that there is different long-term memory store for practised skills. The term 'procedural memory' has been used to describe our memory for practised skills such as riding a bicycle. The case study of HM also supports the idea of a long-term memory store for practised skills. HM could learn new skills but could not remember learning them. For example, HM would get quicker at completing jigsaw puzzles even though he couldn't recall doing them.

Explanation-A criticism of Tulving's idea of separate episodic and semantic memory systems is that there needs to be communication between the systems. Episodic memory cannot work without semantic memory because in order to understand episodes in our lives we need to relate it to our general knowledge. Anderson and Ross (1980) found that semantic memory is also affected by episodic memory. They asked participants to decide whether a sentence was true or false, a test of semantic memory, and the results showed that their ability to verify the sentences was affected by prior episodic information. Such evidence suggests that episodic and semantic memory are not separate. Semantic memories may form through an abstraction of information from episodic memories.

Application to real life-Tulving's idea of episodic memory as being context dependent can explain why people forget information in the absence of the right cues (cue-dependent forgetting). The police often use cues during interviewing to reinstate the context of an incident to improve witness' memory of events.

You need to be able to describe and evaluate reconstructive memory (Bartlett, 1932)

Description:

Bartlett suggested that memory is an imaginative reconstruction of past events. We do not remember information accurately like a DVD recording but instead we are influenced by our prior knowledge. Schemas are 'packets of information' we have about the world and they affect how we interpret events. For example, we might have classroom schema and that might include the idea of a teacher, a whiteboard and some students being taught. If we are shown a film of a classroom situation, we might recall that the students were set homework even though they weren't because homework forms part of our classroom schema. When we retrieve stored memories, we use previous experiences to interpret the information and so the information is reconstructed. If there are any gaps in our memory, we may use schema to organise the information. Therefore, schemas may lead us to distort unfamiliar information so that it fits in with our existing knowledge.

Evaluation:

Studies- Bartlett carried out a number of repeated reproduction experiments to show that participants will reconstruct their memories. The repeated reproduction method involved participants being asked to recall a story or object after increasing time intervals. For example, in his 'War of the Ghosts' study, participants read the story twice and were then asked to recall it after several minutes, weeks, months and then years. Bartlett used eight unfamiliar stories altogether and a number of different pictures as well. He found that participants' memories were distorted. When participants were asked to recall the stories, they often shortened the stories and made them more coherent.

Explanation- Bartlett focused on memory being reconstructed at recall. However, our schema may also affect the way we perceive and understand information before it is stored. We may not store information exactly as it is presented to us but in a way that it makes sense to us. Bartlett may also have overemphasised the inaccuracy of our memory. Research into flashbulb memory has shown that we can remember emotionally significant events very accurately.

Application to real life-The concept of reconstructive memory has been used to explain why eyewitness testimony can be inaccurate. Innocent people have been convicted on the basis of eyewitness testimony alone and later been found innocent based on DNA evidence.

You need to be able to describe and evaluate the classic study Baddeley (1966b) 'The influence of acoustic and semantic similarity on long-term memory for word sequences'

Description:

Aim: To see whether words that sound similar (acoustically similar) or are similar in meaning (semantically similar) affect participants' ability to recall them in order (sequential recall).

Procedure: Male and female participants were divided into four conditions: In condition 1, they had to recall a list of acoustically similar words; in condition 2, they had to recall a list of acoustically dissimilar words; in condition 3, they had to recall a list of semantically similar words and in condition 4, they had to recall a list of semantically dissimilar words. Each list had 10 words and each word was displayed via a projector to the participants for a few seconds. Participants were then asked to remember some numbers to remove the words from their short-term memory. Then to test participants' sequential recall for their list of words, they were shown the words and asked to write them down in the order they had been presented. This was repeated four times. Participants were then given a 15 minute interference task where they had to copy some number sequences. Finally, participants were asked to recall their word list in order again to test their long-term memory for the words.

Results: Participants' sequential recall of semantically similar words was significantly worse than for semantically dissimilar words during the final stage of the experiment. Participants' sequential recall of acoustically similar words was not significantly different to acoustically dissimilar words during the final stage. However, initially participants' memory for the acoustically similar sounding words was worse compared to the acoustically dissimilar words.

Conclusion: It was difficult for participants to recall semantically similar words during the final stage as information is encoded in long-term memory semantically. Sequential recall of the acoustically similar words was worse at the beginning because information is encoded in short-term memory acoustically.

Evaluation:

Generalisability-Participants were all undergraduate students so were not representative of the wider population as they may have been more used to learning and recalling information.

Reliability-The study was conducted under controlled conditions and followed a standardised procedure. This makes the study easy to replicate and the reliability of the study can be tested. Studies that are reliable are considered more scientific.

Application to real life-The study suggests that information is encoded into short-term memory and long-term memory differently and so supports the idea of separate stores. This helps us to understand case studies of brain-damaged patients and why they have problems remembering some things but not others.

Validity-The study lacks ecological validity because the situation was artificial and does not relate to how we use memory in everyday life. The task lacked mundane realism as people are not usually asked to learn and recall a list of words. Furthermore, participants were asked to rehearse the words during four trials, which may have enhanced their memory for the words and is unlike how we remember things in real life.
Songs can be encoded in LTM without people thinking about their meaning, which suggests that some information in LTM can be encoded acoustically.

Ethics-There are no ethical issues so you don't need to comment on the ethics of this study at all.

You need to be able to discuss individual differences in memory including processing speed and schemas

People process information at different speeds. Some people can take longer to take in information than others. Children who have a slower 'processing speed' can get extra time in examinations to allow them process what they are being asked to do. There can also be individual differences in memory capacity. Sebastien and Hernandez-Gil (2012) found that younger children had shorter digit spans than older children.

Individuals may have slightly different schemas (packets of information) about the world. For example, one person's idea about what a criminal looks like may be different to another person's. Our perceptions can affect our outlook on a situation and also how we recall information. It has been shown that stereotypes can affect a witness' recall of a crime incident.

You need to be able to discuss individual differences in autobiographical memory

Autobiographical memory is our memory for the events that have happened during our lives. Our clearest memories tend to be recent ones or ones that occurred between 15 and 25-years-old (the remininscence bump). It has been argued that we remember things well from our teenage years and early twenties because it is when we form our identity. Palombo et al. (2012) found individual differences in autobiographical memory. They questioned people about different aspects of their memory including episodic memory (memory for events) and semantic memory (memory for facts). They found that people who had poor episodic memories also had poor semantic memories. This suggests that the different types of memory are interlinked.

You need to be able to discuss how dyslexia affects children's memory, span and working memory (one area of developmental psychology)

Dyslexia is a developmental disorder that affects the way a person processes written material. People with dyslexia read at a level lower than would be expected for the age and intelligence. There is often a discrepancy between their oral and written abilities.

Dyslexia affects up to 10% of the population. More boys are affected than girls. Research has found the children with dyslexia have problems recognising similar sounding words (the phonological similarity effect). They also find it harder to remember strings of longer words relative to shorter words (the word length effect). This suggests that children with dyslexia have a poor verbal short-term memory.

Breznitz (2008) argues that dyslexia is caused by slow processing during the decoding of words. Breznitz and Horowitz (2007) found that children with dyslexia could be trained to process information at a faster speed.
However, there is still no universally accepted explanation of what constitutes dyslexia as there are wide variations in symptoms. It seems to have a genetic basis and it may be a neurological syndrome. Stein (2008) found that the development of magnocellular neurones is impaired in children with dyslexia. Furthermore, dyslexia can coincide with other learning difficulties such as attention hyperactivity disorder (ADHD) suggesting it is more than just a phonological issue.

The most effective intervention programmes in schools seem to focus on phonological awareness. Children with poor phonological awareness may not understand that if you change the letter 'c' in the word 'cat' to 'h', the word would become 'hat'.

Practising phoneme deletion is one technique that can improve dyslexic children's phonological awareness. For example, a teacher might use two cards with the word 'mice' on one and 'ice' on the other. They might then ask the child, 'If you take away 'm' from the word mice, what is left then?' Another technique is phoneme identification. For example, the teacher might say a single speech sound such as 't' and show six pictured words. The child then has to pick the picture that begins with 't'. Phoneme discrimination is another method of helping children with dyslexia to really listen to speech sounds. This is when two pictures of similar sounding words are presented together such as 'cat' and 'hat'. The teacher would then say such just one of the words and the child has to pick the correct picture.

Retgvoort and van der Leij (2007) used a 14 week home- and computer-based training in phonemic awareness and letter-sound relationships with children who were genetically at risk of dyslexia. Initially, the trained at-risk children kept up with untrained not-at-risk controls in reading ability. However, once the children started school, the trained at-risk children had delayed reading relative to the not-at-risk control children. This study shows the importance of support at school as well as at home and how the advantages of early intervention can be undone unless on-going help is provided.

You need to be able to describe and evaluate one contemporary study in cognitive psychology. For example, Steyvers and Hemmer (2012) 'Reconstruction from memory in naturalistic environments'

Description:

Aim-To see whether there is a link between episodic memory (memory for events) and semantic memory (memory for objects and facts) in everyday, natural environments. They wanted to see how prior knowledge (semantic memory) was used to reconstruct memory for photographs of normal everyday settings (episodic recall).

Procedure-The researchers found 25 images of everyday scenes. There were 5 types of scenes: kitchens, dining rooms, offices, hotels and urban scenes. 5 images were chosen of each of the 5 scene types.

The researchers wanted to find out what people might expect to see in a particular scene so 22 participants from the University of California were asked to list objects that might be in a kitchen, dining room, office, hotel and urban scene. As participants were asked to say what they expected to be in a scene, this was called the expectation test. In this condition, the participants were not shown any stimulus image.

25 other participants were shown the 5 scenes and asked to name any objects they could see. This was to check whether the people could see all the objects in the photographs that the researchers had placed there. This was called the perception test as it was used to check what participants could perceive.

In the main experiment, a separate group of 49 participants were shown a set of 5 images (there were 2 sets of 5 images altogether). The participants saw the images for either 2 seconds or 10 seconds and this was chosen randomly. For example, one participant might be allocated the following timings: Urban 10s, Office 10s, Dining 10s, Kitchen 2s, Hotel 2s. The participants were then asked to free recall all the objects that they could remember. The researchers believed that when participants only saw a scene for 2s, they would have to rely on prior knowledge (semantic knowledge) to help them recall it. In contrast, they believed that when participants saw the scene for 10s then they could use their episodic memory to recall the scene and would be better able to recall unusual objects in the scene.

The effect of prior knowledge (semantic memory) on recall was also tested by comparing participants' recall of the objects in the 2s and 10s conditions with the expectation test.

Results-The mean number of objects recalled when participants saw a scene for 2 seconds was 7.75 compared to 10.05 when participants had seen a scene for 10 seconds. Participants made very few errors in their recall. Incorrect recall of objects that would be expected to be in such as scene was only 9%. Incorrect recall of low probability objects was 18%, which suggests that participants were reasonably good at recalling unusual items.

Participants were able to guess many of the objects using prior knowledge (semantic memory). More than 55% of accurate object guesses were based on semantic memory. Participants were able to recall 80% of the objects in the 2s and 10s conditions, suggesting that episodic memory helped them to recall the rest of the objects.

Conclusion-Memory of naturalistic scenes can be accurate and reliable. Prior knowledge (semantic memory) can enhance recall.

Evaluation:

Generalisability-All the participants were university students, who are not representative of the wider population. However, as the study was looking at memory, which is similar across the general population except for the very young or very old, it could be deemed to be generalisable.

Reliability-The study had a clear standardised procedure with good controls. For example, the participants saw the photos for a certain amount of time under controlled conditions. The researchers could then compare recall in the 2s and 10s conditions fairly. Participants also only viewed one image of any scene such as the kitchen scene to make sure that photos of the same scene did not interfere with recall. These controls make the study replicable and reliable.

Application to real life-The study suggests that eyewitness memory is real life may be better than previous laboratory research has shown. Prior knowledge (semantic memory) may actually enhance recall and allow people to notice unusual features of the situation.

Validity-The study presented naturalistic scenes to participants, which enhances the ecological validity of the study. However, the study was still a laboratory experiment and involved an artificial situation. Seeing photographs of a scene is not the same as seeing it in real life.

Ethics-No ethical issues so no there is no need to discuss this.

An alternative contemporary study you could learn is Sebastián and Hernández-Gil's (2012) study of the developmental pattern of digit span

Description

Aim-To see whether digit span (a measure of phonological capacity) increases with age. To investigate whether there are any differences in digit span in Spanish culture compared to Anglo-Saxon culture. To compare digit span in children between 5- and 17-years-old and adults, older people and patients with dementia.

Procedure-570 participants were recruited from Madrid schools. All the participants were Spanish and between 5- and 17-years old. They were selected by school year and their cognitive functioning was controlled for. None of the participants had repeated a year and none of them had hearing, reading or writing difficulties. The participants were divided into five different age groups and they were all given a digit span test. Random sequences of digits were read aloud to participants at a rate of one digit per second. Initially, participants were given three sequences of three digits. Participants were then asked to recall the digits in the same order. The number of digits the participants had to recall increased each time by one digit. The digit span recorded for each participant was the maximum number of digits they could recall in the right order without any errors. The results were analysed by school year and by developmental period (5 years; 6-8 years; 9-11 years; 12-14 years and 15-17 years). Sebastián and Hernández-Gil also compared the data with results from their 2010 study looking at digit span amongst healthy older people and patients with Alzheimer's disease and frontotemporal dementia.

Results-Digit span increases with age from 3.76 at 5-years-old to 5.91 at 17-years-old. There was a steady increase in digit span with age amongst their Spanish participants. This contrasts with Anglo-Saxon research, which suggests that digit span does not increase past 15-years-old.

They also found that Spanish children's digit span was lower than Anglo-Saxon children of a comparable age.

When they compared the digit span of healthy older people (4.44) with those with Alzheimer's disease (4.20) and Frontotemporal dementia (4.22), they found a decreased digit span in all groups compared to the 17-year-olds. The healthy older people had a digit span of the average 7-year-old and the patients with Alzheimer's disease and Frontotemporal dementia had the digit span of the average 6-year-old. This suggests that the phonological loop is more affected by age than dementia.

Conclusion-Spanish digit words have more syllables e.g. cuatro, cinco, siete compared to English digit words e.g. four, five, six. Words with more syllables take longer to rehearse. This can explain why the Spanish children's digit span was lower than the Anglo-Saxon children of a comparable age.

Evaluation:

Generalisability-570 participants were used, which makes the sample representative of the wider Spanish population.

Reliability-The study had a standardised procedure involving participants being tested individually on their digit span under controlled conditions. This makes the study easy to repeat, which allows it to be tested for reliability.

Application to real life-Digit span can be used to make comparisons between individuals in terms of their verbal memory. This study shows that when comparisons are made using digit span, cultural differences should be accounted for.

Validity-The study lacks ecological validity because the situation was artificial. The task also lacked mundane realism. People are not usually asked to learn a list of digits in everyday life. Furthermore, testing participants' digit span may not be a good way of understanding how verbal memory is used in real situations.

However, the experiment has internal validity. Digit span tests have been shown to be a good indicator of reading ability, which relates to verbal memory.

Ethics-There are no ethical issues with this study so there is no need to discuss this.

You need to be able to discuss case studies of brain-damaged patients, including Henry Molaison (HM) and the use of qualitative data, including strengths and weaknesses of the case study as a research method

Cognitive neuropsychology studies brain-damaged patients to understand how the damage affects their behaviour and cognitive processes such as object recognition, memory and problem solving. Cognitive neuropsychologists use this information to understand how the brain works. For example, some brain-damaged patients have problems remembering information beyond 30 seconds. This provides support for the idea that we have a separate short- and long-term memory.

Henry Molaison (HM) suffered from severe epilepsy. In order to stop his seizures, an operation was carried out to remove his hippocampus. This stopped his seizures but led to damage to his long term memory. HM could remember items for a few minutes but not for long periods of time. This suggests a dissociation between two types of memory and supports Atkinson and Schiffrin's (1968) theory of a separate short-term memory (STM) and long-term memory (LTM) stores. However, a single dissociation does not provide enough evidence for separate memory stores as an alternative theory of HM's deficits would be that more effort is required to retain information for longer periods of time. On the other hand, the contrasting case of KF when looked at beside HM's case study provides further support for the idea of a separate short- and long-term memory. In contrast to HM, KF had impaired STM but his LTM was normal. The double dissociation shown by HM and KF provides support for Atkinson and Schiffrin's multi-store model of memory and the idea of a separate STM and LTM. However, although KF had a severely impaired STM, KF was able to perform a large range of cognitive tasks and had no problems understanding spoken language (Shallice and Warrington, 1970). This challenges the idea of a single STM store and led Baddeley and Hitch (1974) to develop a multi-component working memory model. The working memory model suggests that KF only had damage to the phonological loop component of his working memory and so although he had an auditory digit span of only two items, his visuo-spatial sketchpad and central executive were intact allowing him to process information.

Case studies of brain damaged patients include interviews with them about their experiences. The case studies also include description of how the amnesia has affected the patients' abilities and memory. For example, patients with anterograde amnesia report problems forming new memories and patients with retrograde amnesia have problems recalling past events. This means that qualitative data (descriptive data in words) is collected.

Evaluation:

Single case studies have contributed to our understanding of cognitive processes but they do have limitations. Brain-damaged patients may not be representative of the normal population so neuropsychologists need to be careful about making inferences about intact cognitive processes from such case studies. If brain damage occurs in early childhood, the brain can show plasticity and the damage can have different consequences for the patient. Bates (1998) found that babies who had suffered severe strokes to their left hemisphere could sometimes develop language processing in their right hemisphere.
There are also strengths and weaknesses of the qualitative data collected from case studies. Qualitative data can give rich, detailed information about brain-damaged patients' experiences and functioning. Such data is often considered more valid. However, qualitative data is harder to replicate and can lack reliability. Interpretation of qualitative can be subjective, and therefore, unscientific.

You need to be able to discuss a key question in the cognitive approach.
One possible key question 'How can knowledge of working memory be used to inform the treatment of dyslexia?

Dyslexia is a developmental disorder that affects the way a person processes written material. People with dyslexia read at a level lower than would be expected for the age and intelligence. There is often a discrepancy between their oral and written abilities.

Children with dyslexia have problems recognising similar sounding words (the phonological similarity effect) suggesting they have deficits in the phonological loop component of their working memory. They also find it harder to remember strings of longer words relative to shorter words (the word length effect). This suggests that children with dyslexia have a poor verbal short-term memory. A key question is whether knowing about working memory can help children with dyslexia.

The concept of working memory can be helpful in understanding the difficulties that children with dyslexia face. Working memory is important in reading and understanding words and so deficits in working memory can lead to the problems in these areas. Many children with dyslexia can also have difficulties with following a sequence of instructions and focusing their attention. This can be understood through them having a low working memory capacity. Children's performance at school is likely to be affected by these problems so it is important to provide suitable interventions so that they can achieve their full potential.

Loosli et al. (2011) used a computer-based working memory training programme with 9- to 11-year-old typically developing children and found that they had significantly enhanced reading performance after training compared to a control group. This study supports the idea that working memory is involved in reading ability. Dunning et al. (2012) also found that practising memory tasks on a computer could improve verbal working memory.

Alloway used a training programmed to develop children's working memory. The found that children who practised memory skills four times a week for 30 minutes had higher IQ and working memory scores compared to those who only practised once a week or not at all. When she followed them up 8 months later, they still showed the same improvements in grades, working memory, and IQ.

Breznitz (2008) argues that dyslexia is caused by slow processing during the decoding of words. This may be because their working memory has a low capacity. Breznitz and Horowitz (2007) found that children with dyslexia could be trained to process information at a faster speed.

Understanding that children with dyslexia may find it difficult to do a number of different things at the same time can inform teaching practice. For example, teachers should avoid talking and explaining concepts whilst the students are making notes. Tasks should also be broken down into smaller steps so that students' working memory is not overloaded with instructions.

Some of the most effective intervention programmes in schools seem to focus on phonological awareness. Children with poor phonological awareness may not understand that if you change the letter 'c' in the word 'cat' to 'h', the word would become 'hat'. This may because children need strategies to overcome deficits with the phonological loop component of their working memory.

Retgvoort and van der Leij (2007) used a 14 week home- and computer-based training in phonemic awareness and letter-sound relationships with children who were genetically at risk of dyslexia. They found that the trained at-risk children kept up with untrained not-at-risk controls in reading ability short-term.

Alternative key question: 'Is eyewitness testimony reliable?'

Eyewitness testimony refers to the recalled memory of a witness to a crime or incident. Innocent people have been convicted on the basis of eyewitness testimony alone and have later been found innocent using DNA evidence. Cases like this call into question the reliability of eyewitness testimony. There is also the issue that juries tend to trust eyewitness testimony perhaps disproportionately.

Eyewitness Testimony is unreliable because:

Witnesses' memories for events are not accurate video recordings but subject to errors. If witnesses have gaps in their memory, they may use schema to reconstruct their memories. Schemas may also influence the way a memory is encoded.

Leading questions can influence eyewitness memory and produce errors in recall. Loftus and Palmer (1974) found that they could affect participants recall by changing the way a question is worded. Participants were asked how fast a car was going when it 'hit', 'smashed', 'collided' or 'bumped'. Participants gave a higher estimate of speed if the word was 'smashed' rather than 'collided', they were also more likely to report seeing broken glass in the 'smashed' condition when asked back a week later.

Weapon focus effect: Studies show that when a weapon is used by a criminal, witnesses focus on the weapon rather than the criminal's face or their environment, probably because a weapon is a major threat. Loftus et al. (1987) showed half their participants a film with a customer in a restaurant holding a cheque, and the other half were shown a film with a customer holding a gun. They found that participants had worse recall for a the customer's face when they were holding a weapon.

Yarmey's (2004) study supports the view that jurors should question the reliability of witness identification from line-ups. They found that when participants had actually spoken to a female target, only 49% of them could identify her in a photo line-up when she was present and when she was not present 38% of them decided than one of the filler photos was the target.

Poor line-up procedures may lead to misidentification of a suspect. Simultaneous line-ups (where all the people are presented together in the line-up) may lead to witnesses using a relative judgement strategy (choosing a person who looks most like the perpetrator of the crime rather than really looking at the person's individual characteristics to see whether they match up).

Meissner and Brigham (2001) found that people are less able to recognise people from a different ethnic background to them so this can lead to problems in eyewitness identification.

Buckout (1974) highlighted that photo line-ups can be biased if the suspect's photo is physically different from the fillers.

Busey and Loftus (2006) pointed out that lack of double-blind procedures can mislead witnesses. They gave the example of a police officer who knew who the suspect was in a line-up and when a witness identified the suspect, the police officer said sign here as if to confirm their identification was correct.

Wells and Bradfield found that if a participant was given confirming feedback about an identification they became more confident that their identification was correct. Therefore, by the time a case gets to court, a witness who has had their identification confirmed by a police officer, may be overly confident even if they are wrong.

If there is a long period of time between recall and the incident, people are likely to forget details.

Stereotypes can affect eyewitness memory. People's views on what type of person commits a crime can affect recall. People are less likely to believe that a man is a suit committed a crime compared to someone who is scruffily dressed.

The memory conformity effect can affect witnesses' memory for events. For example, if witnesses discuss a crime incident together, their memory for events becomes more similar. Wright et al. (2000) placed people in pairs to investigate the memory conformity effect under controlled conditions. One of the pair saw pictures of a man entering with the thief, the other saw pictures without the man. They were then asked to recount the story together but fill out questionnaires separately. About half of the participants who had not seen the picture with the man conformed to their partner's account.

Eyewitness Testimony is reliable because:

Yuille and Cutshall (1986) examined the recall of witnesses to a real life gun shooting in Canada. 21 witnesses saw a man try to rob a gun shop and then shoot the shop owner. The shop owner shot back and killed the thief. After the witnesses had been interviewed by police, the researcher used the opportunity to ask them whether they would like to take part in their research into eyewitness testimony. 13 of the 21 witnesses agreed to take part in their research 5 months later. They found that even 5 months after the incident, witnesses had good recall of events and were not affected by the leading questions asked. This study suggests that eyewitness memory in real life is not as likely to be distorted as laboratory experiments suggest.

Rinolo et al. (2003) questioned 20 survivors of the shipwrecked Titanic shipwreck and found that 15 of the 20 witnesses were able to recall details accurately many years later despite inaccurate media coverage.

Cognitive interviews can improve eyewitness testimony: this involves getting the witness to freely describe events without the risk of leading questions. Eyewitnesses are asked to not leave out any detail even if they think it is unimportant and they may be asked to recall the incident in reverse order. Questions can be asked at the end in order for information to be un-altered.

Flashbulb memory may lead witnesses to recall crime incidents very clearly as they are likely to have strong emotions related to the incident and may replay events in their mind.

You need to be able to describe and evaluate the laboratory, field and natural experiments

Laboratory Experiments involve manipulating an independent variable to see the effects on a dependent variable. The dependent variable is measured. Extraneous variables are controlled so that a cause and effect relationship can be established.

Evaluation:

Laboratory experiments have standardised procedures and good controls. This makes them easily replicable and reliable. They can establish cause and effect. However, laboratory experiments lack ecological validity as they are carried out in artificial situations and often involve artificial tasks.

Field experiments looks at participants in their natural environment whilst manipulating the independent variable. The dependent variable is measured. As field experiments take place in a natural environment, extraneous variables are hard to control.

Evaluation:

Field experiments take place in the participants' natural environment. This means that not all the extraneous variables can be controlled and the findings might not be reliable. However, as field experiments have carefully controlled and planned procedures, they often give the same results when repeated. This means that they can be as reliable as laboratory experiments. Field experiments are carried out in the participants' natural environment so they have ecological validity in terms of setting. However, the independent variable(s) is still carefully manipulated to see the effect on the dependent variable, and therefore, the procedure may not be valid. On the other hand, researchers try to make the procedure as realistic as possible to enhance validity.

Natural Experiments are studies carried out in real-life setting where the independent variable occurs naturally. A dependent variable is still measured. Participants cannot be allocated to conditions so it is not a true experiment.

Evaluation:
Natural experiments have high ecological validity as they are carried out in participants' natural environments. However, it can be difficult to establish cause and effect as the extraneous variables are not controlled.

You need to be able to discuss how quantitative data is obtained from experiments

Experiments involve measuring a dependent variable such a number of words recalled, speed estimates and number of aggressive behaviours shown. This is quantitative data, which can be statistically analysed to see how significant the results are or whether they may be due to chance. If quantitative research is repeated, often the same data will be found. This shows that quantitative data is reliable. However, the careful operationalising of variables in quantitative research means that real life events and interactions are not being measured so there can be a problem with validity.

You need to understand and be able to write one-tailed, two-tailed and null hypotheses

An experimental hypothesis predicts what change(s) will take place in the dependent variable when the independent variable is manipulated.

A two-tailed (non-directional) hypothesis predicts that there will be a change in the DV when the IV is manipulated.
e.g. There will be a difference in the number of words recalled when words are processed semantically compared to when they are processed phonetically.

A one-tailed (directional) hypothesis predicts in which direction the change will take place.
e.g. There will be more words recalled when they are processed semantically compared to when they are processed phonetically.

The null hypothesis states that there will be no changes due to the manipulation of the IV.
e.g.There will be no difference in the number of words recalled when processed semantically or phonetically.

Operationalisation: When you operationalise a hypothesis you make it clear what you are going to measure. Try and refer to something numerical. For example, if you are measuring recall, you might say number of words recalled.

You need to be able to describe and evaluate different types of design. You need to be to describe order effects, counterbalancing and randomisation in relation to the repeated measures design

An independent groups design involves testing separate groups of participants. Each group is tested in a different condition. For example, a researcher might ask one group to process words semantically and a second group to process words phonetically.

Advantages: An independent groups design avoids order effects. Each participant only takes part in one condition so they are less likely to become bored and tired (a fatigue effect) and less likely to become practiced at the task (a practice effect). There is also less likelihood of demand characteristics (where the participant guesses the aim of the study and changes their behaviour to please the experimenter) as they do only one condition.

Disadvantages: More people are needed than with the repeated measures design. Differences between participants in the groups may affect results, for example; variations in age, sex or social background. These differences are known as participant variables.

A repeated measures design involves testing the same group of people in different conditions. For example, the same group of people might be asked to process words semantically and phonetically.

Advantages: A repeated measures design avoids the problem of participant variables as the same participants do all conditions. Fewer people are needed.

Disadvantages: There are more likely to be demand characteristics as participants might guess the aim of the study as they take as they take part in more than one condition of the experiment.

Order effects are also more likely to occur with a repeated measures design. There are two types of order effects: practice effects and fatigue effects. Practice effects are when participants become better at a task such as learning a list of words in the second condition compared to the first condition. Fatigue effects are when participants might become bored or tired in the second condition.

Counterbalancing can overcome order effects in a repeated measured design. Counterbalancing is when the experimenter alters the order in which participants perform the different conditions of an experiment. For example, group 1 does condition A first then condition B, group 2 does condition B first then condition A.

Randomisation can overcome order effects as well. Randomisation is when the experimenter asks the participants to carry out the different conditions of the experiment in a random order.

A matched pairs design involves testing separate groups of people who are matched on certain characteristics. For example, each member of one group is same age, gender, race and or socioeconomic status as a member of the other group.

Advantages: A matched pairs design overcomes some of the problems of both an independent groups design and a repeated measures design. As the participants in the different conditions are matched, there is a reduced chance of participant variables affecting the results unlike an independent groups design. A matched pairs design also avoids the problem of order effects as there are different participants in each condition.

Disadvantages: A matched pairs design can be very time-consuming as the researcher need find closely matched pairs of participants. It is also impossible to match people exactly.

You need to be able to describe operationalisation of variables, extraneous variables and confounding variables

Operationalisation of variables refers to clearly defining what your independent and dependent variables are. For example, if you are investigating whether cues affect memory, you need to explain what type of cue you are looking at and how you will measure memory. In this example, the independent variable might be 'Whether participants are in the same room or a not when learning and recalling a list of words' and the dependent variable might be 'number of words recalled from a list of 20 words'.

Extraneous variables are are unwanted variables that can influence the results of an experiment.

Confounding variables are extraneous variables which affect the results of the experiment to the extent that you can't clearly see how the independent variable has affected the dependent variable. For example, a researcher may want to investigate whether mindmaps or flashcards are better at aiding recall of unfamiliar material such as Arabic. A confounding variable in this experiment would be if some of participants were already familiar with Arabic.

You need to be able to describe situation and participant variables

Situation variables and participant variables are types of extraneous variable.

Situation variables are environmental differences such as temperature, noise, other people etc. that can affect how participants respond in an experiment. For example, if an experiment is carried out over a number of days and one of the days there is a lot of noise from building work, this could affect participants' responses.

Participant variables are individual differences between participants, in terms of intelligence, mood, anxiety levels, age, IQ etc. For example, a policeman might be able to judge the speed of a car much better than a young student with no driving experience.

You need to be able to discuss objectivity, reliability and validity (internal, predictive and ecological)

Objectivity

An experiment is more likely to be objective if the data is collected in a strictly controlled environment. Quantitative (numerical) data is less open to interpretation than qualitative (descriptive) data and is viewed as more objective. Such data is also viewed as more credible, reliable and scientific.

Validity

A study has **internal validity** when the material or procedures used in the research measured what they were supposed to measure. For example, if an experimenter uses digit span to measure verbal memory and it has been found that digit span is a good indicator of this, then the study has internal validity.
Studies that avoid demand characteristics and experimenter effects have good internal validity.

A study has **predictive validity** if it accurately predicts a result in the future. For example, ALIS tests have predictive validity if they are good at predicting who will perform well at A-level.

A study has **ecological validity** if it is done in participants' natural environment and involves a situation that they might experience in real life. For example, if you get participants to come to a university and learn lists of words as test of memory, then you are not capturing how memory is used in real life and the study will lack ecological validity.

When discussing ecological validity you may also want to talk about mundane realism. If the study involves an artificial task like learning a list of words in two minutes, the study lacks mundane realism.

Reliability

If a study has a standardised procedure and was done under controlled conditions, then it is easy to replicate. A study is reliable if it has been replicated and similar results have been found. For example, if students are given an ALIS test on two different occasions and their results are similar, then the test can be seen as reliable.

You need to be able to describe experimenter effects and demand characteristics

Participants may try to guess what a psychological experiment is about. Demand characteristics refer to when participants change their behaviour based on what they think the experimenter wants to find from the research. In order to avoid demand characteristics, participants are sometimes not told they are in an experiment or they may be deceived about the true aims of the study (a single-blind experiment).

Experimenters can affect the behaviour of their participants and the results of their study. This is called experimenter effects. For example, the researcher might unwittingly communicate his expectations to the participants. Researchers can also interpret data in a biased way to match their expectations. To avoid experimenter effects, an experimenter may ask another researcher who doesn't know the aim of the study to carry out the actual experiment on participants (a double-blind procedure).

You need to be able to discuss control issues with experiments

One way an experiment can be controlled is through standardisation. This is when an experiment is set up so that all participants experience exactly the same procedure. For example, participants are given exactly the same instructions and carry out the tasks they have been given under the same controlled conditions. The only difference that participants may experience is the manipulation of the independent variable.

You need to understand when to use the inferential tests

One problem with the mean is that it doesn't tell you whether the difference between two conditions is significant or not. For example, you might do an experiment to test whether cues affect recall and your results show that the mean number of words recalled with a cue is 11.2 and the mean number of words recalled without a cue is 12.3. These figures suggest that the participants can recall more words with a cue and so you might conclude that cues do aid recall. However, it is difficult to judge whether the difference in the number of words recalled with a cue or without a cue is big enough to be certain of this conclusion. Perhaps on a different day or with different participants, you might have found less of a difference between the two conditions. An inferential test is a statistical test that shows you whether the difference between the two conditions is significant or not.

You choose an inferential test based on the design of the experiment and the level of data you collected.

You need to be able to recognise levels of data

Nominal data is made up of discrete categories. For example, you might categorise participants as either 'extroverts' or 'introverts'.

Ordinal data are ranked data. For example, you might rank participants on how well they recognise emotional expressions. Helen came first, Alex came second and Philippa came third.

Interval data are measurements along a scale with no true zero. For example, IQ can be measured along a scale but there is no true zero for IQ. Most people have an IQ between 70 and 130. For example, Helen has an IQ of 120, Alex has an IQ of 117 and Philippa has an IQ of 115.

Ratio data are measurements along a scale with a true zero. For example, time can be measured along a scale and there is a true zero. For example, Helen completed a spatial awareness task in 90s, Alex completed the task in 97s and Philippa completed the task in 105s.

**You need to understand about probability and level of significance
($p \leq 0.10$ $p \leq 0.05$ $p \leq 0.01$)**

In psychology, a significance level of $p \leq 0.05$ is chosen.

$p \leq 0.05$ means that there is an equal or less than 5% probability that the results could have occurred due to chance.

> p = the probability of the results being due to chance
>
> $\leq$ = less than or equal to
>
> $0.05 = 1$ in $20 = 5\%$

Psychologists prefer to use the significance level: $p \leq 0.05$ to judge whether to accept a hypothesis or not. This means that there is an equal or less than 5% probability that the results are due to chance e.g. the group that received a cue recalled more words than the group that did not receive a cue and there is a less than 5% chance that the difference between the two groups could have been due to chance (random differences between the groups).

Sometimes researchers use the significance level: $p \leq 0.1$ to judge whether to accept a hypothesis or not. This means that there is an equal or less than 10% probability that the results are due to chance. You can see that this is less conservative than $p \leq 0.05$. It is easier for the hypothesis to be accepted even though the null hypothesis might be true. This leads to a type 1 error. Type 1 errors can lead to false positive results; accepting a hypothesis even though it is incorrect. This could lead to psychologists thinking that there is a significant difference between participant's recall when they are given a cue and not given a cue when there isn't a significant difference in recall.

Sometimes researchers use the significance level: $p \leq 0.01$ to judge whether to accept a hypothesis or not. This means that there is an equal or less than 1% probability that the results are due to chance. You can see that this is stricter than $p \leq 0.05$. It is harder for the hypothesis to be accepted even though it might actually be correct. This leads to a type 2 error. Type 2 errors can lead to false negative results; rejecting a hypothesis when it is correct. This could lead to psychologists thinking that there was no difference between participants recall when given a cue compared to no cue, when there was a significant difference.

You need to be able to use a Mann-Whitney U test and a Wilcoxon test and to understand what observed and critical values are

You use a Mann-Whitney U test when you have an independent groups design and you are testing for a difference between groups. At A2, you need to understand that a Mann-Whitney U test is usually used when you have ordinal data as well.

You use a Wilcoxon test when you have a repeated measures design and you are testing for a difference between conditions. At A2, you need to know that a Wilcoxon U test is usually used when you have ordinal data as well.

To decide whether the results are significant there must be an equal or less than 5% probability that the results are due to chance. If the results are significant, then psychologists say that they are rejecting the null hypothesis. In essence, they mean that they are accepting the experimental hypothesis but it is standard form to refer to rejecting the null hypothesis.

In order to decide whether the results are significant or not the observed value (the result obtained from the data collected) is compared to the critical value.

The critical value is a statistical 'cut-off' point. It is a number presented on a table of critical values that determines whether the result is significant enough for the null hypothesis not to be accepted.

The observed value relates to the data that has been collected in an experiment. You calculate an observed value by using the relevant formula for the statistical test you have decided to you use and inputting your collected data. The observed value that you calculate is compared with the relevant critical value to see if a null hypothesis should be rejected or not.

Note: You don't need to remember the formula of the Mann-Whitney U test or Wilcoxon as they will be given on your data sheet. However, you do need to understand how to input data into them and calculate an observed value.

You need to be able to use a Mann-Whitney U or Wilcoxon T Critical Values Table

In order to interpret the critical values tables, you need to know whether the hypothesis was one-tailed or two-tailed; the number of participants in each condition (shown as 'N' on the table) and the significance level. The values in the Mann-Whitney test are termed 'U' and the values in the Wilcoxon test are termed 'T'. Unlike the Spearman-rank and Chi-squared tests the observed value has to be equal to or less than the critical value for the results to be significant (i.e. to accept the experimental hypothesis and reject the null hypothesis).

You need to be able to describe a practical in the cognitive approach. Example practical: A dual task experiment to test the working memory model

Aim: To test the limited capacity of the phonological loop by carrying out a dual task experiment. To see whether carrying out two verbal tasks at the same time is harder than doing one verbal task and one visuo-spatial task.

One-tailed Hypothesis: Participants will recall fewer words from a list when they are asked to recite the song 'twinkle twinkle little star' than when they are asked to complete a puzzle.

Null Hypothesis: The number of words recalled will not be affected by whether participants are asked to do another verbal task or a visuo-spatial task.

Independent Variable: Type of task. Whether participants are asked to carry out a second verbal task or a visuo-spatial task.

Dependent Variable: The number of words recalled.

Sampling Method: Opportunity Sampling

Design: Independent Groups

Procedure:
20 participants were recruited using opportunity sampling due to the limited timescale. All the participants were from the sixth form and were over 16 years old. An independent measures design was employed and the participants were divided into two groups of ten. All the participants were told that they had to recall a list of twenty unrelated words. Group 1 was asked to recite 'Twinkle Twinkle Little Star' at the same time as learning the list of words. This was to see whether carrying out two verbal tasks at the same time would interfere with recall of the word list. The working memory model suggests that the phonological loop has limited capacity. Group 2 was asked to complete a twenty-four-piece puzzle of Thomas the tank engine (a visual spatial task) at the same time as learning the word list. The working memory model suggests that a visuo-spatial task should not interfere with a verbal task as it involves a different component of working memory. Standardised instructions were read to each participant and they were informed of their right to withdraw from the study at any time. The experiment was carried out individually in a classroom. Participants were debriefed at the end of the experiment.

Results:

	Visuo-spatial task	Verbal task
Mean	12.4	9.9
Median	12	10.5
Mode	12	11
Range	6	5

Participants had a mean recall of 12.4 words when completing the puzzle a visuo-spatial task) compared to 9.9 words when reciting 'Twinkle Twinkle Little Star' (a verbal task).

Conclusion:
Two verbal tasks will interfere with each other more than a verbal task combined with a visuo-spatial task. This provides evidence for the different components of working memory.

Evaluation:

Generalisability: We used an opportunity sample of 16-17 year olds in our sixth form. Therefore, our sample is not representative of the wider population. However, as most people's cognitive abilities are similar, this study on memory could be considered generalisable.

Reliability: This experiment is reliable, because the extraneous variables were controlled and we used a standardised procedure. However, as an opportunity sample was used, it would be hard for someone else to obtain the same sample and repeat the findings making the study less reliable.

Validity: The experiment lacks ecological validity because learning and recalling a list of words is an artificial task.

You need to be able to discuss ethical issues in cognitive psychology

Experiments investigating memory tend to follow BPS ethical guidelines and rarely cause psychological harm. However, some research does deceive participants and it is important that participants are fully debriefed and given the right to withdraw at the end. Case studies of brain-damaged patients can be criticised for subjecting vulnerable individuals to intensive testing and violating their right to privacy. However, the patients' anonymity is ensured by giving them pseudonyms.

You need to be able to discuss practical issues in the design and implementation of research in cognitive psychology

A practical issue with memory research is that many experiments lack ecological validity as they are often conducted in artificial settings. Testing memory using lists of words or trigrams does not reflect how we use memory in real life and so the tasks lack mundane realism.

You need to be able to discuss reductionism in cognitive psychology

Many memory theories reduce memory down to separate parts. For example, the multi-store model of memory reduces memory down to sensory memory, short-term memory and long-term memory without taking into account the interactions between each memory store. More recently brain scans have shown the interactions between different brain regions when processing information.

You need to be able to compare different explanations of memory in cognitive psychology

The multi-store model of memory is more simplistic than the working memory model as it suggests that we only have three memory stores: sensory memory, short-term memory (STM) and long-term memory (LTM). It is now widely believed that both STM and LTM have several separate storage systems. The working memory model argues that there are separate short-term memory systems to handle visual and verbal information.

Both the multi-store model of memory and the working memory model focus on the idea of memory consisting of different stores. Therefore, they are both structural models of memory. There are other theories of memory that emphasise information processing rather than structure. The levels of processing theory of memory says we remember information better if we process it deeply rather than at a shallow level. Bartlett's reconstructive theory of memory focuses on how we construct memories using schemas.

You need to be able to discuss cognitive psychology as a science

The cognitive approach often uses experimental methods to investigate topics such as memory and forgetting. Laboratory experiments have good controls and are able to establish cause and effect relationships. This makes such research more scientific. Therefore, the cognitive approach is considered one of the more scientific approaches in psychology.

You need to able to discuss the nature nurture debate in cognitive psychology

The cognitive approach supports the nature side of the debate because it believes that we are born with certain structures such as short-term memory and long-term memory that allow us to process information. However, it also believes that our environment (nurture) affects our cognitive functioning. For example, our schema are affected by our experiences.

You need to be able to discuss how psychological knowledge has developed over time in cognitive psychology

In the 1880s, Ebbinghaus used experiments to study memory. He suggested that there are three types of memory: sensory, short-term and long-term. Bartlett's research in the 1930s led to the theory of reconstructive memory and has influenced later ideas on how the brain stores information.

In the 1950s and 1960s, psychologists started to compare computer processes with how the human brain process information. The led to advances in the understanding of encoding, storage and retrieval.

In 1968, Atkinson and Schiffrin developed the multi-store model of memory, which became the popular model for studying memory for many years although it is now viewed as overly simplistic. Tulving elaborated on the nature of long-term memory in 1972 by making a distinction between episodic and semantic memory. In 1974, Baddeley and Hitch proposed the working memory model, which gave a better explanation for short-term memory. The episodic buffer was added to this model in 2000 to explain how the different components of the model could integrate information.

You need to be able to discuss the use of psychological knowledge from the cognitive approach within society

Memory research has helped psychologists explain some of the memory problems which people with anterograde amnesia have and to develop appropriate therapies. Understanding memory has also helped in the treatment of people with Alzheimers.
The concept of working memory can be helpful in understanding the difficulties that children with dyslexia face. Working memory is important in reading and understanding words and so deficits in working memory can lead to the problems in these areas. Many children with dyslexia can also have difficulties with following a sequence of instructions and focusing their attention. Understanding that children with dyslexia may find it difficult to do a number of different things at the same time can inform teaching practice.
The theory of reconstructive memory has been used to explain why eyewitness testimony can be inaccurate. Research into the effect of leading questions, weapon focus effect, memory conformity effect and anxiety on witnesses has led to improvements in the legal system. The police use cues to aid witnesses' recall of incidents during interviews and avoid leading questions.

Exemplar exam question:

Describe and evaluate one model of memory other than working memory. (12 marks)

Student answer:

The multi-store model of memory suggests there are three stores of information in the brain. Information is taken in by the senses and held briefly in the sensory store. Information is then either retained in short-term memory (STM) or is forgotten. The STM can hold up to 7 chunks of information for a short amount of time. The information is encoded by the way it was processed in the sensory store i.e. if it was seen it will remain as visual information. In the STM, information can be encoded acoustically, visually or semantically. Information can then either be forgotten or retained in the long-term memory (LTM). In the LTM, the capacity is unlimited and the length of time it is held for is potentially unlimited also. The information can be encoded in any form. Information can be rehearsed by the rehearsal loop, which brings information into the STM from the LTM and back again.

The multi-store model of memory may be too simplistic. The working memory model describes short-term memory as an active store that holds and manipulates information consisting of the visuo-spatial sketchpad and the phonological loop. Tulving's theory of episodic and semantic memory suggests that there are different types of long-term memory too. This is backed up by case studies of brain-damaged patients who cannot form new long-term memories off episodes in their lives but can get better at practised skills. However, the multi-store model was a breakthrough into memory theories and led to research and theories that are now accepted today. It can be applied to real life as it suggests that we can only attempt to remember 7 chunks of information for a short time. This has been supported by studies as 7 chunks of random trigrams could be remembered as 7 chunks but not all in one go. Peterson and Peterson showed that information is encoded by the senses. They used a table of letters and found that participants could not recall the letters after being briefly shown them. The multi-store model does not explain cases such as Clive Wearing who has brain damage and extreme memory loss but can still remember how to play the piano.

6/12 marks

Commentary:

There is a reasonable description of the multi-store model of memory here. However, this student does not describe how information flows through the system. For information to go from sensory memory to STM, attention is needed. For information to go from STM to LTM, rehearsal is required. It can be helpful to draw a flow diagram in the exam. The description would also have benefited from a description of the capacity of each store. Information that is stored in the sensory memory is only stored for a fraction of a second whereas information in STM can last between 18 and 30 seconds. The capacity of LTM is unlimited and information can last a lifetime. There were a couple of errors in the description. The STM does not hold seven chunks of information but plus or minus 7 items or chunks. STM, information is held in acoustic form while in LTM it is held in semantic form. Information is encoded acoustically in STM not visually or semantically. Visual information is changed to sounds.

There is a reasonable attempt at an evaluation. There is a good comparison with the working memory model and Tulving's explanation of long-term memory. However, the Peterson and Peterson study has been mixed up with a different study. Peterson and Peterson (1959) investigated the duration of short-term memory using 3 consonant trigrams (e.g. MCR). Participants were asked to recall the trigrams after 3, 6, 9, 12, 15 or 18 seconds. They found that after a 3 second delay, 80% of the trigrams could be recalled but after an 18 second delay, less than 10% of the trigrams could be recalled. This study provides support for the limited duration of STM. The case study of Clive Wearing is not well explained. Clive Wearing has difficulty forming new long term memories but his short term memory is relatively normal. Therefore, the study supports the existence of a separate STM and LTM. However, the case study also highlights problems with the multi-store model of memory. Although Clive Wearing cannot remember a conversation he had 30 seconds ago, he can form new procedural memories. Procedural memory refers to the memory for performing certain kinds of tasks such as tying shoe laces or riding a bike. Procedural memories are usually automatically accessed. The multi-store model is too simplistic because it does not take into account different types of LTM such as procedural memory.

Chapter 3-Biological Psychology

You need to be able to describe what the biological approach is about

The biological approach is about how our genes, hormones and nervous system affect our behaviour.

You need to be able to describe how the central nervous system (CNS) and neurotransmitters affect human behaviour, including the structure and role of the neuron, the function of neurotransmitters and synaptic transmission

A Neuron: is a nerve cell. They send electrical messages, called nerve impulses, along their length.

A Synapse: is the tiny gap between two neurons. When a nerve impulse travels along a pre-synaptic neuron (a sending neuron), it triggers the nerve ending to release neurotransmitters across the synapse. The neurotransmitters diffuse across the synapse and bind with receptors on the post-synaptic neuron (the receiving neuron). This causes the post-synaptic neuron to transmit a nerve impulse.

Neurotransmitters: are chemical messengers that carry a signal across a synapse from one neuron to another. Examples of neurotransmitters are dopamine and serotonin.

Receptors: are sites on the post-synaptic neuron (the receiving neuron) that bind with neurotransmitters.

The central nervous system (CNS) consists of the brain and spinal cord. Sensory neurons are nerves that carry information from the sensory organs (such as our skin or ears) to the CNS. The brain processes this information and sends a message back to the motor neurons. These neurons then carry information to parts of our body to produce a response such as moving our leg. For example, if we see that the TV remote control is on the other side of the room, sensory neurons send this information to the CNS. The brain processes where the TV remote control is in the room and it sends a message to the parts of the body involved in movement.

Messages travel along neurons via nerve impulses (electrical impulses). The tiny gap between two neurons is called a synapse. When a nerve impulse travels along a pre-synaptic neuron (a sending neuron), it triggers the nerve ending to release neurotransmitters across the synapse. Neurotransmitters are chemicals messengers that carry a signal across a synapse from one neuron to another. Examples of neurotransmitters are dopamine and serotonin. The neurotransmitters diffuse across the synapse and bind with receptors on the post-synaptic neuron (the receiving neuron). This causes the post-synaptic neuron to transmit the message onwards via a nerve impulse.

Behaviour is strongly influenced by the nervous system. For example, high levels of serotonin, a neurotransmitter, make us feel happy. Low levels of serotonin are thought to reduce the ability to control aggressive impulses.

You need to be able to describe and evaluate the effect of recreational drugs on the transmission process in the central nervous system

Description:

Recreational drugs refer to substances that are taken for pleasure. These include legal drugs such as alcohol, caffeine and nicotine and illegal drugs such as cannabis, cocaine, heroin and ecstasy.

Nicotine affects the reward pathway in the brain. When a person smokes nicotine it binds to nicotinic receptors and excites the neuron leading to the release of dopamine into the synapse. Dopamine is related to feelings of pleasure so smoking nicotine can be addictive. However, increased dopamine in the synapse leads to over-stimulation of the dopamine receptors on the post-synaptic neuron and they can become damaged. When there are fewer dopamine receptors on the post-synaptic neuron, a person can become desensitised to the effects of dopamine. As a result, over time more nicotine is needed to produce the same pleasurable feelings. This is called tolerance and can lead to addiction. A person may need to take nicotine just to maintain the same levels of dopamine that were in the brain before they started taking it. Addiction is when person finds a drug so rewarding that they feel they must have it.

Cocaine also leads to an increase in dopamine and feelings of pleasure. It works by binding to the receptors on the pre-synaptic neuron stopping reuptake of dopamine. As a result, there is an excess of dopamine in the synapse. The post-synaptic dopamine receptors are over-stimulated by dopamine leading to feelings of pleasure. As with nicotine, the over-stimulation of the post-synaptic dopamine receptors can lead to damage and desensitisation. In turn, this causes tolerance and addiction.

Cannabis works by binding to cannabinoid receptors. This blocks the activity of the neurons in the hippocampus area of the brain. As the hippocampus is involved in memory, taking cannabis can lead to memory loss. Cannabis also leads to an increase in dopamine leading to feelings of pleasure. One explanation is that cannabis inhibits the GABA neurons, which then increases the activity of the dopamine neurons and releases more dopamine into the synapses in the reward pathway of the brain.

Evaluation:

Studies-Li et al. (2013) found that the brains of heroin addicts respond differently to heroin-related images compared to non-addicts. Heroin-related images can trigger activity in the PCC and other brain areas linked to rewards and cravings in heroin addicts. This study supports the theory that recreational drugs affect the dopamine reward system.

Explanation- The idea that recreational drugs affect dopamine levels in the reward area of the brain, leading to feelings of pleasure is supported by people's experiences of taking the drugs. This gives the theory face validity. Research also shows that people develop a tolerance to drugs over time and that they can become addicted. This supports the idea of the desensitising effect of recreational drugs.

However, it may be too simplistic to say that recreational drugs affect just dopamine levels in the brain and one reward pathway as the brain is complex.

Application to real life-Understanding how recreational drugs work can help health professionals in preventing drug use and helping those who are already drug users.

You need to be able to describe and evaluate how the structure of the brain, different brain areas (e.g. pre-frontal cortex) and brain functioning can be used to explain aggression as a human behaviour

Description:

The prefrontal cortex is involved in regulating emotions and behaviour. If a person's prefrontal cortex is damaged or dysfunctioning, they may not be able to regulate their anger and are more likely to show aggressive behaviour.

The limbic system is also associated with aggressive behaviour. It includes the amygdala and hypothalamus. The amygdala is believed to play an important role in aggression and the hypothalamus is involved in regulating our arousal levels (the fight or flight response).

Evaluation:

Studies- Phineas Gage was a railway worker whose brain was damaged in a railway accident. After the accident, he became much more aggressive. This suggests that certain parts of the brain are linked to aggression. However, this is a unique study and it is difficult to generalise the findings.

Bard (1940) lesioned the brains of cats and found that the hypothalamus and amygdala were responsible for aggression.
However, there are problems with generalising animal research to humans as humans are more complex. For example, the prefrontal cortex in animals is smaller than in humans.

Swantje et al. (2012) found that women with smaller amygdalas were more likely to have higher aggression scores. This supports the idea that the amygdala plays an important role in aggression.

Explanation-The idea that brain structure affects aggression has scientific credibility as brain scans (e.g. PET, MRI) show differences in brain activity in those who are particularly prone to aggression.

Application to real life-Understanding how brain structure affects aggression can be helpful in criminal cases. For example, Raine et al. found that murderers who were pleading not guilty due to reasons of insanity did have different levels of activity in the brain compared to non-murderers.

You need to be able to describe and evaluate the role of evolution and natural selection to explain behaviour, including aggression

Description:

Evolutionary psychology focuses on how humans have adapted to show certain behaviours through the process of natural selection. The theory of natural selection says that traits that aid our survival are more likely to be passed on through our genes.

For example, aggressive behaviour may have been an important behaviour in ensuring our survival amongst our ancestors so these traits are more likely to be passed down the generations. Females may have selected males who were more aggressive to provide greater protection for them and their offspring. Male aggression may have been driven by the desire to find a suitable partner. Aggression can be used to assert dominance and power amongst same sex rivals and females are said to be attracted to dominant and powerful men.

Evolutionary psychology can also explain the aggression as a response to sexual jealousy. People may behave aggressively out of the desire to keep their mate. For example, a person may be jealous of their partner flirting with a rival and respond with aggression. Some research suggests that men are more likely than women to use aggression against a rival.

Evaluation:

Studies-Buss and Shackleton (1997) found that men would try to intimidate other males if they felt their relationship was threatened. This supports the idea that men may use aggression to maintain their relationships with women and to ensure their genes are passed on.
Dobash and Dobash (1984) found that sexual jealousy could lead to violence against women. This suggests that male aggression may be a trait that has evolved to ensure survival of their genes.

Explanation-A limitation of the evolutionary explanation of aggression is that it does not explain why some people who are provoked will respond with aggression whereas others will not. Aggression may also be counter-productive in ensuring a person's survival. If a person is aggressive and gets into fights with other people, their behaviour may decrease their chance of survival.

Application to real life-If women notice mate retention strategies in their partners such as jealousy when they speak to other men, they may be at risk of violence and should be cautious about continuing the relationship.

You need to be able to describe and evaluate Freud's psychodynamic explanation of the personality (id, ego, superego), the importance of the unconscious, and catharsis

Freud suggested that there are three aspects to the personality, the id, ego and superego. The **id** is the part of the personality that is present from birth. It consists of our instincts and desires. As the id wants instant wish fulfilment, it is said to operate on the pleasure principle. From birth onwards, the **ego** develops. The job of this part of the personality is to balance the demands of the id and superego. For this reason, it is said to operate on the reality principle. The **superego** is the part of the personality that develops at around age 6. It represents our conscience and is said to operate on the morality principle.

The ego sometimes finds it difficult to respond to the id's drives whilst balancing the demands of the superego. As a result, it may repress unacceptable thoughts in the unconscious mind. The unconscious is the part of the mind that we cannot access. It holds hidden fears, anxieties and conflicts that our ego had difficulties dealing with. For example, an attraction to our best friend's boyfriend or girlfriend may be hidden in our unconscious to stop us feeling guilty.

Aggression is one of our drives. Freud believed that we all have a death instinct (thanatos), which is the desire to go back to before being born and a life instinct (eros), which is the desire to live. Aggression allows us to release frustration and move forward with life. Freud believed that frustration can occur when we can't get something that we desire or when we can't avoid pain. We may show aggression when our id is frustrated by the demands of our superego.

Catharsis refers to the release of emotions such as aggression. Psychodynamic theorists argue that pent up aggression can be released through watching violent TV or playing violent computer games. Playing sport may also release aggression and can be cathartic.

Evaluation:

Studies-Research suggests that when people react in an aggressive way to a frustrating situation, although they may experience less tension at first, it makes them more aggressive later. This contradicts the concept of catharsis. Verona and Sullivan (2008) found that participants who were allowed to press a 'shock' button after being annoyed by a confederate, had a reduced heart rate at first compared to a participants who pressed a 'non-shock' button but then they displayed more aggression later to a blast of hot air. Research by Bandura has found that watching aggressive media can make children more aggressive not less, which contradicts the idea of catharsis.

Explanation-The idea that we can experience aggression as a result of unmet desires has face validity.

Application to real life-Psychoanalysis is a therapy that has developed out of Freud's ideas about unconscious conflicts. This therapy has been used to help people with mental health problems.

You need to be able to compare the biological explanation of aggression with the psychodynamic explanation of aggression

Both the psychodynamic and biological approaches look at how internal factors are involved in aggression. The psychodynamic approach says that aggression occurs due to internal drives and unconscious conflicts whereas the biological approach says that aggression occurs due internal structures such as the amygdala.

There is more scientific evidence for biological explanation of aggression than the psychodynamic explanation. Brain scans such as PET and MRI scans provide evidence for certain physical structures being involved in aggression. In contrast, the psychodynamic approach based its theories on evidence from case studies of unique people. These case studies are not generalisable to the wider population.

Some biological evidence supports the psychodynamic approach. Brain scans show that the limbic system is involved in emotions and aggression. This relates to Freud's theory that our unconscious desires are related to aggression.

You need to be able to describe and evaluate the role of hormones (e.g. testosterone) to explain human behaviour such as aggression

Description:

Hormones are chemical substances that are produced by glands in the body. They travel in the blood to target organs. They are similar to neurotransmitters in terms of carrying messages but they move more slowly. For example, the adrenal glands produce the hormone adrenaline, which moves to target organs such as the heart. Heart rate increases to prepare the body for fight or flight. The testes produce the hormone testosterone, which moves to the male reproductive organs and is needed to produce sperm. It also causes changes at puberty in males such as facial hair, a deep voice and increased aggression. Males often have raised testosterone levels, when aggressive behaviour is shown. Animals that have been injected with testosterone show increased aggression and animals that have had their testes removed display decreased aggression. This supports the link between testosterone and aggression.

Evaluation:

Studies- Brook et al (2001) conducted a meta-analysis of 45 studies and found a mean correlation of + 0.14 between testosterone and aggression. However, much of the research is correlational and cannot establish cause and effect. On the other hand, Bain et al (1987) found no significant differences in testosterone levels in men convicted of violent compared to men convicted of non-violent crimes. Kreuz and Rose (1972) also found no difference in testosterone levels in a group of 21 prisoners who had been classified as violent and non-violent.

Explanation-It is difficult to establish whether testosterone is directly linked to aggression. Higher levels of testosterone may be related to dominant behaviour rather than aggression.

Application to real life-If testosterone levels are linked to violent behaviour, then this has implications for the way we treat violent offenders.

You need to be able to describe and evaluate whether case studies of brain-damaged patients can be used to explain individual differences in behaviour

Description:

Phineas Gage was a railway worker who ended up with an iron rod through his head as a result of an explosion. The rod went through the top of his head and out of the left frontal lobe of his brain. Prior to the accident, he was a quiet, polite man but after the accident he became rude and aggressive. This case study suggests that aggression may be linked to frontal lobe.

Evaluation:

We need to be careful about generalising from case studies of unique individuals to the wider population. The effect of damage to the frontal lobe in Phineas Gage may not be the same in other people.

You need to be able to describe correlational research in psychology. You need to be able to describe types of correlation: positive, negative and including the use of scatter diagrams.

Correlational studies look for a relationship between two variables (called co-variables). For example, it may look for a relationship between the number of hours of violent TV watched and levels of aggression. An example of a positive correlation is: the more hours of violent TV watched, the more aggressive people are. An example of a negative correlation is: the more hours of violent computer games played, the less helpful people are.

Positive correlations occur when two variables rise together. An example would be the higher the happiness rating, the longer the relationship.

Negative correlations occur when one variable rises and the other falls. For example, the higher the age, the lower the number of items recalled from a list.

A correlation coefficient refers to a number between -1 and +1 and states how strong a correlation is. If the number is close to +1 then there is a positive correlation. If the number is close to -1 then there is a negative correlation. If the number is close to 0 then the variables are uncorrelated. For example, +0.9 refers to a strong positive correlation, 0 is no correlation and -0.2 is a weak negative correlation.

Evaluation:

Correlational studies can demonstrate a relationship between two variables, which was not noticed before. They can also be used to look for relationships between variables that cannot be investigated by other means. For example, researchers can look to see whether there is a relationship between parents having low expectations of their children and the children's later academic performance. Manipulating such variables would be unethical. However, correlational studies cannot establish cause and effect relationships. A third factor may affect both variables under investigation. For example, although a correlational study might show a relationship between the number of hours of violent TV watched and levels of aggression, we cannot be certain that the violent TV programmes led to the aggression. It may be that children who watch violent TV programmes are naturally more aggressive and so seek such programmes out.

Scatter diagrams can be used to display data from correlational studies.

A positive correlation

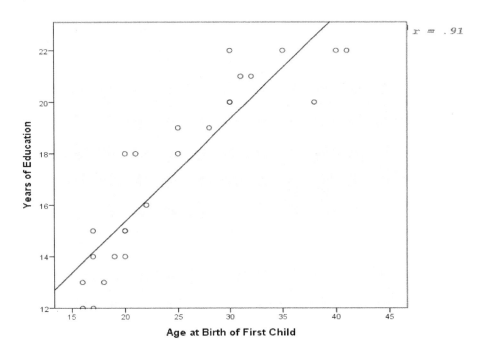

A negative correlation

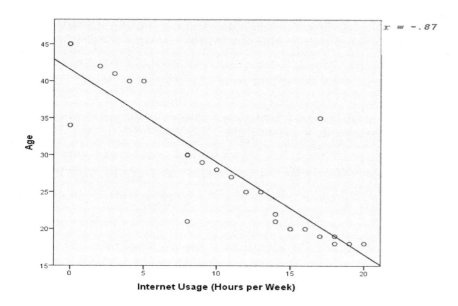

No correlation

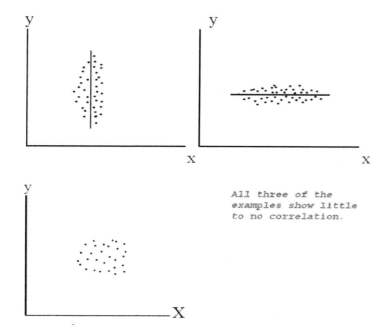

All three of the
examples show little
to no correlation.

You need to be able to understand the use of alternate, experimental and null hypotheses

An experimental hypothesis predicts what change(s) will take place in the dependent variable (DV) when the independent variable (IV) is manipulated in an experiment.

A two-tailed (non-directional) hypothesis predicts that there will be a change in the DV when the IV is manipulated.
e.g. There will be a difference in the number of words recalled when words are processed semantically compared to when they are processed phonetically.

A one-tailed (directional) hypothesis predicts in which direction the change will take place.
e.g. There will be more words recalled when they are processed semantically compared to when they are processed phonetically.

The null hypothesis states that there will be no changes due to the manipulation of the IV.
e.g. There will be no difference in the number of words recalled when processed semantically or phonetically.

Operationalisation: A hypothesis is operationalised when it is clear what is being manipulated and what is being measured. The dependent variable should refer to a numerical value. For example, if you are measuring recall, you might say number of words recalled.

The term 'alternative hypothesis' is used when predicting what will happen for a study that is not an experiment, for example, a correlational study.
A non-directional (two-tailed) alternative hypothesis predicts that there will be a relationship between two variables. For example, there will be a relationship between the hours of computer games played and empathy scores.
A directional (one-tailed) alternative hypothesis for a correlation would predict whether there will be a positive or negative relationship between two variables. For example, the more hours of computer games played, the lower the score for empathy.
Null hypothesis: There will be no relationship between the number of hours of computer games played and empathy scores.

You need to understand the use of control group

It is important to have a control group in an experiment to compare the experimental group against. For example, if you want to measure the effectiveness of a treatment on a group of patients, you should give a control group a placebo treatment and compare the effects. If you want to measure the effects of giving a cue on memory on a group of participants, then you should have a control group who do not receive a cue.

You need to understand the use random assignment

In order to ensure that the experimental and control groups in a psychology experiment are chosen without bias, random assignment is used. This means that each participant has an equal chance of being assigned to a particular group. Researchers may draw names out of a hat, pick straws or use a computer system to randomly decide which participants are placed in a certain group.

You need to be able to give reasons for using the Spearman's Rho statistical test (A2 knowledge)

Spearman's Rho is used when you have a correlational design and the level of data is ordinal.

The observed value needs to be higher than the critical value for the null hypothesis to be rejected (i.e. to accept the alternative hypothesis).

You need to be able to describe and evaluate the following brain-scanning techniques: CAT, PET and fMRI

CAT (Computerised Axial Tomography) scans

CAT scans use x-rays to produce a series of pictures showing slices of tissue in the brain. The pictures can then be combined to build up a 3D image of the brain. CAT scans can highlight brain damage or the position of tumours in the brain.

Evaluation: CAT scans are easy to carry out and can give accurate images of the brain although they are unable to show brain activity. X-rays can be harmful so CAT scans are only done when there are clear benefits.

Positron emission tomography (PET)

PET scans can be used to produce 3D computer-generated images of the brain. A radioactive substance, called a tracer, is injected into the bloodstream and travels to the brain. As the tracer breaks down it releases energy waves called gamma rays, which are picked up by the PET scanner. More active areas of the brain break down the radioactive substance more quickly. Areas of high activity in the brain produce more gamma rays and this is shown up in red and yellow on the 3D computer image. Areas of low activity are shown in blue and darker colours on the 3D computer image. Psychologists can use PET scanning to find out which parts of the brain are active when performing certain tasks such as a language or spatial task. Raine et al. used PET scans to compare the brain activity of murderers and non-murderers.

Evaluation: PET scans are able to highlight areas of brain activity and can be used to identify parts of the brain that are not functioning normally. However, they require a patient to be injected with a radioactive substance, which although low risk could have potentially harmful effects if done too many times.

fMRI (Functional Magnetic Resonance Imaging)

More active areas of the brain use more oxygen. Our blood carries oxygen so when a specific part of the brain is active, blood flow increases to that area. fMRI works by detecting changes in blood oxygenation and flow in order to measure brain activity. fMRI scans have been used to investigate learning, emotion and memory.

The fMRI scanner is able to detect changes in blood oxygenation and flow because it contains a powerful electromagnet. The magnetic properties of blood differ depending on whether it is oxygenated or deoxygenated. More active areas of the brain receive more oxygenated blood. The fMRI scanner picks up on this.

Evaluation: fMRI scans are useful at showing brain activity when a person is asked to carry out different tasks. They are also non-invasive and do not involve injecting someone with a radioactive substance or exposing them to potentially harmful x-rays. On the other hand, as a strong magnetic field is used, people with pacemakers or metal implants cannot have fMRI scans. Some people can also find the scanners claustrophobic.

You need to be able to describe and evaluate the use of brain scanning techniques to investigate human behaviour e.g. aggression

Bufkin and Luttrell (2005) reviewed 17 neuroimaging studies and found that the prefrontal and medial temporal regions are associated with aggressive behaviour and impulsive acts. Evaluation:

Brain scans might show that certain aggressive traits correlate with a particular brain area but they cannot prove causation. It may be that a third factor is involved such as drug abuse or brain trauma. Furthermore, many brain areas involved in aggression have multiple functions.

You need to be able to describe and evaluate twin studies and give an example of one.

Description:

MZ twins are compared to each other to see whether they share the same characteristics. Concordance rates are used to see the similarity between the twins for a certain characteristic such as IQ, personality or mental disorder. For example, Gottesman (1991) found that if one MZ twin has schizophrenia, there is a 48% chance (0.48 concordance) that the other twin will have it too.
In a twin study, DZ twins are also compared to each other to see what the concordance rates are for certain characteristics in them. For example, Gottesman found that if one DZ twin has schizophrenia, there is a 17% chance (0.17 concordance) that the other one will have it too.
MZ twins share 100% of their genes whereas DZ twins only share 50% of their genes. Therefore, if MZ twins have a higher concordance rate than DZ twins for a certain characteristic such as schizophrenia, this suggests that genes are important in determining this characteristic.

Evaluation:

An assumption with twin studies is that MZ twins and DZ twins share similar environments and the only difference between MZ twins and DZ twins is that MZ twins share 100% of their genes whereas DZ twins share 50% of their genes. However, this assumption can be questioned. MZ twins are often treated more similarly than DZ twins, for example, they are often dressed the same and people may respond to them in similar ways because they look the same. Therefore, it may be the more similar experiences of MZ twins rather than genes, which leads to them having higher concordance rates for IQ, personality characteristics and mental disorders. Studying separated twins make it easier to assess the influence of genes versus environment. However, separated twins may still have shared the same environment for a certain amount of time before separation. Another problem with twin studies is that most people are not twins so it is hard to generalise from twins to the wider population.

An example of a twin study is Lacourse et al. (2014)

Description:

Aim-To see whether genetic factors affect physical aggression in young children.
Procedure-Researchers used 254 MZ twins and 413 DZ twins born between 1995 and 1998 who were part of the Quebec Newborn Twin Study. Mothers were asked to rate their twins on physical aggression at 20,32 and 50 months using a questionnaire with a three point scale – 0 = never; 1 = sometimes; 3 = often for frequency of: hitting / biting / kicking; fighting and attacking another person.
Results-The correlation between MZ twins for physical aggression was 0.7 compared to 0.4 for DZ twins.
Conclusion-Genes play an important role in children's physical aggression.

Evaluation:

Generalisability-The study looked at twins so the findings are difficult to generalise to non-twins.

Reliability-The children were rated for aggression by their mothers only so the study lacks inter-rater reliability.

Application to real life-The study helps us to understand the role of genes in aggression and could be used to identify those children at risk of aggression.

Validity-The mothers of MZ twins may have rated their children with more similar levels of aggression than mothers of DZ twins.

Ethics-Asking mothers to rate their children for aggression could potentially cause problems in their relationships with their children.

You need to be able to describe and evaluate adoption studies and give an example of one.

Description:

Children who have been adopted are compared to their biological parents and adoptive parents for a certain characteristic. If there is greater similarity between the child and their biological parents, this suggests that genes are important for this characteristic. Heston found that 10% of adopted children whose biological mothers had schizophrenia went on to develop it themselves compared to none in the control group. Heston's study suggests a genetic basis for schizophrenia.

Evaluation:

A problem with adoption studies is that adoption agencies usually try to place children in families that are similar to the biological family. Therefore, it is difficult to separate out the influence of genes and the environment. Furthermore, most people are not adopted so it is hard to generalise findings from adoptees to the wider population.

An example of an adoption study: Mednick et al. (2008)

Description:

Aim-To see whether there is an effect of genes on criminality amongst adoptees.

Procedure-14,427 people who had been adopted between 1924 and 1947 in Denmark were studied. The court conviction histories of the adoptees, their biological mothers and fathers and their adoptive mothers and fathers were examined. The researchers used the court convictions to determine the individual's criminal involvement and the occupation was used to determine the person's socioeconomic status.

Results-If neither the biological or adoptive parents of the adoptee had a criminal conviction, then only 13.5% of the adoptees had a conviction themselves. If the adoptive parents had a conviction but the biological parents did not, then 14.7% of the adoptees had a conviction. In contrast, if the biological parents had a conviction, 20% of the adoptees had a conviction. The rate of convictions amongst male adoptees whose biological parents had three or more convictions, was three times that of those adoptees whose biological parents did not have a criminal conviction.

Conclusion-Genes do play a role in criminality.

Evaluation:

Generalisability-It is hard to generalise from adoptees to the wider population as most people are not adopted.

Reliability-Criminal convictions are an objective measure of criminality and this makes the study more replicable and reliable. Cloninger and Gottesman (1987) carried out a similar study and found similar results. This suggests that the findings of this study are reliable.

Application to real life-If genes predispose certain individuals to criminality, then those at risk can be identified and preventative measures can be used.

Validity-It can be hard to separate out the effects of genes and environment. Mednick points out that the biological mothers of the adoptees may not have given their developing baby an ideal environment in the womb, which may have made them more susceptible to criminality.

Ethics-Looking at the court convictions of adoptees and their families may be seen as intrusion on privacy.

Note: Genes are units of information that pass on genetic traits such as personality and intelligence from parents to offspring. 50% of our genes come from our mother and 50% of our genes come from our father. Genes are found in our chromosomes. Chromosomes consist of long strands of DNA (deoxyribonucleic acid).

You need to understand that the biological approach mainly supports the nature side of the nature-nurture debate

The biological approach mainly supports the nature side of the debate. It says that we are born with certain genes and a nervous system that affect the way we think, feel and behave. However, the biological approach accepts that our environment, for example, our diet can affect our development.

Note: The learning approach mainly supports the nurture side of the nature-nurture debate. It says that most of our behaviour is learnt from our environment through operant conditioning, classical conditioning and social learning theory. However, it accepts that we are born with some natural behaviours such as automatic reflexes.

The psychodynamic approach supports the nature and nurture side of debate. It supports the nature side of the debate because it says we are born with certain drives and instincts. On the other hand, it supports the nurture side of the debate because it says our experiences in childhood, our environment, affect us later in life.

You need to be able to describe and evaluate the classic study: Raine et al. (1997) 'Brain abnormalities in murderers indicated by positron emission tomography'

Description:

Aim-To see if murderers who plead not guilty by reason of insanity (NGRI) have localised brain impairments.

Procedure-The experimental group consisted of 41 people (39 men and 2 women) who had been charged with murder or manslaughter in California, USA and were in custody.

They were chosen because they had reasons for pleading not guilty by reason of insanity (NGRI). Reasons included schizophrenia, head injury, substance abuse and learning disabilities. They were matched with a control group of non-murderers based on age and sex. All the participants were asked to carry out a task whilst in a PET scanner.

Results-The PET scans showed that the 41 murderers had lower activity in the prefrontal cortex, parietal cortex and corpus callosum than the non-murderers. They also had higher activity in the occipital lobe. In addition, there were abnormal imbalances of activity in the amygdala, thalamus and medial temporal gyrus including the hippocampus.

Conclusion-Brain dysfunction may predispose a person to violence. Damage to the prefrontal cortex is associated with impulsivity, loss of self-control and the inability to modify behaviour. An imbalance of activity in the amygdala , thalamus and hippocampus could lead to increased aggression.

Note: The sample consisted of people who had been charged with murder and manslaughter but they are all called murderers for ease of reference in this study.

Evaluation:

Generalisability-The study only looked at brain differences in NGRIs so it is difficult to generalise the findings to other types of violent offenders.

Reliability-The researchers tried to control many of the variables. For example, the murderers were carefully matched with a control group based on age and sex. In addition, a PET scan was carried out on all the participants, which is a scientific and objective way of measuring brain activity. This means that the study is replicable and can be tested for reliability.

Application to real life-The study has important implications for the type of sentencing given to NGRIs and to what degree they are responsible for their actions.

Validity-The researchers made inferences from the brain scans and so the results need to be treated with caution.

The PET scan involved participants carrying out a task that had no relation to violence so it is difficult to generalise brain activity during the task to brain activity during a violent act. This questions the validity of the findings.

It is also difficult to establish cause and effect in this study. Although differences in brain activity were found between the murderers and the non-murderers, we cannot be certain that the murderers had these differences before they carried out the murder. It is possible that changes in brain activity occurred as a consequence of carrying out their crime. Furthermore, environmental factors such as a poor home life may have led to the differences in brain activity and the violent behaviour.

Ethics- The research is socially sensitive because it suggests that violent behaviour is biologically determined.

You need to be able to describe and evaluate one contemporary study. For example, Brendgen et al. (2005) 'Examining genetic and environmental effects on social aggression: A study of 6-year-old twins'

Description:

Aim-To look at the relationship between genetic and environmental factors on social and physical aggression.

Procedure-234 six-year old Canadian twins were used from an ongoing longitudinal study (Quebec Newborn Twin Study). Teachers rated the children's levels of physical and social aggression using questionnaires. Indicators of social aggression were the extent to which the children might try to socially exclude another child or spread rumours. The social aggression questions included: to what extent the child 'tries to make other dislike a child', 'becomes friends with another child for revenge' and 'says bad things or spreads nasty rumours about another child'. The physical aggression questions included: to what extent 'the child gets into fights', 'physically attacks others' and 'hits, bites or kicks others'. Responses were given on a 3-point scale (5 never, 15 sometimes, 25 often). For each child, a total social aggression score and total physical aggression score were calculated. Peer ratings of the children's social and physical aggression were also obtained. This was carried out by giving booklets of photographs of all the children in particular class to them. The children were then asked to circle the faces of children who fitted a certain characteristic. The two behavioural descriptors for social aggression were 'tells others not to play with a child' and 'tells mean secrets about another child'. The two behavioural descriptors for physical aggression were 'gets into fights' and 'hits, bites or kicks others'. The total number of nominations for social and physical aggression were then calculated for the twins in the classes. Taking into account different class sizes, a total score for social and physical aggression was worked out.

Results-According to teachers, boys were more physically aggressive than girls but girls were more socially aggressive than boys. However, according to peer ratings, boys were more physically and more socially aggressive than girls. The correlation between the teacher and peer ratings were moderate for physical and social aggression.
The correlations for physical aggression in the MZ twins were almost twice as high as the DZ twins. This suggests that genetic factors play an important role in physical aggression. In contrast, the correlations for social aggression were similar in MZ and DZ twins, which suggests that environmental factors play a greater role in social aggression than genetic factors.

Conclusion-50% to 60% of individual differences in physical aggression in related to genes and the rest to environmental factors. Social aggression is more influenced by environmental factors.

Evaluation:

Generalisability-The study focused on twins, who are not representative of the wider population. It also focused on a specific age group and other age groups may demonstrate their aggression differently. For example, older children may display more social aggression and less physical aggression.

Reliability-The teachers rated the children using a questionnaire with a 3-point scale. The children rated their peers by circling photos of children from a booklet that fitted behavioural descriptions. Therefore, the procedure is replicable and can be tested for reliability.

Application to real life- The study suggests that it is important to target and reduce physical aggression in young children as this can help prevent the development of social aggression later on.

Validity-The study used teacher and peer ratings, which gives the findings greater validity especially as there was moderate concordance between the ratings for social and physical aggression for both groups.

Ethics-Asking children to rate their peers on physical and social aggression could potentially cause conflict between the children.

An alternative contemporary study is: Li et al. (2013) 'Abnormal function of the posterior cingulate cortex in heroin addicted users during resting state and drug-cue stimulation task'

Description:

Aim-To see whether the activation of the posterior cingulate cortex (PCC) of heroin addicts is different to non-addicts when shown drug-related images. To investigate the connectivity between the PCC and different areas of the brain linked to addiction such as the bilateral insula and the bilateral dorsal striatum.

Procedure-14 male detoxed, chronic heroin users were matched with 15 healthy participants based on age and gender. Both groups were giving an fMRI scan when resting. They were also given an fMRI scan during a cue-related task. This task involved 48 pictures, half of which were related to heroin and half of which were neutral. The participants' cravings were measured before and after the images.

Results-There was a significant difference in brain activity between the two groups. The activation of the PCC was greater in the heroin users compared to the non-addicts when shown the heroin-related images. The connectivity between the PCC and bilateral insula and bilateral dorsal striatum was greater in the heroin users as well. The correlation between activity in the PCC and bilateral insula was r=0.60. The correlation between activity in the PCC and the bilateral dorsal stratum was r=0.58.

Conclusion-The brains of heroin addicts respond differently to heroin-related images compared to non-addicts. Heroin-related images can trigger activity in the PCC and other brain areas linked to rewards and cravings in heroin addicts.

Note: The PCC is involved in autobiographical memories and what we pay attention to emotionally. Therefore, if drug addicts looks at heroin-related images, this may trigger their memories of the heroin use and the emotional cravings.

The bilateral insula is related to our emotions in social situations.

The bilateral dorsal striatum is a critical part of the dopamine reward system, which is activated when people take drugs such as heroin.

Evaluation:

Generalisability-It is hard to generalise from this small, all male sample to the wider population.

Reliability-The heroin addicts were well-matched with a control group of healthy participants, which makes the study more reliable. The fMRI scans measured brain activity in the resting state and when the participants were shown various images under controlled conditions, which makes the study more replicable and reliable.

Application to real life-Understanding how drug addicts' brains respond to drug-related cues could help in their treatment. Recovering drug addicts should be encouraged to avoid any cues that might trigger their desire for the drugs.

Validity-fMRI has been shown to be a good technique for measuring brain activity, which makes the study more valid.

Ethics-The heroin addicts were shown heroin related images and this might have triggered a desire to use the drug, which is unethical.

You need to be able to describe one key question in the biological approach. For example, 'What are the implications for society if aggression is found to be caused by nature not nurture?'

If a person is born to be aggressive due to their genes, hormones, neurotransmitters, brain structure or central nervous system then it could be argued that they don't have a choice in behaving aggressively. This has implications for society. On the other hand, if a person's environment and experiences affect whether they are aggressive or not, then it could be argued that they have a choice whether to behave aggressively or not. A person who has learnt aggression from their environment can also unlearn that behaviour or avoid situations that cause it. In contrast, if aggression stems from biological factors, it is harder to change and it could be argued that people should not be blamed or punished for it. Being criminalised or put in prison for behaviour that is outside a person's control could be considered unfair and unethical.
Applications of concepts and ideas

Brendgen et al. (2005) found that 50% to 60% of individual differences in physical aggression related to genes. This study suggests that certain individuals may be predisposed to showing aggression.

Raine et al. (1997) found differences in brain activity between murderers and non-murderers. Brain dysfunction may predispose a person to violence. Damage to the prefrontal cortex is associated with impulsivity, loss of self-control and the inability to modify behaviour. An imbalance of activity in the amygdala, thalamus and hippocampus could lead to increased aggression.

Phineas Gage was a railway worker whose brain was damaged in a railway accident. After the accident, he became much more aggressive. This suggests that certain parts of the brain are linked to aggression. However, this is a unique study and it is difficult to generalise the findings.

Bard (1940) lesioned the brains of cats and found that the hypothalamus and amygdala were responsible for aggression. However, there are problems with generalising animal research to humans as humans are more complex. For example, the prefrontal cortex in animals is smaller than in humans.

Swantje et al. (2012) found that women with smaller amygdalas were more likely to have higher aggression scores. This supports the idea that the amygdala plays an important role in aggression.

We may have evolved to show aggression. For example, aggressive behaviour may have been an important behaviour in ensuring our survival amongst our ancestors so these traits are more likely to be passed down the generations. Females may have selected males who were more aggressive to provide greater protection for them and their offspring. Male aggression may have been driven by the desire to find a suitable partner. Buss and Shackleton (1997) found that men would try to intimidate other males if they felt their relationship was threatened. This supports the idea that men may use aggression to maintain their relationships with women and to ensure their genes are passed on.

Brook et al (2001) conducted a meta-analysis of 45 studies and found a mean correlation of + 0.14 between testosterone and aggression. However, much of the research is correlational and cannot establish cause and effect. Higher levels of testosterone may be related to dominant behaviour rather than aggression.

McDermott et al. (2009) found that people with a particular version of the MAOA gene (the 'warrior gene'), which shows low activity were more likely to be aggressive and impulsive especially if they have high levels of testosterone too.

Research which show that aggression is linked to differences in genes, brain functioning or hormones suggest that people who display aggression may not be in control of their behaviour and so cannot be blamed for it. If a person's biology is leading to their aggressive behaviour, then a key question is should they be criminalised or punished for it?

You need to be able to describe a practical you carried out in the biological approach. Example practical: To see whether there is a correlation between brain sex and aggression

Aim: To see whether there is a correlation between brain sex and aggression

Alternative directional hypothesis: The higher the male brain score, the high the aggression score.

Null hypothesis: There will be no relationship between male brain score and aggression score.

Procedure: Participants were briefed about the aims of the study and what they would be asked to do at the beginning. An opportunity sample of 10 female participants between 16-17 years old was used. They were asked to complete an online quiz on brain sex in a silent computer room. Their percentage score for having a male brain was recorded. They were then asked to complete a questionnaire which measures aggression levels. Participants were asked to note down their aggression scores and male brain scores on a sheet of paper without their name on and to fold it to be collected in to ensure anonymity. A Spearman's rho statistical test was carried out on the data to see whether there was a relationship between the male brain score and aggression score. Participants were debriefed at the end. They were given the right to withdraw throughout.

Results:

Participant number	Male brain score (A)	Aggression score (B)	Rank A	Rank B	d=Rank A- Rank B	d^2
1	56	66	9	4	5	25
2	75	70	3	2	1	1
3	45	40	10	10	0	0
4	71	60	4	7	3	9
5	62	65	6	5	1	1
6	64	56	5	9	4	16
7	58	59	8	8	0	0
8	80	77	1	1	0	0
9	76	67	2	3	1	1
10	61	63	7	6	1	1

d=the difference between the ranks
d^2= the difference between the ranks squared

The formula for Spearman's rho is:

$$r_s = 1 - \frac{6\sum d^2}{n(n^2 - 1)}$$

Step 1: Work out the sum of d^2. Note the symbol, $\sum$, means 'sum of'.

$\sum d^2 = 25+1+9+1+16+1+1=54$

Step 2: We then substitute this into the main equation with the other information. Remember n=10 as there were 10 participants.
$r^s = 1 - 6 \sum d_i^2 / n (n^2-1)$
$r^s = 1 - 6 \times 54/10(10^2-1)$
$r^s = 1 - (324/990)$
$r^s = 1 - 0.33$
$r^s = 0.67$

The r^s value of 0.67 indicates a strong positive relationship between the male brain score and aggression. That is, the higher you ranked for male brain score, the higher you ranked in aggression.

Note: The Spearman correlation coefficient, r_s, can take values from +1 to -1. A r_s of +1 indicates a perfect positive correlation, a r_s of zero indicates no relationship and a r_s of -1 indicates a perfect negative correlation. The closer r_s is to zero, the weaker the relationship between the co-variables.

You need to be able to compare the observed value of r^s with the critical value. To find the critical value in a critical values table, you need to look for n=10 as there were 10 participants and $p \leq 0.05$. For Spearman's rho, the observed value of r^s need to be bigger than the critical value for the result to be significant.

Conclusion: There is a relationship between male brain score and aggression score.

Evaluation:

Generalisability-An opportunity sample of 10 female students was used. As only females were used, the sample is not representative of the wider population.

Reliability-As questionnaires were used to measure brain sex and aggression, it is possible to replicate the procedure. This makes the study more reliable. However, on a different day, participants might have answered the questions differently.

Application to real life-Understanding how brain sex affects aggression, could lead to greater understanding of the causes of aggressive behaviour.

Validity-The online brain sex quiz may have lacked validity. The questions asked may not have been a true reflection of brain sex. The questionnaire measuring aggression may not have reflected real life aggression and participants may have given socially desirable answers. Correlational studies cannot establish cause and effect relationships. There may be other factors involved affecting both co-variables.

Ethics-Participants may have felt distressed if they scored highly for aggression and may have felt uncomfortable writing their scores down.

You need to be able to discuss ethical issues in biological psychology

Animals have been used to investigate biological aspects of behaviour. However, there are ethical issues in using animals in research. For example, Rechstaffen et al (1983) aimed to see the effects of sleep deprivation on rats. In this laboratory experiment, researchers placed rats on a disc above a bucket of water. When the rats fell asleep the disc would rotate and in order to not fall into the water, the rats had to stay awake and walk on the disc. The rats eventually died after severe sleep deprivation. It is questionable whether there is any clear benefit to this research and it certainly caused the rats to suffer distress and die. One ethical guideline for animal research says that experimenters should avoid or minimise stress and suffering for all living animals, which was not done in this study.

There are ethical issues with some studies using humans as well. For example, in Li et al.'s study, the heroin addicts were shown heroin related images and this might have triggered a desire to use the drug, which is unethical. PET scans have been used to highlight areas of brain activity and to identify parts of the brain that are not functioning normally. However, they require a patient to be injected with a radioactive substance, which although low risk could have potentially harmful effects if done too many times.

You need to be able to discuss practical issues in the design and implementation of research in biological psychology

Twin and adoption studies have been used in biological psychological to establish a genetic basis for behaviour. An assumption with twin studies is that MZ twins and DZ twins share similar environments and the only difference between MZ twins and DZ twins is that MZ twins share 100% of their genes whereas DZ twins share 50% of their genes. However, this assumption can be questioned. MZ twins are often treated more similarly than DZ twins, for example, they are often dressed the same and people may respond to them in similar ways because they look the same. Therefore, it may be the more similar experiences of MZ twins rather than genes, which leads to them having higher concordance rates for IQ, personality characteristics and mental disorders. Studying separated twins makes it easier to assess the influence of genes versus environment. However, separated twins may still have shared the same environment for a certain amount of time before separation. Another problem with twin studies is that most people are not twins so it is hard to generalise from twins to the wider population.

A problem with adoption studies is that adoption agencies usually try to place children in families that are similar to the biological family. Therefore, it is difficult to separate out the influence of genes and the environment. Furthermore, most people are not adopted so it is hard to generalise findings from adoptees to the wider population.

Brains scans are used in biological psychology to look at the function of different brain regions. They are considered to be a scientific method but researchers still have to make inferences about what certain brain regions are used for and so the results need to be treated with caution. In Raine et al.'s study, differences in brain activity were found between the murderers and the non-murderers but we cannot be certain that the murderers had these differences before they carried out the murder. It is possible that changes in brain activity occurred as a consequence of carrying out their crime. Furthermore, environmental factors such as a poor home life may have led to the differences in brain activity and the violent behaviour rather than biological factors.

You need to be able to discuss reductionism in biological psychology

Biological psychology reduces behaviour down to genes, brain structure and the nervous system. However, most psychologists believe that human behaviour is affected by the interaction of genes and environment. For example, genetic factors may influence aggression but so does growing up with aggressive role models.

You need to be able to discuss biological psychology as a science

The biological approach is considered scientific as it usually collects data from controlled experiments. It uses theories to develop hypotheses, which are then tested to see whether they are supported or not by empirical evidence. Therefore the biological approach is able to build a body of scientific knowledge from the data collected. The biological approach also uses brains scans to understand more about how the brain works. However, inferences are made from brain scans which may not be valid. Twin studies and adoption studies try to establish genetic links for mental disorders and developmental disorders. However, twin and adoption studies are correlational and cannot separate out the influence of genes from the environment.

You need to be able to discuss the nature-nurture debate in biological psychology

The biological approach mainly supports the nature side of the debate. It says that we are born with certain genes and a nervous system that affect the way we think, feel and behave. However, the biological approach accepts that our environment, for example, our diet can affect our development.

You need to be able to show an understanding of how psychological knowledge has developed over time

In 1859, Charles Darwin introduced ideas about natural selection and evolution . This led to link between genetic inheritance and behaviour. In 1861, Paul Broca showed that brain damage affected language and behaviour by studying a man who had suffered a brain injury. William James argued in 1890 that psychology should be grounded in an understanding of biology. Twin studies and adoption studies have been used to investigate the effect of genetics on behaviour. Advances in brain scanning techniques have given us a better understanding of how brain structure and brain activity affect behaviour. For example, Raine et al. (1997) used PET scans to look at the differences in brain activity between murderers and non-murderers.

You need to be able to discuss issues of social control in biological psychology

When biological understanding is used to control behaviour then this is a form of social control. An example of this is when drugs are given to people who have committed an offence in order to change their behaviour. For example, sex offenders have been given drugs which reduce their male hormone levels and hence their sexually deviant behaviour. Some people argue that this is a good use of biological knowledge whereas others feel it is unethical.
Research into aggression could be used to control people in our society. For example, those who are identified as at risk of aggression as a result of brain scans or genetic testing might have some of their rights taken away.

You need to be able to discuss the use of psychological knowledge from the biological approach

The biological approach has contributed to our understanding of aggression by explaining it in terms of biological concepts. Understanding that aggression has a biological basis can take the blame away from the individual and has implications for society. Raine et al compared the brains of murderers and non-murderers using PET scans and found that the 41 murderers who were pleading not guilty by reason of insanity had lower activity in the prefrontal cortex, parietal cortex and corpus callosum than the non-murderers. Such findings can affect the type of sentencing
given.

You need to be able to discuss issues related to socially sensitive research in biological psychology

Research showing a biological basis for aggression is socially sensitive as it has implications for society. If biological factors are involved in aggression, it suggests that individuals are not responsible for their actions. This leads to the question of whether people should be criminalised for behaviour that is outside of their control. It also means that biological markers can be used to identify those people who are at risk of aggressive behaviour and some groups might want to control those individuals as a preventative measure. This is an ethical issue.

Exemplar Exam Question

A 9-year-old boy gets into a fight with his friends at school and his mother says, 'Boys will be boys'.

Discuss the role of hormones in aggression with reference to the statement 'boys will be boys'.

Student Answer:

Testosterone is produced in the testes and is needed to produce sperm and leads to male secondary sex characteristics such as facial hair and a deep voice. At puberty, when testosterone levels rise in males, aggression often increases. Furthermore, there is a rise in testosterone levels, when men display aggression. This provides support for the theory that testosterone relates to aggression. However, it is difficult to know whether testosterone leads to aggression or whether aggression produces higher testosterone levels.

Animals that have been injected with testosterone show increased aggression and animals that have had their testes removed display decreased aggression. This supports the link between testosterone and aggression.

Many correlational studies have found a relationship between testosterone and aggression. However, much of the research is correlational and cannot establish cause and effect. There is also conflicting evidence. Bain et al (1987) found no significant differences in testosterone levels in men convicted of violent crimes compared to men convicted of non-violent crimes. Kreuz and Rose (1972) also found no difference in testosterone levels in violent and non-violent offenders. Higher levels of testosterone may be related to dominant behaviour rather than aggression.

Testosterone has been shown to influence levels of the neurotransmitter serotonin, which is linked to mood. Low levels of serotonin are linked with aggression. Therefore, testosterone may have an indirect effect on aggression by modulating serotonin levels.

9/12 marks

Commentary:

This student has covered a wide range of points related to hormone levels and aggression. However, they have not related it to the comment, 'boys will be boys'. It is important to relate your answer to the scenario given in the exam. For example, this student could have said that boys have higher testosterone levels than girls and as testosterone is linked with aggression this may have led to the comment 'boys will be boys'.

Chapter 4-Learning Theories

You need to be able describe what the learning approach is about

The learning approach focuses on how our behaviour is influenced by the environment. It makes the following assumptions: we respond to stimuli in our environment and behaviour is affected by our experiences.

You need to be able to describe and evaluate classical conditioning

Description:

Classical conditioning refers to the process of learning through association. When a neutral stimulus is paired with an unconditioned stimulus, we can become 'conditioned' to respond to the neutral stimulus. The neutral stimulus becomes a conditioned stimulus and produces a conditioned response.

E.G. Pavlov's dog study
Food (UCS) ⟶ Salivation (UCR)
Food (UCS) + Bell (NS) ⟶ Salivation (UCR)
Bell (CS) ⟶ Salivation (CR)

Extinction: When a conditioned response is suppressed. This occurs when the conditioned stimulus is no longer paired with the unconditioned stimulus. For example, if a dog is no longer given food (unconditioned stimulus) when it hears a bell (conditioned stimulus), it will stop salivating (conditioned response) to the sound of the bell. Extinction does not mean that the behaviour has been unlearnt; it just means that the behaviour has become dormant.

Spontaneous recovery: A conditioned response may be dormant but suddenly reappear again. For example, a dog's conditioned response of salivating to a bell may extinguish but then reappear later when the dog hears the sound of a bell.

Stimulus Generalisation is when someone becomes conditioned to respond to not only the conditioned stimulus but also similar stimuli. For example, Little Albert became conditioned to not only fear white rats but also other white furry objects.

Note:

A stimulus is something that causes a response. For example, a spider might be a stimulus that causes a fear response.

A response is a reaction to a specific stimulus. For example, salivation might be the response to the stimulus of food.

Evaluation:

Studies-Watson and Rayner's Little Albert study showed how a baby could learn to fear a white rat through classical conditioning. This study supports the idea that behaviours can be learnt through association.

Pavlov's study on dogs showed that dogs would learn to salivate to the sound of a bell through the association of food and a bell. This study supports the idea that behaviours can be learnt through association.

Explanation-Classical conditioning is reductionist because it focuses on how behaviour is learnt through association and does not take into account other factors involved in behaviour e.g. genes and social factors.

Note: Reductionist means reducing behaviour down to one thing and not taking into account other factors.

Application to real life-Classical conditioning can explain how we learn phobias and other behaviours through association. For example, it can explain why dogs get excited when their owners get their leads out because they have associated it with going for a walk.

You need to be able to describe and evaluate Pavlov (1927) experiment with salivation in dogs

Description:

Aim-To investigate digestion in dogs by measuring the amount of saliva produced by a dog when it eats. (Pavlov had not aimed to investigate classical conditioning)

Procedure-Meat powder was placed directly on the dog's tongue or in a bowl. A tube was surgically attached to the dog's cheek near one of the salivary glands and a fistula was made so that the saliva drained straight out into a measuring device. Pavlov measured the amount of saliva that occurred naturally whenever food was placed in the dog's mouth as salivation is an involuntary, reflex response.

Results-He observed that the dogs salivated not only at the sight of the food, but also at the sight or sound of the laboratory technician who had been preparing the food.

Conclusion-He concluded that salivation is a natural, reflexive response to food and that this involuntary response can become associated with a neutral stimulus such as the laboratory technician.

Further experiments: Pavlov was intrigued by these unintentional observations and carried out further experiments. He conducted a study to see whether a dog would salivate to the sound of a bell if it had become associated with food.

UCS (Food)   →   UCR (Salivation)
NS (Bell) + UCS (Food)   →   UCR(Salivation)
CS (Bell)   →   CR (Salivation)

An UCS (unconditioned stimulus) is something that naturally causes you to respond in some way.

An UCR (an unconditioned response) is a natural, involuntary response. For example, salivating to food is a reflexive response.

A NS (a neutral response) is a stimulus that you feel neutral towards (it can becomes a CS)

A CS (a conditioned stimulus) is something that you would not normally respond to but since being paired with an UCS makes you respond in a certain way

A CR (a conditioned response) is learnt response that has occurred as a result of classical conditioning. For example, salivating to the sound of a bell is not a natural response but a learnt/ programmed response.

Evaluation:

Generalisability-Humans have more complex cognitive (thinking) capacities than animals so it is hard to generalise the research to humans. However, numerous studies have since found that classical conditioning occurs in humans as well as animals.

Reliability-Pavlov carried out a standardised procedure that he replicated with different dogs to test for reliability. He used a number of different stimuli to see whether he could create an association and found the same results, which shows the study is reliable. He controlled the extraneous variables to find out the causes of the dogs 'salivation and this ensured he had established a cause and effect relationship.

Application to real life-The study can explain many learnt behaviours. For example, dogs get excited when their owners get their leads out because they have associated this with going for a walk.

Validity-The study was carried out in an artificial setting of a laboratory so it lacks ecological validity. However, because the study was carried out on dogs, it could be argued that they would have responded naturally irrespective of the artificial environment. The dogs displayed natural, involuntary responses to the stimuli, which are valid.

Ethics-Pavlov surgically altered the dogs so that he could collect their saliva outside of their bodies. This caused physical harm to the dogs. The dogs were strapped/tied down during the experiments, which would have caused them distress.

You need to be able to describe and evaluate Watson and Rayner (1920) 'Little Albert: Conditioned emotional reactions'

Description:

Aim-To see whether Little Albert could be classically conditioned to be afraid of a stimulus he was originally unafraid of.

Procedure-Little Albert was chosen for the study because he was an emotionally stable child who was not easily frightened. He was also familiar with the hospital environment as his mother worked there. At 9 months old, he was tested to see whether he was afraid of a variety of stimuli. He was unafraid of a white rat but was afraid of the sound of a metal bar being banged. When Albert was 11 months old, the researchers decided to classically condition him to be afraid of a white rat. Albert was shown the white rat and when he reached out to touch it, a loud noise was made with a metal bar behind his head. This was repeated several times.

UCS (banging of bar) ⟶ UCR (Fear)

UCS(banging of bar) + NS(rat) ⟶ UCR(fear)

CS (rat) ⟶ CR (fear)

Originally the rat is a neutral stimulus (NS) but once it begins to cause fear, it becomes a conditioned stimulus (CS)

Results-Little Albert showed a fear response to the rat on its own after a number of pairings of the rat and the banging bar over a period of a week. At 11 months 15 days old, Little Albert was happy to play with some toy blocks but showed fear towards the rat. He also showed a negative response to a rabbit and a fur coat suggesting he had transferred his fear of the white rat onto similar objects.

Conclusion-This study showed that Little Albert was classically conditioned to be afraid of a stimulus he was originally unafraid of. It also showed that conditioned responses can be generalised to other similar objects.

Evaluation:

Generalisability-The study was carried out on only one boy so it is hard to generalise it to the wider population.

Reliability-This laboratory experiment had good controls and a procedure that would be easy to replicate. The researchers carefully observed and recorded Little Albert's responses to the stimuli, which makes it reliable. They also made sure Little Albert was not afraid of furry things and rats before the study. However, if the study was repeated with other children, it may be difficult to replicate the findings as other children might be afraid of a white rat but unafraid of a banging metal bar.

Application to real life-This study can explain how humans learn phobias through association. For example, a child may be initially afraid of spiders but unafraid of going into a shed. However, they may become afraid of the shed after a spider runs across their shoe in the shed.

Validity-The study lacks ecological validity because it was an artificial situation. In real life, stimuli are not carefully paired together under controlled conditions as the white rat and banging bar were in this study.

Ethics- Little Albert was not protected from psychological harm. He was only 11 months old when he took part in the experiments and he was caused distress. For example, he showed fear and cried when shown the white rat. They also did not extinguish his fear.

You need to be able to describe how phobias may occur through classical conditioning

Anxiety and fear can become associated with neutral stimuli leading to anxiety disorders and phobias. For example, you might observe someone being mugged on a certain street and afterwards have a phobia of walking down this street.

UCS (Mugging) → UCR (Fear)
NS (Street) + UCS (Mugging) → UCR(Fear)
CS (Street) → CR (Fear)

You need to be able to describe and evaluate treatments for phobias based on classical conditioning principles: flooding and systematic sensitisation

Systematic desensitisation description:

Systematic desensitisation is based on classical conditioning principles. It can be used to get rid of phobias. There are four processes in systematic desensitisation: functional analysis, constructing an anxiety hierarchy, relaxation techniques and gradual exposure. Functional analysis involves discussing triggers for the phobia with the therapist. The therapist and client then construct an anxiety hierarchy. The idea is to help a person overcome their phobia by starting with something less fearful and working up to the real fear. For example, a student with a fear of attending school might have a picture of their school at the bottom of their anxiety hierarchy. One step up their hierarchy might be driving past their school. Next it might be going into the school playground and finally at the top of the hierarchy would be going into a classroom. The third process in systematic desensitisation is teaching the client relaxation techniques such as deep breathing and visualising being in a safe comfortable place. The final process is gradual exposure. The client moves up their anxiety hierarchy at their own pace using relaxation techniques at each stage. The person learns to associate being relaxed with their feared stimulus instead of fear response. For example, the student begins to associate school with feeling relaxed rather than feeling anxious.

Evaluation:

Directive-The therapist guides the treatment but the patient has a lot of control over the treatment. They only progress up the hierarchy when they feel confident enough. Therefore, the treatment can be considered less directive and more ethical.

Effectiveness-Systematic desensitisation helps people get over phobias especially of animals and objects. The positive effects seem to last for longer than some other therapies.

Side effects-None. It is less stressful than flooding.

Expense-It can take a long time for the patient to make progress in overcoming their phobia. Therefore, systematic desensitisation can be expensive in terms of both time and money.

Reasons-Systematic desensitisation does not look at the underlying causes of a phobia. For example, a person may suffer from a certain phobia due to a traumatic experience, which is not addressed during the therapy.

Types of people-Systematic desensitisation tends to be better for people with phobias of animals or objects rather than those with social phobias.

Flooding description:

Flooding is a therapy used to get rid of phobias. It is based on the principles of classical conditioning. During the therapy, patients are forced to confront the object or situation that is causing them distress and they are not allowed to escape. For example, a person with a fear of heights might be taken up to the top of a very tall building and told to stay there until their distress diminishes. The idea is that continued exposure to the feared stimulus weakens and extinguishes the fear as the initial anxiety cannot be sustained.

Evaluation:

Directive-During flooding, the therapist forces the patient to confront their phobia and may even stop them running away. The therapist therefore has a lot of control over the treatment and it can be viewed a directive.

Effectiveness-Wolpe (1973) used flooding to help a young woman overcome her phobia of cars. She was made to sit in the back of a car and was driven around continuously for four hours. Initially she was hysterical with fear but the fear response eventually subsided. This study supports flooding as a technique for overcoming phobias.

Side effects-Flooding can cause patients to become very distressed, which raises ethical issues. Some people may find the approach too difficult and withdraw from the therapy before it's finished. This could lead to the fear or phobia becoming worse.

Expense-Flooding can work quickly, and therefore, it is cheaper than systematic desensitisation in terms of both time and money.

Reasons-Flooding does not look at the underlying causes of a phobia. For example, a person may suffer from a certain phobia due to a traumatic experience, which is not addressed during the therapy.

Types of people-Flooding works by getting people to confront a feared stimulus so it is helpful for people with a fear of objects or animals. However, it is less useful for people with less concrete fears such as fear of failure. Flooding works better on people who are motivated to change and prepared to experience highly stressful situations.

You need to be able to describe and evaluate operant conditioning

Operant conditioning refers to the process of learning through consequences: Positive reinforcement (rewards), negative reinforcement (removing something unpleasant) and punishment (providing something nasty or removing something nice).

Positive reinforcement refers to giving a reward for a desired behaviour. For example, a dog might be given a treat for sitting down when their owner says 'sit'. Behaviour that is positively reinforced is more likely to be repeated.

Negative reinforcement refers to taking away something unpleasant for a desired behaviour. For example, a teacher might take away homework for particularly good work in class. Behaviour that is negatively reinforced is more likely to be repeated.

Positive punishment refers to giving a nasty consequence (such as a detention) for an undesired behaviour. For example, a child might be told to sit on the naughty step for pinching another child. Behaviour that is positively punished is less likely to be repeated.

Negative punishment refers to taking away something nice for an undesired behaviour. For example, a parent might take away a child's toy for bad behaviour. Behaviour that in negatively punished is less likely to be repeated.

Note: Reinforcement increases the frequency of desired behaviours. Punishment decreases the frequency of undesired behaviours. Reinforcement and punishment can be both positive and negative. Think positive (+) means adding or giving something and negative (-) means taking away or removing something.

Primary reinforcers are rewards that satisfy a basic need, such as food, drink, warmth and shelter. Fizzy drinks, sweets, chocolate and cake are all types of primary reinforcer.

Secondary reinforcers are rewards that are not fulfilling on their own but can be exchanged for something that satisfies a basic need. Secondary reinforcers are only fulfilling because they are associated with a primary reinforcer e.g. money can be used to buy food. Merits, tokens and vouchers are types of secondary reinforcers.

Shaping is when a behaviour is learnt by rewarding moves towards the desired behaviour (successive approximations of the desired behaviour). First of all behaviour that is on the way to the desired behaviour is rewarded and then later on only behaviours that are nearer and nearer to the desired behaviour are rewarded. For example, shaping helps children acquire language. When a child first vocalises, their parents are delighted and give the child lots of attention and praise. The attention is rewarding and so the child repeats vocalisations. The parents then begin to only praise (positively reinforce) vocalisations sounding like words so the child begins to only repeat word sounds. Later the parents only reinforce the child when they produce real words so that word sounds (e.g. gadad) are shaped into words (e.g. granddad).

Evaluation:

Studies-Skinner found that rats would press a lever to receive a reward. This supports operant conditioning as it shows how behaviour can be learnt through consequences. However, this study is not generalizable to humans as humans are more complex. For example, humans have language and can adapt their behaviour based on what they are told rather than just through consequences.

Explanation-Operant conditioning is useful at explaining how behaviours such as addictions and language are learnt through consequences. However, it is reductionist because it focuses on learning through consequences and does not take into account other factors.

Application to real life-Token economy programmes are based on operant conditioning. Operant conditioning principles can be applied to help children behave better through rewards and punishment. Language acquisition can be explained through shaping.

You need to be able to describe different schedules of reinforcement and their effects on learning: continuous reinforcement; fixed interval; variable interval; fixed ratio and variable ratio

There are different ways to arrange the delivery of reinforcement/rewards: Continuous reinforcement and partial/intermittent reinforcement.

Continuous reinforcement is when every desired behaviour is reinforced/rewarded. It is useful when you are trying to teach a new behaviour. However, behaviour that is continuously reinforced can become extinct quickly if the reinforcement is no longer given. Furthermore, if the same reward is given all the time, then there is a risk of reinforcer satiation (the reward is no longer desired so the behaviour may no longer be performed).

Intermittent reinforcement is when some, but not all, desired behaviours are rewarded. Behaviour that is only intermittently reinforced is more resistant to extinction and so intermittent schedules of reinforcement are useful in maintaining established behaviours. There is also less risk of reinforcer satiation with an intermittent schedule.

There are different types of intermittent reinforcement schedules: fixed ratio (FR), fixed interval (FI), variable ratio (VR) and variable interval (VI).

Ratio schedules are based on giving reinforcement after a certain number of desired behaviours.

Fixed ratio (FR) schedules involve reinforcement being given after a set number of responses/behaviours. For example, you might give a reward every fourth time a child tidies their toys up (FR-4). Fixed ratio schedules result in a high rate of desired responses but it can lead to a drop in the desired behaviour straight after the reinforcement is given. Another problem with fixed ratio schedules is that if a person has to wait too long for reinforcement, they might stop performing the desired behaviour. Therefore, if you are changing from a continuous reinforcement schedule and moving to a fixed ratio schedule, you should reinforce behaviour quite frequently. For example, you might start by offering a reward every two behaviours and move up to offering a reward every four behaviours and so on.

Variable ratio (VR) schedules involve reinforcement being given after a varying number of responses. For example, with a VR-6 schedule, rewards are given on average every six desired behaviours but reinforcement might come after three behaviours one time, after nine behaviours another time and after six behaviours the time after that. Variable ratio schedules are good at encouraging desired behaviour long-term with no post-reinforcement pauses. As reinforcement can occur at any time, extinction is not likely. It is possible to move from a continuous reinforcement schedule to a low reinforcement variable ratio schedule easily.

Interval schedules involve reinforcement being given for desired behaviour after a certain amount of time has elapsed.

Fixed interval (FI) schedules involve reinforcement being given for desired behaviour after a set amount of time has passed. For example with a FI-2 minute schedule, reinforcement is given after 2 minutes if the behaviour has already occurred or as soon as the behaviour occurs after the 2 minutes has elapsed. For example, you might try to use a fixed interval schedule to get your child to stay seated at dinner time. After 2 minutes, if your child has not got out of their seat yet, you might give them praise or a star on a chart. However, extinction can occur if schedule is thinned too quickly. For example, if you start giving rewards only every 20 minutes too early in the process, then the desired behaviour may become extinct.

Variable interval (VI) schedules involve reinforcement being given for desired behaviour after varying time intervals. For example, with a VI-10 minute schedule, reinforcement is given for the desired behaviour at varying time intervals with an average of 10 minutes. For example, a teacher could set a timer that goes off at varying intervals to encourage the students to stay on task. The timer might go off after 5 minutes, 15 minutes and then 10 minutes (an average of 10 minutes) and the teacher could praise the students if they are on task at these varying intervals. Variable interval schedules have the most resistance to extinction of any schedule. There are also no post-reinforcement pauses, because intervals between reinforcement are not predictable.

You need to be able to describe how some techniques based upon the principles of operant conditioning can be used to modify problem behaviour. For example, Token Economy Programmes

Description:

Token Economy Programmes (TEPs) are used in mental health institutions, schools and prisons to modify problem behaviour. TEPs are based on the principles of operant conditioning. Tokens (secondary reinforcers) are given for desired behaviour and these can then be exchanged for primary reinforcers. For example, in schools a pupil might be rewarded with merits for good behaviour. Once the pupil has a certain number of merits they might be able to exchange them for a book voucher. In prisons, cooperative and non-aggressive behaviour is rewarded. Prisoners may need to collect a certain number of tokens, which they can then exchange for something they actually want such as a phone card (a primary reinforcer). In mental health institutions, patients are rewarded for more adaptive behaviour. For example, anorexic patients are given tokens if they gain a certain amount of weight each week and these tokens can be exchanged for outings.

Evaluation:

Directive: Staff implementing a token economy programme have a lot of power. It is important that staff do not favour or ignore certain individuals if the programme is to work. Therefore, staff need to be trained to give tokens fairly and consistently even when there are shift changes such as in a prison or in a psychiatric hospital.

Effectiveness- TEPs can quickly change behaviour. Hobbs and Holt found direct short-term success in using TEPs with youth offenders. They recorded the effects of introducing a TEP to youth offenders in three institutions, while a fourth acted as a control. They found the TEP led to a significant increase in the targeted behaviours compared to the group not involved. On the other hand, although TEPs may be effective whilst an offender is in an institution, it may only change behaviour temporarily. Once the offender leaves the prison and goes into the outside world, there may be no real change in thinking or behaviour. Pearson et al. found that behavioural treatments such as TEPs were not good at stopping reoffending. TEPs can be useful with those with mental health issues. TEPs have been useful at getting sufferers of anorexia nervosa to a reasonable weight after which issues can be addressed. TEPs can also be effective with schizophrenics who lack the motivation to perform self-care tasks. Allyon and Azrin (1968) used a TEP to change the behaviour of 45 chronic schizophrenics who had been institutionalised for an average of 16 years. They were given tokens for making their beds or combing their hair. After the TEP, the schizophrenics were much better at looking after themselves.

Side effects- TEPs can lead to learned helplessness where prisoners or patients feel that they have no choice about taking part in the programme. TEPs may also stop people looking inside themselves for the problem.

Expense-TEPs are relatively cheap to implement as staff do not need much training to deliver them. However, staff need to give the rewards and punishments consistently and this can be difficult to achieve especially with shift changes.

Reasons-TEPs do not address the underlying causes of the person's behaviour such as family issues and traumatic experiences.

Types of people-TEPs can be used effectively in institutions such as schools, hospitals and prisons but they may be viewed as patronising by people outside an institution.

You need to be able to describe how phobias can be maintained through operant conditioning

Phobias may be maintained through coping techniques such as avoidance and escape. Avoidance refers to behaviours that attempt to prevent exposure to a fear-provoking stimulus. Escape means to quickly exit a fear-provoking situation. For example, a person who has a phobia of heights may avoid going to high places. This coping strategy rewards them by reducing their feelings of stress and anxiety. Another person may feel uncomfortable in a crowded room, so they leave to reduce their anxiety. Both avoidance and escape are highly reinforcing because they remove or diminish the unpleasant feelings. However, they do not stop the anxiety from re-occurring again and again in the future. So the principles of operant conditioning can explain how a phobia is maintained.

You need to be able to describe and evaluate social learning theory

Social learning refers to learning through observation and imitation. For social learning to occur, the learner must pay **attention** to and **retain** the model's behaviour. The learner must have the physical abilities to **reproduce** the behaviour and the learner must be **motivated** to imitate the behaviour. If the model is rewarded this increases the likelihood that the learner will imitate the behaviour. This is called **vicarious reinforcement**. For example, a girl may observe her older sister bake a cake and get praise for it. She is more likely to copy her sister's behaviour because she has seen her sister be rewarded for it.

Observation with reference to social learning theory refers to watching a model's behaviour. For example, a girl may watch her older sister put on make-up.

Imitation refers to copying a behaviour after it has been modelled. For example, a boy may play with a toy gun in the same way his friend does.

Modelling refers to learning new behaviours by observing other people. The modelling process involves the following processes: attention, retention, reproduction and motivation. For example, a boy may pay attention to his father playing the guitar and retain the behaviour. In order to reproduce the behaviour, he will need to practise the guitar. Finally, to successfully imitate his father's playing ability, he needs to be motivated to copy the behaviour.

Vicarious reinforcement refers to a behaviour being reinforced because another person has been observed receiving a reward for it. For example, a boy is more likely to work hard on his sums at school, after seeing another boy get rewarded with a sticker for completing a set of sums quickly.

Models of the same gender and age are more powerful (are more likely to be imitated). Models of higher status such as celebrities are also more likely to be copied.

Exam tip: Use ARRM to help you describe social learning theory. Attention, Retention, Reproduction and Motivation.

Evaluation:

Studies-Bandura's Bobo doll experiments found that children will copy aggressive behaviour shown by a model. This supports the idea that behaviour can be learnt through observation and imitation.

Explanation-Social learning theory is reductionist because it focuses on how behaviour is learnt through observation and it does not take into account other factors that affect our behaviour e.g. genes. However, social learning theory can explain how our thoughts and motivations affect behaviour. For example, people will have increased motivation to copy high status models who are rewarded for their behaviour. They are also more likely to imitate the behaviours of a role model if they feel confident in their abilities to reproduce the behaviour (self-efficacy).

Application to real life-Modelling-based therapies are based on the principles of social learning theory. Positive role models can be used to encourage people to change their behaviour.

You need to be able to describe and evaluate Bandura, Ross and Ross (1961) original Bobo doll experiment

Description:

Aim-1)To see if children might observe aggressive behaviour and then model their own actions on it. 2) To investigate the impact of gender on modelling.

Procedure- The study involved 72 children from one nursery in the USA. There was an equal mix of boys and girls and they were between 3- to 5-years-old. 24 of the children were put in a control group and did not observe a model at all. The remaining 48 children were divided into eight conditions: Condition 1-Boys watch aggressive, male model; Condition 2-Boys watch non-aggressive male model; Condition 3-Boys watch aggressive, female model; Condition 4-Boys watch non-aggressive female model; Condition 5-Girls watch aggressive, male model; Condition 6-Girls watch non-aggressive male model; Condition 7-Girls watch aggressive, female model and Condition 8-Girls watch non-aggressive, female model.

The children in the different conditions were matched individually on the basis of ratings of their aggressive behaviour in social interactions in the nursery school. During the experiment, the children were taken individually into a room by the experimenter and seated at a table where they could design pictures with potato prints and picture stickers provided. The experimenter then brought the adult model to the opposite corner of the room where there was a tinker toy set, a mallet, and a 5-foot inflated Bobo doll. The experimenter then left the room. Children in the non-aggressive condition saw a model quietly play with some tinker toys in the corner. Children in the aggressive condition, saw the model play with the tinker toys and then after one minute behave aggressively to the Bobo doll. The model sat on the Bobo doll and punched it repeatedly in the nose. The model then raised the Bobo doll, picked up the mallet and struck the doll on the head. The final aggressive act in the sequence was throwing the model into the air and kicking it around the room. The model then repeated this sequence of aggressive acts approximately three times. The model also made verbally aggressive comments such as, "Sock him in the nose . . . ," "Hit him down . . . ," "Throw him in the air . . . ," "Kick him . . . ," "Pow . . . ," and two non-aggressive comments, "He keeps coming back for more" and "He sure is a tough fella."

After 10 minutes, the experimenter entered the room and took the child to a different room to play after saying goodbye to the model. When they got to the new room, the children were all put into a slightly aggressive state by being told that they could not play with certain toys. This was to make sure that all the children were at the same level of aggression. The children were then observed playing. The researchers scored any behaviour to the Bobo doll that was imitative of the specific aggressive acts shown by the model to the Bobo doll.

Results-The children who had watched the aggressive models were more aggressive. In the non-aggressive and control conditions, approximately 70% of the children had a zero score for aggressive acts. Boys were more physically aggressive than girls but there was little difference for verbal aggression. The children were more likely to imitate same sex models. The mean number of aggressive acts committed by the boys was 25.8 after observing the male model and 12.4 after observing the female model. The boys showed more than double the number of aggressive acts towards the Bobo doll after observing a male model compared to a female model.

Conclusion-When children watch adults being aggressive they are likely to imitate that aggression, so it shows that observational learning takes places (social learning theory). Children are more likely to copy same-sex models. Boys, in particular, are more likely to be aggressive after observing a same-sex model be aggressive.

Evaluation:

Generalisability-All the children were from one nursery in the USA so it is hard to generalise from the study to the wider population.

Reliability- The study was a laboratory experiment with good controls so it is replicable and reliable. The researchers matched the children on levels of aggression at start. Inter-observer reliability was established by having more than one observer.

Application to real life-This study suggests that children are likely to copy violence shown by models. Therefore, children's exposure to violent role models in real life, on TV or in computer games should be limited.

Validity-The study involved an artificial situation so it lacks ecological validity. The children who saw the model behave aggressively to the Bobo doll, may have thought that they were supposed to behave that way towards the Bobo doll. If they had seen a model behave aggressively to a real person, they may have been much less likely to copy the behaviour. The children knew that the plastic Bobo doll could not be hurt so the study does not measure real aggression.

Ethics-The children who watched the aggressive model may have been made more aggressive and this is an ethical issue.

Credibility-Although the study showed that children will copy aggressive behaviour shown by a model immediately, it does not establish any link between watching violence and long-term aggressive behaviour.

To be able to describe and evaluate Bandura, Ross and Ross (1963) Bobo Doll experiment

Description:

Aim-To compare imitative behaviours when children watch an aggressive model in the same room as them, on film and using a cartoon character.

Procedure-48 boys and 48 girls from one nursery school in the USA were used. They ranged in age from 35 to 69 months. The children were divided into three experimental groups and one control group with 24 participants in each group. In one experimental group, children watched a real life aggressive model, in the second group, they watched a human model be aggressive in a film and in the third group, they watched an aggressive cartoon character in a film. As in the 1961 study, the children were sub-divided further into male and female participants so that half the children saw same-sex models and half the children saw opposite sex models. The control group saw no aggressive model at all. Participants in the experimental and control groups were matched for aggression on the basis of their social interactions in the nursery school by the experimenter and nursery school teacher. Children who had been assigned to the real life aggression group, were sat at a table at one corner of a room with potato prints, stickers and coloured paper, while an adult model was taken to the opposite corner of the room, which contained a small table and chair, a tinker toy set, a mallet and a 5-foot inflated Bobo doll. The experimenter left and then the model played with the tinker toy set for approximately one minute before behaving aggressively to the Bobo doll. In order, to measure imitative aggression, the model carried out the following distinctive acts of aggression: the model sat on the Bobo doll and punched it repeatedly in the nose, the model raised the Bobo doll and hit it on the head with a mallet and finally the model tossed the Bobo doll up into the air and kicked it about the room. This sequence of aggressive acts was repeated three times. The model also made verbally aggressive comments such as, "Sock him in the nose . . . ," "Hit him down . . . ," "Throw him in the air . . . ," "Kick him . . . ," "Pow . . . ," and two non-aggressive comments, "He keeps coming back for more" and "He sure is a tough fella."

Children in the human-model film group were sat at a table with potato prints and shown a film for 10 minutes with the same models as in the real life aggression condition displaying the same aggressive acts towards the Bobo doll.

Children in the cartoon film group were sat at a table with potato prints, coloured paper and stickers while being shown a film of a female model dressed up as a black cat performing aggressive acts. The cat was similar to many cartoon cats and to make it more like a cartoon, the backdrop was composed of brightly coloured trees, birds and butterflies and there was cartoon music in the background. The cat performed the same aggressive acts to the Bobo doll as the human models had but the movements were done in a more feline way. The same verbally aggressive comments were made but in a high-pitched animated voice.

After the children had seen the aggressive models, the children were brought to an anteroom with a number of attractive toys. They were then told that they couldn't play with these toys but they could play with the toys in the next room. This was to make them all feel equally frustrated and aggressive. They were then brought to an experimental room, which contained a mixture of aggressive and non-aggressive toys. The aggressive toys included a 3-foot Bobo doll, a mallet and two dart guns. The children's behaviour was observed through a one-way mirror for a period of twenty minutes. There was more than one observer to establish inter-observer reliability.

Results-The mean total aggression scores for participants in the real-life, human film, cartoon film and control groups were 83, 92, 99 and 54 respectively. The children who had observed the human models displayed more imitative aggression than those who had seen the cartoon model. However, the children who had observed the cartoon model demonstrated many partially-imitative acts such as carrying out the aggression towards an object other than the Bobo doll. The children who watched the aggressive models exhibited nearly twice the amount of aggression than children in the control group. The boys performed more imitative aggression than the girls.

Conclusion-Exposure to aggressive human and cartoon models in film and real life increases aggressive behaviour in children.

Evaluation:

Many of the same evaluative points can be made as for Bandura, Ross and Ross' (1961) study.

An additional point that can be made about this study is that it provides further evidence that media violence can lead to aggression. The results suggest that there should be a watershed and films should have ratings.

You need to be able to describe and evaluate Bandura (1965) Bobo doll experiment with vicarious reinforcement

Bandura's (1965) study was different to the original study in three ways: The children observed an adult be aggressive to a Bobo doll on a film rather than in the same room as them; the study looked at vicarious reinforcement and the children were offered rewards (stickers and juice) for each behaviour they copied.

Description:

Aims-To see whether children will copy an aggressive model shown in a film clip. To see whether the model being punished, rewarded or having no consequences for the behaviour affects the children's desire to imitate the aggressive behaviour. To see how many of the aggressive behaviours the child will imitate when given rewards.

Procedure-33 boys and 33 girls aged between 3 and 6 years old were split into to three conditions: Model rewarded; model punished and model receives no consequences. The children watched a film showing an adult be aggressive to a plastic Bobo doll. The film ended in three different ways: The model was rewarded by being praised for their aggressive behaviour; the model was punished by being told off and spanked with a rolled up newspaper and the model experienced no consequences for their aggressive behaviour. After watching the film, the children spent 10 minutes in the same room with a Bobo doll and other toys. Two observers recorded the number of imitative behaviours the children displayed. The children were asked to copy what Rocky did in the film and offered stickers and juice for each physical or verbal response they copied.

Results-The children who saw the model receive rewards or no consequences for the aggressive behaviour were more likely to copy it. The same number of imitative behaviours were shown by these two groups. The children who saw the model punished copied the aggressive behaviours less. When the children were offered rewards for copying, there was no difference between the groups.

Conclusion-Children are less likely to copy a model's behaviour if they see the model punished. However, the children all learnt the behaviours even in the model-punished condition and they were able to copy the behaviour when given rewards for doing so.

Evaluation:

Many of the same points can be made as for the 1961 study.
An additional point is that the children not only watched aggressive behaviour in this study but were also rewarded for aggressive behaviour, which may have made them more aggressive. Therefore, this study is more unethical than the original study.

You need to be able to describe and evaluate one contemporary study. For example, Becker et al. (2002) 'Eating behaviours and attitudes following prolonged exposure to television among ethnic Fijian adolescent girls'

Background:

The researchers were interested in whether increased exposure to television would affect eating behaviours amongst Fijian girls. Fiji was chosen because it has an extremely low prevalence of eating disorders. It had only one reported case of anorexia by the mid- 1990s.The Nadroga province of Fiji was selected because of its lack of exposure to television until mid-1995. Furthermore, Fijian culture encourages robust appetites and larger figures.

Description:

Aim-To look at the impact of the introduction of television on eating behaviour and attitudes in Fijian adolescent girls.

Procedure-A cross-sectional design was used to compare two groups of Fijian girls at secondary school in forms 5-7 before and after prolonged television exposure. The first group of girls were tested in 1995, within weeks of the introduction of television to Nadroga, Fiji. 63 girls took part (mean age 17.3 years). The second group of girls were tested in 1998, after the area had been exposed to television for three years. 65 girls took part (mean age 16.9 years). There was no significant difference between the girls in terms of mean age or body mass index. 41.3% of the sample had television sets in their homes in 1995 compared to 70.8% in 1998. The girls were asked to complete a 26-item eating attitudes test (EAT-26), which included questions on bingeing and purging behaviour. A score greater than 20 was considered high. Girls who self-reported bingeing or purging on the test were asked to respond to a semi-structured interview to confirm their symptoms.

Results-The percentage of participants with EAT-26 scores greater than 20 was 12.6% in 1995 compared with 29.2% in 1998. The percentage of participants reporting self-induced vomiting to control weight was 0% in 1995 compared to 11.3% in 1998. Respondents living in a household with a television set were three times as likely to have a EAT-26 score greater than 20. 74% of the 1998 group reported feeling 'too big or too fat' at least some of the time. 62% of the 1998 group reported dieting in the four weeks prior to the study and 77% reported that television had influenced their own body image. In 1998, they frequently said during the interviews that they wanted to lose weight or reshape their bodies to be more like a Western Television characters.

Conclusion-This study suggests that television can have a negative impact on eating attitudes and behaviours.

Evaluation:

Generalisability-It is hard to generalise from Fijians to other cultures. The marked disparity between normal Fijian body shapes and the slender figures shown on TV may make Fijians particularly vulnerable to developing eating disorders due exposure to TV images. Fijians may also associate thinness with glamour as the characters on TV often have expensive clothing and good careers.

Reliability-The EAT-26 test was replicable. This increases the reliability and objectivity of the study. The interviews would be hard to repeat and are open to interpretation. This makes this element of the study more subjective.

Application to real life-It has helped us to understand how thin media celebrities can be connected to disordered eating attitudes.

Validity-This naturalistic experiment has good ecological validity as it was able to assess the impact of television on a traditional society. Qualitative data was collected via interviews, which gives the study greater validity.

Ethics-Interviewing vulnerable adolescent girls with high EAT-26 scores regarding their eating behaviour may have caused them distress.

Credibility-Scores on the EAT-26 test cannot be equated with a clinical diagnosis of an eating disorder. However, high EAT-26 scores and induced vomiting are associated with eating disorders.

You need to be able to describe and evaluate one key question. For example, 'Is the influence of role models and celebrities something that causes anorexia?'

In our society, images of the female body in magazines, on TV and in films all suggest that being thin is beautiful. These images and thin celebrities in the media act as models for women in our society. There is an argument over whether these images lead to anorexia nervosa or whether anorexia nervosa is caused by other factors such as genes or family issues.

Social learning theory suggests anorexia nervosa may be due to role models in the media. Young people may feel they have to get to around the same weight as thin celebrities in order to be accepted. Teenagers pay attention to the fact that many celebrity role models are extremely thin and are likely to retain this information. They have the ability to reproduce being thin if they diet excessively and will do it if they are motivated to do so. They can see that their role models are famous and rich and this may motivate them to be thin too. Teenagers may also think that they need to be thin in order to be accepted by their peers, which may also provide motivation for excessive dieting.

Evaluation:

There are a number of studies which support social learning theory as an explanation of anorexia nervosa. Becker et al. (2002) found that the women living on the island of Fiji started developing eating disorder symptoms after the introduction of Western TV channels. Nasser (1986) compared Egyptian women studying in Cairo with similar Egyptian women studying in London and found that 12% of those living in London developed eating disorder symptoms, compared to 0% in Cairo. Lai (2000) found that the rate of anorexia increased for Chinese residents in Hong Kong as the culture slowly became more westernised. Mumford et al. (1991) found that Arab and Asian women were more likely to develop eating disorders if they moved to the West. These studies suggest that it is Western media images that lead girls and women to diet excessively and develop eating disorders. However, Eysenck and Flanagan (2000) point out that although all young women in the West are exposed to the media, only 3-4% of them develop an eating disorder. Therefore, there must be other factors other than media images that play a role in the development of anorexia.

Social learning theory cannot explain why anorexia nervosa usually develops in adolescence. A psychodynamic explanation for anorexia nervosa is that the disorder develops due to fears about growing up. Family issues may also contribute to the development of anorexia. Parents of anorexics may be too controlling and not allow their child to explain their own needs. Some anorexic sufferers report that they started dieting as method of gaining control over their lives. Genetics may also predispose someone to anorexia as the disorder does run in families. Relatives of people with eating disorders are four or five times more likely to also suffer (Strober and Humphrey, 1987).

You need to be able to describe how phobias can be learnt through social learning theory

Phobias can be learnt through observation and imitation. For example, a young boy may develop a phobia of spiders because his father has one. The young boy pays attention to the fact that his father shows signs of fear in the presence of spiders. He remembers this behaviour and because he views his father as a role model and wants to be like him, the next time he sees a spider he may copy his father's behaviour. In this way, the boy may develop a phobia of spiders.

You need to be able to describe and evaluate observations

There are structured laboratory observations and naturalistic observations. Structured laboratory observations involve careful controls and a set-up situation that can be repeated. There is often more than one observer and observations tend to be carried out through a one-way mirror to avoid the researchers' presence affecting participants' behaviour. Naturalistic observations involve observing participants in their natural environment. For example, observing children's behaviour in a playground.

Observations can be overt or covert. Covert observations involve observing a person or group of people without their knowledge. Overt observations involve observing a person or group of people with their knowledge.

Observations can also be participant or non-participant. A participant observation involves the researcher interacting with the person or group of people that they are observing. A non-participant observation involves the researcher observing behaviour from a distance without having any influence or getting involved.

An observation can be carried out by counting the frequency of certain behaviours during a fixed period of time.
Event sampling-when you record every time an event such as a kick occurs
Time sampling-when you record what is happening every set amount of time e.g. every 5 minutes.
Point sampling- The behaviour of just one individual in the group at a time is recorded.
Inter-observer reliability-Comparing the ratings of a number of observers as an individual observer may be biased. This would increase the reliability of the data collected if all the observers agree.

Evaluation:

Researchers may find it difficult to record all the behaviours shown, although event sampling, time sampling and point sampling can help. Video recordings can be used to record participants' behaviour and played back later so that all actions can be noted. It may also be difficult to analyse or interpret all the data collected. Observers often have to be specially trained so that they can record behaviours quickly and to avoid bias.

Participant observations allow researchers to experience the same environment as their participants. However, the researcher's involvement can affect the behaviour of participants. In contrast, non-participant observations allow researchers to observe participants' behaviour more objectively as they are not directly involved in the action. However, if participants are aware they are being observed, they may still change their behaviour.

Covert observations enable researchers to observe participants behave naturally as the participants do not know they are being observed. However, there are ethical issues with observing participants without their consent. They do not have the right to withdraw, they have not given informed consent and there also issues of confidentiality especially if their behaviour has been video-recorded. The British Psychological Society advises that it is only suitable to conduct a covert observation in a place where people might reasonably be expected to be observed by other people such as a shopping centre or other public place. Overt observations do not have as many ethical issues as covert observations. However, when participants know they are being observed they may change their behaviour so that it appears socially desirable. Therefore, overt observations can be less valid.

You need to be able to describe and evaluate the laboratory experiment as a research method

The learning approach uses laboratory experiments with both animal and human participants.

A laboratory experiment involves manipulating an independent variable to see the effect on a dependent variable. The dependent variable is measured. The extraneous variables are controlled in order to establish a cause and effect relationship.

For example, in Bandura, Ross and Ross (1961), the researchers manipulated whether the children saw an aggressive model, a non-aggressive model or no model at all. They then measured the number of aggressive behaviours shown by the children. This meant that they collected quantitative data, which could be statistically analysed to see how significant the results were.

Evaluation:

Laboratory experiments have standardised procedures, which are easy to replicate so that reliability can be tested. Data from laboratory experiments is quantitative and objective. Due to the careful manipulation and control of variables in a laboratory experiment, a cause and effect relationship can be established. Such evidence is considered scientific.

However, laboratory experiments lack ecological validity because they take place in artificial environments and often involve artificial tasks. Participants may behave unnaturally in an artificial situation. Experimenter effects can also affect laboratory experiments. The characteristics of the researcher may affect participants' responses. Furthermore, demand characteristics can affect results. Participants may guess what the study is about and give responses that they think the researcher wants.

You need to be able to describe, evaluate and carry out a content analysis

A content analysis involves changing qualitative data into quantitative data. This often means tallying how many times certain themes occur within a source such as a newspaper article, magazine article, journal article, radio programme or television programme. The source may be coded or broken down into manageable categories, for example, by words, phrases, sentences or themes. The researcher then analyses the presence and meaning of these categories and draws conclusions. For example, a researcher might tally how often negative or positive comments about daycare occur within two newspaper articles and draw conclusions about how daycare is portrayed in the media.

Evaluation:

As the data comes from secondary sources such as newspaper articles or television programmes, it does not change. Therefore, other researchers can check whether any conclusions are correct or not. The quantitative tallying of themes allows the data to be statistically analysed. There are unlikely to be any ethical issues with a content analysis, as it only involves analysing existing sources. However, the categorising and tallying of themes in a content analysis can be subjective.

You need to be able to describe and evaluate the use of animals in psychological research

Animal studies involve studying animal behaviour either in a laboratory or in the field. In an experiment, an independent variable is manipulated and a dependent variable is measured.

Example of laboratory experiments using animals

Skinner wanted to see whether he could get rats to learn behaviours through the principles of operant conditioning. He placed rats in a special cage called a Skinner's box to investigate their behaviour. He found that the rats would learn to press a lever every time they saw a flashing light in order to receive a reward. The flashing light acted as an antecedent (A=Antecedent), the rat's response/behaviour would be to press the lever (B = Behaviour) and the consequence would be that the rat received food (C = Consequences). Skinner called this the ABC of operant conditioning.

Evaluation:

Advantages: Animals are easier to use than humans because of ethical issues. Animals are also smaller on average, which makes certain experiments easier to run. For example, Skinner needed a small animal for his Skinner's box. Some animals such as rats breed quickly, which means that you can see how selective breeding affects behaviour. For example, if you breed rats that are good at finding their way around mazes together, then you can see whether their offspring are particularly good at mazes.

Disadvantages: Humans are more complex than animals and so it is difficult to generalise results from animal studies to humans. There can be ethical issues with carrying out studies on animals.

You need to be able to discuss ethical guidelines in relation to animals (non-human participants)

Caging and Stress: Experimenters should avoid or minimise stress and suffering for all living animals. The cages the animals are kept in during the experiment should be large enough for the animals to be comfortable.

Number or animals used: Researchers should use as few animals as possible.

Wild Animals: Endangered species should not be used, unless the research has direct benefits for that species e.g. conservation.

Qualified Experimenters: The researchers conducting the experiment should have the necessary qualifications. They should also have a licence from the Home office for that particular experiment.

Look for alternatives: Alternatives to using animals must always be sought, such as using humans or computers.

You need to be able to describe the Bateson's cube

Bateson's cube has three labelled sides: quality of research, animal suffering and certainty of medical benefit. These are on a scale high to low. When a research proposal falls into the opaque region, the experiment should not be conducted i.e. when quality of research is low, animal suffering is high and certainty of benefit is low.

You need to know when to use the chi-square test and how to compare the observed and critical values to judge significance

A chi-square test is a test of difference or association. For example, if males and females tend to choose different types of cars we could say that there is a difference between the genders in terms of car choice or an association between gender and car choice. The chi-square test is used when the data level is nominal, there is an independent measures design and when you are looking for an difference between two groups. There must be a minimum of 5 scores in each category, to carry out a chi-squared test.

The experimental or alternative hypothesis should state that there will be a difference between the two groups. An example of a one tailed (directional) hypothesis is: More males will drive large cars than females.

The null hypothesis should state that there is difference between the groups e.g. There will be no difference between males and females in terms of size of car driven.

For a chi-square test, if the observed value is greater than the critical value shown in a table, then the null hypothesis can be rejected.

The formula for the chi-squared test is:

$$\chi^2 = \sum \frac{(O - E)^2}{E}$$

O = the frequencies observed

E = the frequencies expected

$\sum$ *= the 'sum of'*

For example, a researcher might want to show that more males drive large cars than females and they might collect the following data:

	Male	Female	Totals
Car judged large	19	10	29
Car judged small	6	15	21
Totals	25	25	50

First work out the degrees of freedom (df) for this contingency table:

df= (rows-1) x (columns-1)= (2-1) x (2-1) = 1 x1= 1

A table can then be used to help in the process of working out the chi-square value:

O	E	O-E	$(O-E)^2$	$(O-E)^2/E$
19	14.5	4.5	20.25	1.40
10	14.5	-4.5	20.25	1.40
6	10.5	-4.5	20.25	1.93
15	10.5	4.5	20.25	1.93
				=6.65

The calculated value of chi-square is 6.65. This is called the observed value because it has been obtained from the data observed by the researcher.

Note:
O= observed frequencies. This refers to the number of males and females driving large cars and small cars observed by the researcher.
E=expected frequencies. This refers to what the researcher might expect to see if there is no association between gender and size of car driven. For example, if 29 large cars were observed. You would expect half of them to be driven by females and half of them to be driven by males. 29/2=14.5. Therefore the expected frequency is 14.5.

In order to find out if the observed value of 6.65 is significant or not, it must be compared to the critical value. You need to find the correct critical value in a critical values table for chi-square. Make sure you look for the critical value that corresponds for df=1 and $p \leq 0.05$ for a one-tailed hypothesis. This is 2.71.

As observed value of 6.65 is bigger than the critical value of 2.71, we would say that the result is significant and more males do drive large cars than females.

You need to be able to discuss the scientific status of psychology including: replicability, reliability, validity (internal, predictive and ecological), reductionism, falsification, empiricism, hypothesis testing and use of controls

Scientific knowledge is built from testing theories and collecting empirical data. Empirical data is data gathered through our senses. For example, we might time how long it takes males to complete a spatial awareness task versus females. This is empirical data. Empiricism is the theory that experience is of primary importance in giving us knowledge of the world. John Locke said our mind is a tabula rasa, a "blank slate", when we enter the world. At birth we know nothing but then we learn about the world through our senses and experiences.

Scientific research usually follows a hypothetico-deductive model. A researcher may come up with a hypothesis (prediction) based on a theory. For example, the theory of cue-dependent forgetting might lead to the hypothesis: participants will recall more words with a cue than without a cue. The hypothesis is then tested to see whether it is supported by empirical evidence. Based on the evidence collected, the theory is rejected or accepted.

A key concept in science is falsifiability, which refers to whether a theory can actually be tested or not. The concept of schema in the cognitive approach cannot be falsified so it is considered unscientific. However, the concept of short-term memory can be falsified so it is scientific.

Reductionism refers to reducing a theory into parts. This makes it easier to test. For example, the theory of operant conditioning can be broken down into parts, which can be tested. Skinner tested this: Animals were more likely to repeat a behaviour if they were given a reward and less likely to repeat it if they were punished.
The opposite of reductionism is holism. This means looking at a person as a whole rather than in parts. For example, it may be better to look at a range of factors affecting gender behaviour rather than just focusing on biological reasons. However, this is harder to test scientifically.

For research to be considered scientific, other people need to be able to replicate the study and find the same results. If the same or similar results are found, this suggests the study is reliable.

A scientific study should control any extraneous variables that could affect the results. It is important to establish that it is the independent variable that is leading to a change in the dependent variable rather than any other extraneous variables. For example, in Skinner's study on rats the independent variable was whether the rats were given a reward or punishment for pressing a lever and the dependent variable was the repetition of the behaviour. This was done under controlled conditions so that a cause and effect relationship could be established between the independent variable and the dependent variable.

For a study to have internal validity as few of the following must affect results: Extraneous variables; attrition (participants dropping out before the end of the study); non-random assignment; demand characteristics and experimenter effects. Avoiding these problems makes the study more scientific.

Laboratory experiments tend to be more scientific but they can lack ecological validity.

A study has predictive validity if it accurately predicts a result in the future. CATs tests has predictive validity if they predict accurately that those who score highly on the tests, will go on to get good grades at GCSE. A study or test that has predictive validity is more scientific.

The learning approach is considered to be scientific because it uses laboratory experiments with good controls to investigate how behaviour is learnt.

You need to be able to describe an observation you carried out. Example practical: An observation of how gender affects polite behaviour

Background: Social learning theory suggests that learn gender appropriate behaviour through copying same-sex role models. Women in our society are expected to behave in a polite way in public. Younger females may observe their behaviour and then model this behaviour.

Aim: To see whether gender affects polite behaviour.

Independent variable: Gender

Dependent variable: Whether the person thanks the café assistant or not.

Directional hypothesis: More females will thank the café assistant than males.

Design: Independent groups design as two groups: males and females.

Ethical issues: The study can be considered ethical because the participants were observed in a public place and only their gender and whether they thanked the café assistant were recorded.

Procedure: The observation was carried out on in the sixth form café and care was taken so that students did not think they were being observed (so that their behaviour was not affected by the observation at all). Data was gathered by discreetly tallying the number of thank yous given by male and female students on a mobile whilst sat in the café near the serving area. Qualitative data was collected by noting down when a male or female made conversation with the café assistant and what was actually said in shorthand. The amount of eye contact was also added to the notes.

Participants: There were 20 participants altogether. Their age ranged from 16- to 18-years-old.

Results:

Quantitative data

	Male	Female	Totals
Thanked the café assistant	12	16	28
Did not thank the café assistant	18	7	25
Totals	30	23	53

More females (16) said 'Thank you' than males (12). More males (18) did not say 'Thank you' than females (7).

The observed value was 4.567 which is greater than the critical value of 2.71 (for df=1 and p ≤ 0.05) so the results are significant. The null hypothesis can be must be rejected.

Note: A chi-squared test was carried out on the results as the study used an independent groups design and the level of measurement was nominal. The critical value was taken from a table of critical values for the chi-squared test. 2.71 is the critical value for df=1 and p ≤ 0.05 for a one-tailed hypothesis.

Qualitative data

The male students made more conversation with the café assistants. They were more likely make a joke or ask them about their day than the female students. The female students made more eye contact with the café assistants and were more likely to give a simple 'Thank you' when they received their food or drink.

Conclusions:

There was a significant difference in the gender of the student and whether they said thank you to the café assistants. Female students were more likely to say 'Thank you' than male students. However, male students were more likely to talk to the café assistants. Females are more polite than males but males are friendlier.

Evaluation:

Validity: This study took place in participants' natural environment so it has ecological validity. Participants were observed buying food and drink in an everyday situation of a sixth form cafe. Counting the number of times the students said 'Thank you' was an objective measure of politeness, which increases validity. The qualitative data collected from the conversations is subject to interpretation.

Reliability: It would be difficult to replicate the findings of this study as it took place in participants' natural environment and there were no controls over extraneous variables. Results were collected in the middle of day and results might have been very different in the early morning when students might be have been more tired and less likely to engage in conversation. If the study was replicated in a café in a different school or town, findings might be different. Having more than one observer could have improved reliability. If there is a high level of agreement between the observers, then the study can be said to have inter-rater reliability.

Generalisability: The participants may not be representative of the wider population as only sixth form students were used.

Credibility: The study has credibility because it was a naturalistic observation of students in an everyday situation.

You need to be able to discuss ethical issues related to learning theories

Animal experiments have been used in the learning approach to investigate behaviour and many of these studies have ethical issues. For example, Skinner gave electric shocks to rats to investigated negative reinforcement. Ethical guidelines now say that experimenters should avoid or minimise stress and suffering for all living animals.
There have also been ethical issues in experiments involving humans. For example, Watson and Rayner (1920) conditioned a fear response in a baby boy, Little Albert. This experiment caused Little Albert psychological distress, which goes against ethical guidelines.

You need to be able to discuss practical issues in the design and implementation of research related to learning theories

Humans are more complex than animals and so it is difficult to generalise results from animal studies to humans. The human brain functions in a different way to animals.

A problem with using humans to investigate learning theories is that they are likely to show demand characteristics.

You need to be able to discuss reductionism in relation to learning theories

The theories of classical conditioning and operant conditioning are reductionist because they reduce behaviour down to learned responses. Social learning theory is less reductionist because it takes into account cognitive factors (thought processes) in behaviour as well as learned responses.

You need to be able to make comparisons between different learning theories

Classical conditioning, operant conditioning and social learning theory explain how we learn behaviour from our environment. However, classical conditioning focuses on learning through association, operant conditioning focuses on learning through consequences and social learning theory focuses on learning through observation. The different theories can be applied to different aspects of behaviour. For example, classical conditioning is useful at explaining how we might learn a phobia, operant conditioning is useful at explaining how desired behaviour can be reinforced and social learning theory is useful at explaining the impact of role models.

You need to be able to discuss psychology as a science and learning theories

Learning theories have been developed using a scientific approach. Research in this area has tried to measure responses to certain stimuli using objective, empirical evidence from laboratory experiments. For example, Skinner measured how often a rat would press a lever when given rewards.

You need to be able to discuss cultural issues in relation to learning theories

Learning theories focus on environmental influences on behaviour. Culture is one of the environmental influences that play an important part in how we behave. For example, some cultures are more accepting of aggression than others.

You need to be able to discuss gender issues in relation to learning theories

Learning theories emphasise that gender differences are caused by environmental influences from parents, school, society, peers, TV and other models.

Operant conditioning can be used to explain gender differences. Gender-appropriate behaviour is encouraged from birth and gender-stereotypical behaviours are reinforced. For example, girls may be encouraged to play with dolls and boys with cars. Gender-inappropriate behaviours are punished. For example, when boys play with dolls they may be laughed at or ignored.

Social learning theory argues that gender identification occurs through observing and imitating gender-appropriate behaviour from same-sex models. The theory suggests that children pay more attention to same-sex models, retain their behaviour and then if they are capable of reproducing the behaviour and motivated to do so they will (ARRM). Gender development occurs through imitating gender-appropriate behaviours from same-sex parents, peers and others. For example, a young boy may pay attention to his father fixing a car. He will remember how to do it and reproduce the behaviour when he is motivated to do so.

You need to be able to discuss the nature-nurture debate in the learning approach

Learning theories support the nurture side of the nature-nurture debate. They argue that most of our behaviour is learnt from our environment. However, learning theories accept that we are born with some natural behaviours such as automatic reflexes.

You need to be able to show an understanding of how psychological knowledge had developed over time in relation to learning theories

Learning theories had the most influence on psychological thinking between 1920 and 1950. However, in the 1950s cognitive theories took over. However, many of the principles of learning theories are still used today. For example, behaviour analysts break behaviour down into small components and shape desired behaviour to help those with autism and developmental delays.

You need to be able to discuss issues of social control in relation to learning theories

Learning theories can be used to change and manipulate behaviour and this can be viewed as a form of social control. For example, token economy programmes (TEPs) are used in mental health institutions, schools and prisons to control behaviour. In mental health institutions, patients are rewarded for more adaptive behaviour. For example, anorexic patients are given tokens if they eat well or gain a certain amount of weight each week and these tokens can be exchanged for leisure time or outings. However, if a TEP is the only therapy used it only serves to control their behaviour rather than change it. TEPs may only change behaviour in the short term and learnt behaviour does not transfer easily to the outside world especially if the underlying causes of the disorder have not been dealt with. Token economy programmes are also used with prisoners. Tokens (secondary reinforcers) are given for cooperative and non-aggressive behaviour. Once the prisoners have a certain number of tokens they can exchange them for something they actually wants such as a phone card (a primary reinforcer). However, there are ethical issues with TEPs as staff implementing a token economy programme have a lot of power. It is important that staff do not favour or ignore certain individuals if the programme is to work (the practitioner may have too much influence and power). Therefore, prison staff need to be trained to give tokens fairly and consistently even when there are shift changes.

You need to be able to discuss learning theories and the use of psychological knowledge in society

Learning theories have been applied to many situations. For example, token economy programmes are used in prisons, schools and mental health institutions to improve and change behaviour. Techniques such as flooding and systematic desensitisation have also been used to get rid of phobias.

You need to be able to discuss issues related to socially sensitive research in relation to learning theories

Some treatments based on learning theories are controversial. Aversion Therapy uses classical conditioning to get rid of unwanted behaviours. It works by the association of an unpleasant stimulus with the unwanted behaviour. A paedophile can be conditioned to respond to children with fear rather than sexual arousal by pairing thoughts about children with painful electric shocks. Many people may see this as acceptable as it is performed with the offender's consent and counselling. However, in the past when homosexuality was illegal, aversion therapy was used on homosexual men as an alternative to a prison sentence. This shows how aversion therapy has ethical issues and is open to abuse. Even nowadays, people may only consent to aversion therapy because they feel under pressure to have the treatment and during the treatment they may feel out of control.

Exemplar Exam Questions

Polly has a fear of cotton wool. At university, she will have to share a bathroom with other students. She knows that she needs to overcome her phobia of cotton wool and is deciding between systematic desensitisation and flooding.

Describe how systematic desensitisation and flooding could be used for Polly's phobia. Evaluate the therapies and discuss the things she should consider before choosing between the therapies. (12 marks)

Student Answer:

Systematic desensitisation is based on classical conditioning principles and it can be used to get rid of phobias. It involves helping someone to gradually face up to their fears. During systematic desensitisation, Polly would first discuss her phobia of cotton wool and the triggers with a therapist. Together they could create a hierarchy of anxiety. At the bottom of the hierarchy might be looking at a picture of some cotton wool, then it might be sitting in the same room as some cotton wool, then it might be having the cotton wool on the same seat and finally it might involve touching some cotton wool. Polly can decide the pace at which she'd like to progress up the hierarchy. This will all be made a lot easier by the therapist as they will teach her relaxation techniques to deal with her phobia. She will use these techniques while gradually moving up the anxiety hierarchy.

Flooding is also based on classical conditioning principles. It would involve exposing Polly to cotton wool for a long period of time without letting her escape from the situation. The idea is that Polly's anxiety will reach a peak and then come back down again. She will then realise that the cotton wool is not going to cause any harm to her.

When deciding between flooding and systematic desensitisation, Polly would need to decide how quickly she wants the therapy to work and what degree of stress she is willing to undergo. Systematic desensitisation takes longer than flooding as it is a gradual process of relaxation and moving up the anxiety hierarchy. However, flooding is more stressful than systematic desensitisation as Polly would not be able to escape from the feared stimulus of the cotton wool.

8/12

Commentary:
This student has described systematic desensitisation and flooding well. However, they could have identified the four processes in systematic desensitisation more clearly: functional analysis, developing an anxiety hierarchy, relaxation training and gradual exposure. They should have also spent more time evaluating the therapies. For example, McGrath et al. (1990) found that systematic desensitisation was effective with 75% of people with phobias. Flooding raises ethical issues as the therapist prevents the client escaping from their feared stimulus and may be viewed as having too much control.

Assess token economies as a form of behaviour modification (8 marks)

There are 4 marks here for demonstrating a knowledge and understanding of the different factors involved in token economies (AO1 marks) and 4 marks for considering the significance of different factors and making a balanced judgement (AO3 marks).

Student Answer:

Token Economy Programmes (TEPs) are useful in institutions such as prisons, schools and mental health units to modify problem behaviour through the principles of operant conditioning. They have been found to quickly control unmanageable behaviour. Hobbs and Holt (1976) found that TEPs significantly improved behaviour amongst young offenders in three institutions compared to a fourth institution, which acted as a control. Whitby & Miller (2009) reported that TEPs can be successful at helping children behave in schools leading to a better learning environment.

On the other hand, TEPs are unlikely to help with the underlying aspects of behaviour. TEPs may be effective with an offender whilst they are in prison but this only changes their behaviour temporarily. Once the offender leaves the prison and goes into the outside world, there may be no real change in thinking or behaviour. Pearson et al. found that behavioural treatments such as TEPs were ineffective at preventing reoffending compared to cognitive behavioural therapies such as anger management, which change thinking. Anorexic patients may gain weight under a TEP in order to be allowed to go on outings and have visits home but it is also important to address their distorted thinking and any family issues otherwise their eating disordered symptoms will continue once they leave the institution.

It is important that rewards are motivating in a TEP and that behaviours are agreed upon in advance for a TEP to be effective. TEPs are relatively cheap to implement as staff do not need much training to deliver them. However, in order for a TEP to be successful, tokens need to be given fairly and consistently even when there are shift changes such as in a prison or in a psychiatric hospital. It is also possible for staff to abuse their power by favouring some offenders or patients over others.

TEPs can lead to learned helplessness where prisoners or patients feel that they have no choice about taking part in the programme. TEPs may also stop people looking inside themselves for the problem.

In conclusion, TEPs can be effective at modifying behaviour in institutions short-term but other methods such as cognitive behavioural therapies need to be used to change behaviour long-term. In order for TEPs to work successfully, rewards have to be given consistently by staff and prisoners/patients have to be motivated by the rewards. TEPs are judged to be effective and useful in institutions at modifying behaviour quickly but not at addressing underlying issues.

8/8 marks

Commentary:

This student demonstrates a good knowledge of token economies whilst assessing their effectiveness. They discuss practical or ethical issues related to it and make comparisons with cognitive behavioural treatments, which involve changing faulty thinking. The final paragraph comes to a conclusion and makes a judgement.

Chapter 5-Clinical Psychology

Clinical psychology investigates explanations and treatments for mental disorders. It also studies issues related to the diagnosis. For example, it looks at validity and reliability of different diagnostic systems.

You need to be able to describe and evaluate the diagnosis of mental disorders with reference to deviance, dysfunction, distress and danger

Description:

Clinicians may diagnose someone with a mental disorder based on four dimensions: deviance, dysfunction, distress and danger.
Deviance refers to behaviour that goes against social norms. For example, if a person sits in a restaurant talking to themselves then this can be viewed as deviant behaviour.
Dysfunction refers to behaviour that stops someone living their life normally. For example, their behaviour might be interfering with their job or relationships.
Distress refers to behaviour that causes upset to an individual. It is important that clinicians understand what level of distress a person is feeling before diagnosis.
Danger refers to behaviour that causes personal harm or other people harm. For example, someone may attempt suicide or attack someone else.

Evaluation:

The deviance dimension can lead to the curtailing of people's human rights as social norms can change with time. For example, in the past homosexuality was viewed as a mental disorder and now it is not. The problem with the dysfunction dimension is that people can disagree on what is considered dysfunctional behaviour. The distress dimension takes into account how an individual is feeling. It is important that clinicians consider an individual's subjective experience of distress even if they are functioning normally. The danger dimension can be difficult in diagnosis if a person engages in risky behaviour that does not cause immediate harm. Some risky behaviours can cause personal harm such as extreme sports but these do not usually lead to a diagnosis.
A problem with interviewing patients using the four dimensions is that clinicians may subjectively interpret what their patients say. Clinicians need to use standardised tests to assess symptoms.

Note 1 : Clinical interviews are unstructured or semi-structured interviews used to find out about a person's wellbeing and personal life so that they can be diagnosed correctly.

Note 2: A clinician is a health professional who directly works with patients. This could be a doctor, psychologist or nurse. Doctors who specialise in mental health are called psychiatrists and psychologists who specialise in mental health are called clinical psychologists.

You need to be able to describe the diagnostic systems: DSM V and ICD for mental health

DSM V is a manual used to diagnose mental disorders. It groups mental disorders into 'families'. For example, anorexia nervosa, bulimia nervosa and binge-eating disorder are grouped together under eating disorders. There are three sections in the manual. Section one is an introduction, section two contains the classification of the main mental disorders and section three contains other assessment measures to help with diagnosis. In section two, details are given about specific symptoms for the disorder and how long the person needs to have them before a diagnosis is made. For example, the manual says that for an individual to be diagnosed with schizophrenia, they need to show at least two of the following symptoms: (1) delusions, (2) hallucinations, (3) disorganised speech, (4) grossly disorganised behaviour, (5) negative symptoms (e.g. diminished emotional response or avolition). In addition, one of the symptoms must be delusions, hallucinations or disorganised speech. There needs to be continuous disturbance for 6 months including at least 1 month of symptoms for a diagnosis of schizophrenia to be given.

The American Psychiatric Association (APA) has attempted to make the DSM system more reliable and valid with each new version. DSM-V takes cultural issues in diagnosis into account. For example, people from different cultures and communities may exhibit symptoms of a mental disorder in a different way. DSM-V has been designed to be more comprehensive that previous versions and aims to help doctors make a diagnosis more easily. One of the main changes is that diagnosis of Asperger's syndrome has been removed from the DSM-V and is now part of one umbrella term Autistic Spectrum Disorder (ASD).

ICD-10 covers all health disorders not just mental disorders. Section F of ICD-10 is specifically for mental disorders. Like DSM-V, it groups disorders into 'families' and outlines the symptoms for each disorder. Mental disorders are given an ICD-10 code consisting of the letter F followed by 3 or more digits. For example, F50 refers to eating disorders. F50.0 refers to anorexia nervosa and F50.2 refers to bulimia nervosa.

You need to be able to discuss reliability of diagnoses in relation to diagnostic systems

A diagnosis is reliable when one clinician gives a diagnosis and another clinician gives the same diagnosis. This is called inter-rater reliability.

If different clinicians agree on the same diagnosis for the same patient using the same diagnostic system e.g. DSM then the diagnosis has inter-rater reliability.
If a clinician tests the same patient two or more times and ends up with the same diagnosis, then the diagnosis has test-retest reliability.
Issues of reliability can occur when someone who has previously been diagnosed with a mental disorder, is then re-diagnosed later as not having it. For example, it may be disturbing for a person who has been diagnosed with schizophrenia to be told later told that they do not have it. There can also be problems if one clinician diagnoses a girl as having anorexia nervosa but another disagrees.

Brown et al. (2001) found that good inter-rater reliability for anxiety and mood disorders with DSM IV.

Rosenhan's study found that DSM III was reliable for diagnosing schizophrenia as all the pseudo-patients who said they had schizophrenic symptoms were diagnosed with schizophrenia.

Silverman et al. (2001) found that the Anxiety Disorders Interview Schedule (ADIS) on DSM IV was reliable at diagnosing anxiety disorder in children.

If different diagnostic systems such as the DSM and the ICD come up with the same diagnosis, then the diagnosis can also be considered reliable.

However, Nicholls et al. (2000) looked at inter-rater reliability for eating disorders in children using ICD 10, DSM IV and the Great Ormond Street's criteria (GOS). They found poor inter-rater reliability using ICD 10 (36% only), reasonable agreement for eating disorders in children using DSM IV (64%) but much better agreement with GOS (88%). They concluded that the GOS criteria were much better for diagnosing eating disorders in children because they were developed for use with children.

Goldstein (1988) used DSM-III to re-diagnose 199 patients with schizophrenia who had been originally diagnosed using DSM–II. She found only 169 patients were re-diagnosed with schizophrenia. This suggests some problems in reliability between DSM-II and DSM-III.

Goldstein then picked a random sample of eight patients who had been re-diagnosed as having schizophrenia using DSM-III and asked two experts to re-diagnose them as well. She found a high level of agreement in diagnosis, which suggests DSM-III is reliable.

You need to be able to discuss the validity of diagnoses in relation to diagnostic systems

A diagnosis is valid if different people who are diagnosed with schizophrenia exhibit the same symptoms as each other and respond to the same treatments. A diagnosis has face validity if the person's behaviour matches what most people believe about the mental illness. For example, most people believe that someone with bi-polar disorder can be depressed on some days but hyper on others.

Rosenhan's study showed how diagnosis using DSM III wasn't valid. The pseudo-patients did not have schizophrenia but were still diagnosed with it and all but one were given a diagnosis of schizophrenia in remission on release. In the second study, real patients who did have schizophrenia were diagnosed as normal. However, DSM has been revised many times since the Rosenhan study and its validity has been improved.

A diagnosis has etiological validity if a group of people diagnosed with a mental disorder have the same factors causing it e.g. brain scans should show that most people with schizophrenia have a reduced volume of grey matter in the brain.

A diagnosis has concurrent validity if people who are diagnosed with a mental disorder show symptoms related to their mental disorder e.g. people diagnosed with paranoid schizophrenia should exhibit signs of paranoia.

A diagnosis has predictive validity if it predicts how a person will behave in the future and how they will respond to certain treatments. e.g. if a person is diagnosed with schizophrenia and then goes on to respond well to anti-psychotic drugs, then the diagnosis has predictive validity. Lahey et al. (2006) followed children over six years and found that children diagnosed with ADHD displayed behaviour consistent with their diagnosis. Therefore, their diagnosis can be said to have good predictive validity.

If a person is diagnosed with a mental disorder such as schizophrenia but then does not show any symptoms or respond to treatments for schizophrenia, then the diagnosis lacks validity. There has been a great deal of criticism about the validity of ADHD diagnoses. Some clinicians have suggested that young children who have been diagnosed with ADHD may just be displaying normal behaviour. Issues with validity may arise, if the family or mental health staff disagree with a diagnosis.

Patients may not report their symptoms correctly because they're embarrassed or distrust the clinician. They may also not remember their symptoms correctly. This can cause problems with the validity of the diagnosis.

Clinicians may interpret symptoms differently depending on their clinical background. For example, one clinician may focus on childhood experiences and interpret anorexic behaviour as being related to family relationships whereas another clinician might focus on thoughts patterns and give a more cognitive explanation for anorexia.

You need to be able to describe the symptoms and features of schizophrenia, including thought insertion, hallucinations, delusions, disordered thinking

Features

Approximately 1% of the population suffers from schizophrenia. Goldstein found that males tend to suffer more severely from schizophrenia than females. Schizophrenia tends to onset in men between 16 to 25 years old whereas females tend to develop it about 10 years later on average. The incidence of schizophrenia in males and females is similar.

Symptoms

Schizophrenics may suffer from thought disturbances. For example, they may believe an outside force is putting thoughts into their head (thought insertion).

Another symptom of schizophrenia is hallucinations, which involves a person perceiving something that isn't real. Auditory hallucinations are the most common but people can have hallucinations through all five senses. Auditory hallucinations may involve a person hearing a voice(s) that comment on their behaviour or tell them what to do.

Delusions occur when a person has false beliefs. For example, they may have delusions of grandeur where they imagine they are prime minister or delusions of persecution where they think they are being plotted against.

Disordered thinking is when a person cannot organise their thoughts about a situation and so they behave or talk in a confused way.

Positive symptoms are diagnosed by their presence i.e. a 'normal' person does not hear voices, so hearing voices is a positive symptom. Negative symptoms are diagnosed by their absence i.e. a 'normal' person is able to show appropriate emotions so the absence of being able to show emotions is a negative symptom. Alogia (poverty of speech) and flattened effect (lack of emotional responses) are negative symptoms of schizophrenia.

Exam Tip: Do not just list symptoms of schizophrenia. Instead, explain fewer symptoms in more detail and give examples.

You need to be able to describe and evaluate the function of neurotransmitters as an explanation for schizophrenia

Description

A number of neurotransmitters have been linked to the symptoms of schizophrenia. The dopamine hypothesis says that overactivity in the dopamine neurons leads to excessive dopamine production. Excess production of the neurotransmitter dopamine in the brain is linked to schizophrenic symptoms. The over-activity of dopamine in the synapses is particularly associated with positive symptoms of schizophrenia such as hallucinations. Negative symptoms of schizophrenia such as lack of motivation may be caused by a reduction in dopamine production in the pathway connecting the midbrain to the frontal lobes (the mesocortical pathway).

Note: Neurons are nerve cells that carry messages. The tiny gaps between nerve cells are called synapses. Neurotransmitters are chemicals that transmit messages across synapses. Dopaminergic neurons have dopamine as the neurotransmitter and these may be overactive in people with schizophrenia.

Evaluation

Studies- Autopsies have found that people with schizophrenia have a higher number of dopamine receptors in their brains, which supports the theory that increased dopamine is linked with schizophrenia.
Lieberman et al. (1987) looked at the effects of amphetamines on schizophrenic patients and found that they increased positive symptoms. This supports the dopamine hypothesis as amphetamines mimic the action of dopamine in the brain. Anti-psychotic drugs that reduce the effects of dopamine by blocking dopamine receptors have been useful in treating schizophrenia. This suggests that dopamine plays a role in schizophrenic symptoms. However, not all patients respond to these drugs and more modern drugs for schizophrenia do not block dopamine receptors but still reduce the symptoms of schizophrenia. Clozapine is a newer drug for schizophrenia that works by blocking dopamine D2 receptors and serotonin

receptors with fewer side effects than the older drugs. This suggests that schizophrenic symptoms are not just due to high levels of dopamine.

Explanation- It is difficult to say whether high levels of dopamine cause schizophrenia or whether excess dopamine is a result of having the disorder. Other mental disorders such as mania are linked with high levels of dopamine as well. Furthermore, anti-psychotic drugs can cause up-regulation where the number of dopamine receptors increases in response to the receptors being blocked. This can then increase levels of dopamine in the brain.

Note: Anti-psychotic drugs that block dopamine receptors are called dopamine antagonists.

You need to be able to describe and evaluate one other biological explanation for schizophrenia, for example the genetic explanation

Description

The genetic explanation states that genes can predispose someone to develop schizophrenia. DNA studies suggest that a number of genes are associated with schizophrenia although no single gene has been identified. People who inherit a number of these high risk genes are more likely to develop schizophrenia. The genes that are associated with schizophrenia may lead to biochemical differences in the brain such as high levels of dopamine (a neurotransmitter) in the synapses, which is linked with schizophrenia. Genetic abnormalities may also lead to structural differences in the brain that cause schizophrenia. In addition, genetic abnormalities may lead to damage to neural pathways (nerve cells carrying messages) in the brain. Behaviour that is controlled by these neural pathways may then be abnormal.

Evaluation:

Exam tip-When evaluating an explanation/theory, use studies to support or contradict the explanation and then discuss limitations of the explanation. There is also one mark for listing alternative explanations/theories.

Studies- The International Schizophrenia Consortium (2008) found that schizophrenics were more likely to have DNA missing on chromosomes 1,15 and 22 than non-schizophrenics. Hong et al. (2001) found that variation in the TPH gene (the gene involved in production of the enzyme tryptophan hydroxylase) is more common in schizophrenic patients than controls. Sherrington et al. (1988) found a gene located on chromosome 5 which has been linked in a small number of extended families where they have the disorder.
Twin studies suggest that genes can predispose someone to develop schizophrenia. Gottesman's study showed a 0.48 concordance for schizophrenia in MZ twins compared to only 0.17 concordance for DZ twins. The likelihood of schizophrenia in the general population in only 0.01, so these findings suggest a genetic basis for schizophrenia. McGue (1992) found 0.40 concordance for MZ twins. In twin studies, twins share the same environment as well as genes, so the effects of genes and environment cannot be separated.

Adoption studies also suggest that there is a genetic component in schizophrenia. Heston's study showed that 10% of adoptees who had a biological mother with schizophrenia went on to develop it themselves. However, a problem with adoption studies is that adoptees are often selectively placed into families that are similar to their biological family. Therefore, this can make it difficult to separate out the effects of genes and the environment.

Explanation-As schizophrenia has been linked with a number of different genes, it is hard to pin down a genetic cause. There is more than one type of schizophrenia so there may be more than one cause. Furthermore, if schizophrenia was entirely caused by genetics then if one MZ twin had schizophrenia, the other one would automatically develop it but this is not the case. This suggests there must be environmental factors that lead a person to develop schizophrenia as well as genetic factors.

You need to be able to describe and evaluate one non-biological explanation for schizophrenia. For example, the cognitive explanation.

Description:

A cognitive explanation for schizophrenia is that schizophrenics have difficulties with processing information and irrational beliefs. They also have problems with metarepresentation, which is the ability to recognise one's own thoughts and behaviour as being different to someone else's. For example, a schizophrenic may not be able to distinguish between their own thoughts and someone else's speech. This can lead them to believe that other people are putting thoughts in their head (thought insertion). Schizophrenics can be paranoid and think that they are being persecuted and plotted against. This can be viewed as a metarepresentation problem as they have problems interpreting other people's behaviour and intentions. Schizophrenics can also have problems with central control. This means that they cannot suppress automatic responses to stimuli. Therefore, if they intend to carry out an action or talk on a specific topic, they may be distracted by other stimuli in their environment. For example, if you ask some schizophrenics a question, they may end up talking about a stream of loosely related things because they cannot focus on the question asked. The disorganised speech produced by schizophrenics is sometimes referred to as a 'word salad'.

Evaluation:

Studies-
Daprati et al. (1997) asked schizophrenics and non-schizophrenics to make simple hand movements without them being able to see their actual hand. At the same time, they were shown an image of either their hand or a different hand on a TV-screen. They found that schizophrenics with delusions and hallucinations could not tell the difference between their own hand and someone else's hand. This supports the idea that schizophrenics have problems distinguishing between their own actions and other people's actions (a metarepresentation problem).
Frith and Done (1986) found that schizophrenic patients with negative symptoms did worse on verbal fluency tasks (such as name as many fruits as you can). This supports the idea that schizophrenics have difficulties in information processing.

Frith and Done (1989) found that schizophrenic found it much harder to work out the errors they had made in a computer game compared to non-schizophrenics. This supports the idea that schizophrenics have problems recognising their own actions. Another study that shows that people with schizophrenia have problems with information processing is Bentall et al. (1991). They got schizophrenic and non-schizophrenic participants to come up with words or read words from a list. One week later they got the participants back. They found that schizophrenic participants with hallucinations found it very difficult to remember whether they had come up with words themselves, read them or whether the words were new. Non-schizophrenic participants were much better at this, suggesting schizophrenics suffer from difficulties in information processing.

Explanation- A problem with the cognitive explanation of schizophrenia is that it does not explain the causes of schizophrenia. There are biological explanations for schizophrenia that can explain the causes. For example, genes may predispose someone to develop schizophrenia and high levels of dopamine in the brain may cause schizophrenia.

You need to be able to describe and evaluate one biological treatment for schizophrenia, for example, drug therapy.

Description

Anti-psychotic drugs are used to treat schizophrenia. They help sedate the person and reduce the intensity of hallucinations, delusions and other psychotic behaviours. Anti-psychotics are more effective when given at the onset of symptoms. Typical anti-psychotics were the first generation of the drugs aimed to treat schizophrenia. Chlorpromazine is an example of a first generation anti-psychotic drug. These drugs act by blocking the dopamine receptors (acting antagonistically on D2 receptors). The drugs fit into the dopamine receptors in the brain blocking dopamine and preventing it being picked up (remember that excess of dopamine in the brain is related to schizophrenia). However, they caused severe side effects such as neuroleptic malignant syndrome which is potentially fatal. Atypical antipsychotics are the new generation of drugs for schizophrenia. They tend to work on dopamine and serotonin receptors and they have fewer side effects. The newer anti-psychotics such as rispiridone are effective for the positive and negative symptoms of schizophrenia.

Exam tip: You can use DESERT to help you evaluate a therapy.

Directive- Is the patient reliant on the therapist for all the answers? Is there a power imbalance? If the therapist has too much power then the treatment is directive.
Effectiveness-How effective is the therapy at treating the mental disorder? What do outcome studies show?
Side effects-Are there any side effects to the therapy?
Expense-How expensive is the therapy in terms of time and money?
Reasons-Does the therapy looks at the underlying causes/reasons for the mental disorder?
Types of people-Does the therapy only work on certain types of people?

Evaluation:

Directive-Schizophrenics living in the community are often told to take drugs by their doctors but they have control over when they take it. However, schizophrenics in hospital may be pressurised to take their drugs.

Effectiveness-Anti-psychotics allow patients to live in society avoiding long term hospital care and institutionalisation and it enables them to access other therapies such as CBT which may help cure them. Anti-psychotics also reduce the intensity of symptoms. Kane (1992) found that chlorpromazine was effective with 75% of schizophrenics. Emsley (2008) found that injecting risperidone could reduce both positive and negative symptoms of schizophrenia and led to high remission rates.

Side effects-Anti-psychotics have many side effects such as tightening of muscles, constipation, weight gain and in rare cases neuroleptic malignant syndrome, which can be fatal. Many patients stop taking anti-psychotics due to the side effects. Higher and higher doses may be required as the patient develops a tolerance to the drugs.

Expense-Anti-psychotic drugs can be expensive over the long-term but in the short-term they are not as expensive as talking therapies. Atypical anti-psychotic drugs have fewer side effects but are more expensive than typical anti-psychotic drugs. Reasons-Anti-psychotic drugs just treat the symptoms of the schizophrenia, they don't deal with any underlying issues.

Types of people-Anti-psychotic drugs do not work on all schizophrenics. Around 25% of schizophrenics do not respond to the drugs.

You need to be able to describe and evaluate one psychological treatment for schizophrenia. For example, cognitive behavioural therapy (CBT).

Description

The cognitive part of the cognitive behavioural therapy (CBT) involves questioning and changing a schizophrenic's maladaptive thoughts/distorted beliefs. For example, the therapist might question the schizophrenic's beliefs about how powerful the voices are that they hear in their head. They might also change their faulty interpretations of the world such as the belief that everyone is out to get them. The behavioural part of the therapy involves changing their behaviour, for example, getting them to ignore the voices they hear in their head or to ignore ideas that their thoughts are being put in their head by someone else. The therapist has to accept that the patient has a different perception of reality and the aim of the therapy is to help the patient manage their misperceptions.

Evaluation

Directive-Cognitive behavioural therapy is directive as the therapist tells the patient which thoughts are faulty and how they should change them.

Effectiveness-Chadwick's (2000) study found that only 8 hours of CBT combined with anti-psychotics reduced negative beliefs about how powerful the voices were.

Gould et al.'s (2001) meta-analysis concluded that CBT combined with anti-psychotics reduces positive symptoms of schizophrenia. CBT can also be used to help schizophrenics that do not respond to drugs although it is usually used in combination with drugs.

Side effects-None

Expense-CBT can be expensive as it requires a trained therapist to deliver the treatment. However, CBT can be delivered over a short period of time.

Reasons-CBT does not deal with any underlying causes of schizophrenia such as childhood issues. It just deals with changing the patient's current beliefs.

Types of people-CBT is more effective on those with positive symptoms of schizophrenia as it involves getting schizophrenics to challenge their beliefs. It does not work so well on those with negative symptoms such as poverty of speech.

You need to be able to describe the features and symptoms of anorexia nervosa.

Features

Anorexia nervosa mainly affects girls and women although it has become more common amongst boys and men in recent years. The ratio of females: males with the condition is 10:1. The condition usually develops in adolescence. Prevalence of the disorder is higher in high-income industrialised countries. There are two types of anorexia nervosa: restricting type and binge-eating/purging type. People with a restricting type of anorexia restrict how much they eat and exercise excessively. People with a binge-eating/purging type of anorexia have will eat excessively and then vomit or use laxatives to purge the food.

Symptoms

Anorexia nervosa is a refusal to maintain a minimal normal body weight for age and height. Diagnosis requires bodyweight to be less than 85% of that expected. There is an intense fear of gaining weight despite being underweight. Another factor in diagnosis is amenorrhoea, the absence of menstruation for at least three consecutive menstrual cycles. 90% of sufferers are female. Sufferers have a preoccupation with thinness, dieting and exercise.

You need to be able to describe and evaluate one biological explanation of anorexia nervosa. For example, the genetic explanation of anorexia nervosa.

Description

The genetic explanation of anorexia says that genes can predispose someone to develop schizophrenia and that is why it can run in families. There is an increased risk of developing anorexia if you have a parent, sibling or twin with anorexia. Genes may lead to biochemical imbalances in the brain such as low levels of serotonin, which is associated with anorexia. Genes may also cause structural changes in the hypothalamus, which is involved in the regulation of eating. Genetic abnormalities might also lead to damage to neural pathways (nerve cells carrying messages) in the brain. Eating behaviour that is controlled by these neural pathways may then be abnormal.

Evaluation:

Studies- Kortegaard et al. (2001) found a slightly higher concordance for anorexia nervosa in MZ twins compared to DZ twins. Holland (1984) found a higher concordance rate for eating disorders in MZ twins (55%) than DZ twins. However, MZ twins often share a more similar environment than DZ twins so it is difficult to separate out the effects of genes from environment. The fact that MZ twins do not have a 100% concordance rate for anorexia, suggests that environment plays a significant role in the development of the disorder. Twin studies are correlational so it is difficult to establish cause and effect.

Explanation-The genetic explanation for anorexia nervosa is reductionist as it does not take into account psychological, social and cultural factors.

You need to be able to describe and evaluate one non-biological explanation of anorexia nervosa. For example, social learning theory as an explanation of anorexia nervosa.

Description

Pressure from media images may contribute to the development of anorexia nervosa. Social learning theory can explain this in terms of young people paying attention to the fact that many celebrity role models are extremely thin and retaining this information. Young people have the ability to reproduce being thin if they diet excessively and will do it if they are motivated to do so. They can see that their thin role models are famous and rich and they may think that in order to be successful like their role models they have to be thin too. They may also think that being excessively thin is necessary to be accepted. This provides the motivation to diet excessively.

Evaluation:

Studies-Lai (2000) found that the rate of anorexia increased for chinese residents in Hong Kong as the culture slowly became more westernised. This supports the idea that western thin role models lead to anorexia. Crisp et al. (1976) found that dancers and fashion models were more likely to develop anorexia nervosa, which also supports SLT. Mumford et al. (1991) found that Arab and Asian women were more likely to develop eating disorders if they moved to the West. Becker et al. (2002) found that after the introduction of Western TV channels to the island of Fiji, eating disorders previously unknown on the island began to appear.

Explanation- Social learning theory does not explain why anorexia usually develops in adolescence. Anorexia nervosa may be related to fears about growing up and family issues rather than media images. Another limitation of social learning theory as an explanation of anorexia nervosa is that everyone sees pictures of slim people, but not everyone develops eating disorders.

You need to be able to describe and evaluate one biological treatment for anorexia nervosa. For example, drug therapy.

Description

Drugs do not directly help the symptoms of anorexia but they are used to treat depression and anxiety that often occur at the same time as anorexia. This helps anorexic patients to be in a better frame of mind to respond to psychological therapies. Selective serotonin reuptake inhibitors (SSRIs) and olanzapine have been used with patients with anorexia. SSRIs are a type of anti-depressant drug and they work by inhibiting the reuptake of serotonin at the presynaptic neuron. This increases the amount of serotonin in the synapse so that more serotonin can be passed to the postsynaptic neuron. This reduces any feelings of depression that might co-occur with anorexia. Olanzapine is a more modern anti-psychotic drug (atypical anti-psychotic drug), which can be used to treat anxiety as well as schizophrenia. It is believed to block serotonin and dopamine receptors in specific areas of the brain. The drug can be used to reduce any anxiety that might co-occur with anorexia.

Evaluation

Directive-Anorexic patients in a mental health institution may feel pressurised to take their drugs.

Effectiveness-The National Institute of Health and Care Excellence (NICE) recommends that drugs should not be used as the main treatment for anorexia. The majority of studies show that drugs are not effective in treating anorexia. Ferguson et al. (1999) found no significant differences between patients taking SSRIs and those not taking them. However, Jensen and Mejlhede (2000) carried out case studies on three patients taking olanzapine and found a gradual improvement in the patients' body image.

Side effects-Anorexic patients can have heart problems due to malnutrition. Therefore, clinicians need to be particularly careful when administering drugs as some drugs can cause cardiac side effects. Another side effect of SSRIs and olanzapine is that they can cause weight gain, which can be distressing for anorexic patients.

Expense-Drugs can be expensive over the long-term but in the short-term they are not as expensive as talking therapies.

Reasons-Drugs can be used to treat comorbid conditions such as depression and anxiety but they don't they don't deal with anorexic symptoms.

Types of people-Drugs may be an inappropriate treatment for anorexic patients who don't have any accompanying depression or anxiety.

You need to be able to describe and evaluate one non-biological treatment for anorexia nervosa. For example, Rational Emotive Therapy (RET).

Description

Rational emotive therapy (RET) is based on the idea that negative, irrational thoughts can lead to abnormal (maladaptive) behaviour. It aims to replace a person's irrational thoughts with more realistic ones. It works on an ABC model, where A stands for an activating event, B for the beliefs about A and C for the consequences. For example, with an anorexic, the activating event (A) might have been that they saw their friends make fun of a girl at school for being fat. The beliefs (B) about A might have been that they thought they needed to be thin in order to be accepted and liked. The consequences (C) might be that they have started dieting excessively. During therapy, an anorexic would be questioned about their beliefs so that any irrational thoughts can be identified. The therapist then tries to change the person's beliefs so that they have a more realistic view of the world. For example, they might be asked to identify people who are not thin but well-liked. They may also be set homework, where they have to practice thinking and behaving in a more rational way.

Evaluation:

Directive-RET is directive as the therapist has a lot of power over their client, they argue with them about their beliefs and tell them how to change their thinking.

Effectiveness-RET focuses on changing present irrational thoughts rather than taking into account childhood experiences so it can work quickly to change behaviour. Brandsma et al. (1978) found that RET works well on people who are perfectionist and many anorexics have such tendencies. Silverman et al. (1992) did 89 outcomes studies of RET and found that it was more effective or equal to other types of therapy for a wide range disorders.

Side effects-None

Expense-RET requires a trained professional to deliver the treatment so it can be expensive. However, it is less expensive than psychoanalysis (free association) as it can be delivered relatively quickly.

Reason-RET does not deal with the underlying causes of anorexia. It just tries to change negative, irrational thoughts. It may be better to treats anorexics with a mixture of RET and family systems therapy as it does not take into account family relationships, which may contribute to the anorexia.

Types of people-RET can be used with most anorexics.

You need to be able to discuss how cultural effects can lead to individual differences in mental health disorders

Cultural effects such as someone's gender, race, culture or religion can lead to individual differences in mental health disorders. For example, individuals from

Western cultures tend to report higher rates of social anxiety disorder than individuals from Asian cultures. People with social anxiety disorder fear embarrassing themselves. Hofan and Asnaani (2010) suggest that Taijin Kyofusho (TKS), which is prevalent in Japanese and Korean cultures, is a culture-specific expression of social anxiety disorder. Individuals with TKS are concerned with displeasing or embarrassing other people rather than themselves. As a result, they avoid social situations in the same way that those diagnosed with social anxiety disorder do.

Eating disorders are more prevalent in Western cultures. Hoek et al. (2005) found that the incidence of anorexia was much lower on the island of Curacao as it is more culturally acceptable to be overweight. Becker et al. (2002) found that the girls living on the island of Fiji started developing eating disorder symptoms after the introduction of Western TV channels, suggest that Western media images influenced the girls' body image. Nasser (1986) compared Egyptian women studying in Cairo with similar Egyptian women studying in London and found that 12% of those living in London developed eating disorder symptoms, compared to 0% in Cairo. Lai (2000) found that the rate of anorexia increased for Chinese residents in Hong Kong as the culture slowly became more westernised. Mumford et al. (1991) found that Arab and Asian women were more likely to develop eating disorders if they moved to the West. These studies suggest that the Western view that being slim equates to attractiveness influences the development of eating disorders.

You need to be able to discuss how cultural effects can lead to different diagnoses of mental health disorders affecting reliability and validity.

Cultural effects can lead to different diagnoses. For example, people from different cultures may report their symptoms in a different way. Language barriers might also lead to misdiagnosis. Neighbors et al. (2003) found that African Americans are more likely to be diagnosed with schizophrenia whereas white Americans are more likely to be diagnosed with mood disorders. Such studies suggest that there is a bias in diagnosis.

Different cultures may interpret people's behaviour in different ways, for example hearing voices in Britain would be a symptom of schizophrenia but in another culture they might see it as spiritual.

There can also be problems related to mistrust of mainly white, middle class psychiatrists. Casas (1995) found that a lot of African Americans do not like to share their personal information with people of a different race so this can lead to problems with diagnosis. In fact, African Americans are less likely to seek help from mental health professionals than white Americans (Sussman, Robins and Earls, 1987). Sue and Sue (1992) found that many Asian Americans don't like to talk about their emotions and are less likely to admit they have a problem. Cinnerella and Loewethal (1999) compared cultural influences on mental disorders between white Catholics, black Christians, Muslim Pakistanis, Orthodox Jews and Indian Hindus. They found that all the groups except the white Catholics had a fear of health professionals misunderstanding them. This means that certain groups may be less likely to seek help or talk about their issues openly with a psychiatrist.

DSM-5 aims to take into account people's cultural background when making a diagnosis. It highlights how people from different cultures display symptoms of the same mental disorder differently. For example, uncontrollable crying and headaches are symptoms of panic attacks in some cultures, while difficulty breathing is the main symptom in other cultures. DSM-5 provides clinicians with detailed information about how people from different cultures think and talk about psychological problems.

You need to show an awareness of Health and Care Professions Council (HCPC) guidelines for clinical practitioners.

In order for clinicians such as clinical psychologists to practice they need to be registered with the HCPC. The HCPC checks the character of everyone who applies for registration to make sure that they are safe and effective practitioners. This involves looking at criminal convictions, cautions and character references.

The HCPC also check the health of clinicians as this might affect their ability to practise. For example, someone with a mental health issue might not be in the right state of mind to help someone else.

In addition, the HCPC set standards for education and training.

You need to be able to describe and evaluate longitudinal methods in mental health research.

Description:

Longitudinal studies involve studying the same person or group of people over a long period of time. For example, researchers working in mental health might monitor how a treatment is affecting patients' symptoms over a period of time.

Evaluation:

An advantage of longitudinal studies is that they allow researchers to follow the development and progress of a patient or group of patients over time. There are also less likely to be participant variables as the same patients are used and their progress can be tracked. However, longitudinal studies can be expensive. Furthermore, erosion of the sample (patients dropping out of the study) may cause bias. For example, if the researchers are looking at the effects of family systems therapy on anorexic children in a deprived area over time and some children leave the study to move to a more affluent area, then that can bias the results. It is also difficult to replicate a longitudinal study and establish reliability. Furthermore, new treatments are being rapidly developed in clinical psychology, which could make the findings of longitudinal research irrelevant by the time it is published.

You need to be able to describe and evaluate cross-sectional research in mental health.

Description:

Cross-sectional studies involve gathering data at one moment in time from different groups of people so that one group is compared with another group on the same characteristics, behaviour or task i.e. a cross-sectional study might compare anorexic patients of different ages at the same time.

Evaluation:

Cross-sectional designs tend to be cheaper, quicker and more practical than longitudinal designs as participants are tested at one moment in time. However, as different participants are used in the conditions, participant variables can affect results. For example, 12-year-old anorexic girls may not be comparable with the 16-year-old anorexic girls if the 12-year-old girls had more exposure to media images of thin women.

You need to be able to describe and evaluate the use of meta-analysis in mental health research.

Description:

Meta-analyses look at the findings of a number of different studies and draw conclusions. In mental health research, a meta-analysis might be carried out to look at the effectiveness of anti-psychotics versus talking therapies for schizophrenia. For example, Gould et al.'s (2001) meta-analysis concluded that CBT combined with anti-psychotics reduces positive symptoms of schizophrenia.

Evaluation:

Meta-analyses can be carried out quickly at little cost. They are useful when there is a lot of research on a specific topic such as the effectiveness of CBT and conclusions need to be drawn. However, not all studies are equally reliable and valid and some studies may be included in a meta-analysis that distort results.

You need to be able to describe and evaluate the use of primary and secondary data.

Primary data is data that is gathered first hand. For example, when an experiment, observation or questionnaire is carried out and data is collected.

Evaluation: Primary data can be tested for reliability e.g if you gather data from a laboratory experiment; you can repeat the experiment again to see whether the data can be replicated. You can then see whether the data is reliable. Primary data is also up-to-date as it is data that is collected in the present rather taken from previous research. However, primary data takes more time and money to collect.

Secondary data is data that is gathered from a secondary source e.g. data gathered from books, journals, records etc. that already exist.

Evaluation:

It takes less time and money to gather secondary data as you don't have to carry out any studies yourself, you can just look up the data in books, journals and records.

Studies that are unreliable or with a bad design can be left out in the analysis. However, secondary data can be out-of-date as it involves using data from past studies and records.

You need to be able to describe and evaluate the use of case studies

Description:

A case study is an in-depth study of one person or one group of people. A number of different techniques are used to gather data. For example, the researcher may observe, interview and carry out a number of experiments on the same person. Triangulation is used to pool data together from the different types of research method and to draw conclusions. Case studies can be used in clinical psychology to study the effects of a particular therapy or to look at individuals with unique issues.

Evaluation:

Case studies are not generalisable as they are carried out on only one person or one group of people who are often unique and not representative of the wider population. It is also difficult to replicate case studies because they involve unique individuals and the interpretation of the observations and interviews is subject to bias. Therefore it is hard to establish reliability in case studies. However, triangulation is used to draw conclusions about the same concept so this improves the reliability of the findings. An advantage of case studies is that they gather rich, detailed information about the individuals using a number of different techniques, so this increases their validity. There can be ethical issues with case studies. Often they involve studying unique individuals who are more vulnerable than normal. Therefore, researchers have to be careful to protect them from psychological distress.

You need to be able to describe and evaluate an example of a case study. Lavarenne et al. (2013) Containing psychotic patients with fragile boundaries: a single group case study.

Description:

Aim-To see whether group therapy is useful for psychotic patients with fragile ego boundaries.

Procedure-They looked at a group of six individuals who suffered from schizophrenia or schizoaffective disorder who were attending a weekly support group called the 'Thursday group'. The researchers reported on one specific session, just before Christmas when the individuals were facing a break before their next meeting. They wrote down key points about the session immediately afterwards but did not record the session.

Results- The researchers reported that the individuals showed more fragile ego boundaries during this session.

Conclusion- The patients felt more vulnerable and demonstrated more fragile ego boundaries due the increased time gap between that specific session and the next meeting. Group therapy helps individuals with psychotic disorders to develop healthier ego boundaries and a tolerance to interpersonal proximity (being close to others).

Evaluation:

Generalisability-The study is not generalisable as it was only done on one small group of psychotic patients at one specific session.

Reliability-The group therapy session would be hard to replicate and get the same results. Therefore, the study is not reliable.

Application to real life-The study suggests that group therapy helps individuals with fragile ego boundaries create firmer ego boundaries.

Validity-What the patients said during the session is open to interpretation. The group leaders may also not have remembered the session accurately as the session was not recorded and they only wrote notes at the end of the session.

Ethics-There are ethical issues as the patients in the study were particularly vulnerable and may not have given fully informed consent.

Note 1: The term ego boundary refers to distinction people make between themselves and the world and the real and unreal. Some people with schizophrenia and schizoaffective disorder have fragile ego boundaries. This means that they cannot differentiate between their own perceptions and other people's and what is real and unreal.

Note 2: People with schizoaffective disorder have psychotic symptoms such as hallucinations and delusions combined with mood disturbances such as depression or bipolar disorder.

You need to be able to describe and evaluate the use of interviews in clinical psychology.

Description:

An interview involves asking patients questions verbally. For example, an interview can be used to ask schizophrenics and their families about their symptoms and experiences. It may form the basis of a case study or as a follow-up to other research methods. Structured interviews produce quantitative data. All participants are asked the same questions in the same order. They are very similar to a questionnaire except questions are read out. An unstructured interview involves an informal or in-depth conversation. Little is planned in advance (perhaps the first couple of questions) and this allows the interviewee to explain answers and introduce new issues. Unstructured interviews obtain rich, qualitative data. A semi-structured interview involves some prepared questions but also some opportunities for interviewees to expand on their answers.

Evaluation:

Unstructured interviews tend to be valid because they allow the clinician to explore issues that the patient brings up, so there will be a focus on what the patient wants to reveal. Unstructured interviews gather qualitative data as well which means that the data is detailed and in-depth. Detailed interview data can be analysed by looking for themes but this process can be subjective. The interviewers may affect the data by the way the ask questions about the patient's symptoms or background. Patients may give socially desirable answers or not wanted to admit to certain symptoms. At another time, patients may report different symptoms so there is an issue with the reliability of interviews. Certain characteristics about the interviewer such as their dress or manner can also affect replies.

You need to be able to describe and evaluate an example of an interview. Vallentine et al. (2010) Psycho-educational group for detained offender patients: understanding mental illness.

Description:

Aim-To investigate the usefulness of teaching offender patients about their mental illness via groupwork within a high security psychiatric hospital.

Note: The patients in the study are called offender patients because they had committed a criminal offence and were in Broadmoor high-security hospital.

Procedure-The sample consisted of 42 male patients at Broadmoor high security hospital. The majority of them had psychotic disorders (64% of them had paranoid schizophrenia). They had been referred to an 'Understanding Mental Illness' group as many of them lacked information about their diagnosis. A semi-structured interview was developed to see what the patients thought about the group after they had finished the sessions. Their feedback was examined using a content analysis to pick out important themes in the patients' responses.

Result- All the patients interviewed said that they would recommend the group to others. They said that the group had helped them to understand their own behaviour and that it had been valuable to listen to other people's experiences of mental illness. The information they had been given in the group made them feel more confident about coping with their symptoms in the future.

Conclusion-Psycho-educational groupwork can have a positive impact on patients. Feedback from the patients suggests that it can make them feel more confident and empowered.

Note: Psycho-educational groupwork refers to when patients attend group sessions which teach them about symptoms, treatments, causes of their mental disorder, related difficulties and coping skills.

Evaluation:

Generalisability-Only 21 of the 31 completers of the group sessions took part in the interviews. This may have led to bias in the sample.

Reliability-The use of semi-structured interviews means that it would be difficult to repeat the interviews and get the same results. The patients may answer questions differently on a different day. However, the researchers did record their interviews so that the accuracy of their data could be checked.

Application to real life-The study suggests that psycho-educational groupwork can be helpful for offender patients dealing with a psychiatric disorder.

Validity-The researchers gathered in-depth qualitative data from the patients in semi-structured interviews. This gives the study greater validity as they would have been able to understand more fully the patients' viewpoints.

Ethics-The study dealt with vulnerable people who may have felt they had to take part in the research as they were in a high-security hospital. However, some of the patients chose not to take part in the interviews, which shows that they did feel they had the right to withdraw.

You need to be able to analyse descriptive data. This means you need to be able to to work out the mean, median, mode, range and standard deviation from a set of data.

Measures of central tendency
The mean, median and mode are called measures of central tendency.

The mean

The mean is often referred to as the average of a set of numbers. You calculate the mean by adding up all the numbers and then dividing by the number of numbers.

Consider the following data set: 12, 17, 23, 27

Add the numbers together: 12+17+23+27=79
Divide 79 by 4: 79/4 =19.75

The 'Mean' (Average) is 19.75

The median

The median is the 'middle value' in a list of numbers. To find the median, your numbers have to be listed in numerical order. If you have an odd number of numbers, the median is the middle entry in the list. If you have an even number of numbers, the median is equal to the sum of the two middle numbers divided by two.

Consider the following data set: 13, 17, 21, 8

Sort the numbers into numerical order: 8, 13, 17, 21

There is not a single middle number in this data set as there is an even number of numbers.

Therefore, add the two middle numbers, 13 and 17, and divide by two:

13+17=30
30/2=15

The median is 15

The mode

The mode is the number that occurs most frequently in a set of data. If no number is repeated, then there is no mode for the set of data.

Measures of Dispersion

The range and standard deviation are measures of dispersion. They relate to how the data is spread out or 'dispersed'.

The range

The range is the difference between the largest and smallest numbers.

Consider the following data set: 11, 15, 16, 21

Subtract the smallest number from the largest number: 21-11=10

The range is 10

The standard deviation is a way of telling how far apart or how close together the data is.

Standard deviation

Why are we interested in standard deviation?

Consider the following two data sets:
Data set 1: 28, 29, 30, 31, 32   Mean = (28+29+30+31+32)/5=30
Data set 2: 10, 20, 30, 40, 50   Mean = (10+20+30+40+50)/5=30

Both data sets have a mean of 30 but the data is spread much further apart in data set 2. Therefore, data set 2 has a larger standard deviation.

Standard deviation is a measure of dispersion, which means it's useful in determining how spread out the data is. For example, if one school has students with a high mean number of UCAS points and a very small standard deviation, that means that the all the students at this school got good A-levels. If a second school has students that have an equally high mean number of UCAS points with a very high standard deviation as well, that means that the students had a much wider range of A-level grades with some getting high grades and some getting much worse grades.

Calculating standard deviation

$$S = \sqrt{\frac{\sum(x - \bar{x})^2}{n - 1}}$$

X= each value
$\bar{X}$= mean of the data set
n = the number of values
$\sum$=sum of
For example, for the data set 46, 42, 44, 45 ,43:
1) Calculate the mean: $\bar{X}$ = (46+42+44+45+43)/5=44
2) Take away the mean from each value (x - $\bar{X}$) and then square it.
3) Add up all the (x - $\bar{X}$)^2 values 4+4+0+1+1=10
4) Divide the sum of all the (x - $\bar{X}$)^2 values by n-1: 10/(5-1)=10/4=2.5
5) Square root it all for the standard deviation, s. $\sqrt{}$ 2.5= 1.6

Note: Using a table can help you get your calculation right.

X	$\bar{X}$	(X - $\bar{X}$)	(X - $\bar{X}$)^2
46	44	2	4
42	44	-2	4
44	44	0	0
45	44	1	1
43	44	-1	1
$\bar{X}$ = 44			$\sum$ = 10

$$S = \sqrt{\frac{\sum(X - \bar{X})^2}{n - 1}} = 1.6$$

How can you interpret standard deviation?

For datasets that have a normal distribution the standard deviation can be used to determine the proportion of values that lie within a particular range of the mean value. For such distributions, 68% of values are less than one standard deviation (1SD) away from the mean value, 95% of values are less than two standard deviations (2SD) away from the mean and 99% of values are less than three standard deviations (3SD) away from the mean.
The mean of our data set was 44 and the standard deviation (SD) is 1.6. Therefore, 68% of values in the data set lie between mean-1SD (44-1.6 =42.4) and mean +1SD

(44+1.6=45.6). 99% of the values will lie between mean-3SD (44-4.8=39.2) and mean +3SD (44+4.8=48.8).

If the data set had the same mean of 44 but a larger standard deviation e.g. 2.4, it would suggest that the values were more dispersed.

You need to understand levels of data

In order to carry out an inferential statistical test, you need to know what level of data you have. There are four levels of data: nominal, ordinal, interval and ratio. Nominal data is made up of discrete categories. For example, you have two categories such as 'action toys' and 'soft toys'. Ordinal data refers to ranked data. An example of ordinal data is when athletes' are ranked as first, second and third in race. Interval data refers to data that can be measured along a scale but does not have a true zero. For example, IQ can be measured along a scale but it does not have a true zero. In contrast, ratio data is measured on a scale that has a true zero point. For example, time can be measured along a scale and does have a true zero.

You need to know about level of significance

In psychology, a significance level of $p \leq 0.05$ is chosen.

$p \leq 0.05$ means that there is an equal or less than 5% probability that the results could have occurred due to chance.

p = the probability of the results being due to chance

$\leq$ = less than or equal to

0.05 = 1 in 20 = 5%

Psychologists prefer to use the significance level: $p \leq 0.05$ to judge whether to accept a hypothesis or not. This means that there is an equal or less than 5% probability that the results are due to chance. For example, in an experiment looking at the effect of cues on memory, a researcher might find that the group that received a cue recalled more words than the group that did not receive a cue and there is a less than 5% chance that the difference between the two groups could have been due to chance (random differences between the groups).

Sometimes researchers use the significance level: $p \leq 0.1$ to judge whether to accept a hypothesis or not. This means that there is an equal or less than 10% probability that the results are due to chance. You can see that this is less conservative than $p \leq 0.05$. It is easier for the hypothesis to be accepted even though the null hypothesis might be true. This leads to a type 1 error. Type 1 errors can lead to false positive results; accepting a hypothesis even though it is incorrect. This could lead to psychologists thinking that there is a significant difference between participant's recall when they are given a cue and not given a cue when there isn't a significant difference in recall.

Sometimes researchers use the significance level: $p \leq 0.01$ to judge whether to accept a hypothesis or not. This means that there is an equal or less than 1%

probability that the results are due to chance. You can see that this is stricter than p ≤ 0.05. It is harder for the hypothesis to be accepted even though it might actually be correct. This leads to a type 2 error. Type 2 errors can lead to false negative results; rejecting a hypothesis when it is correct. This could lead to psychologists thinking that there was no difference between participants recall when given a cue compared to no cue, when there was a significant difference.

You need to be able to use the chi-square test and understand how to compare the observed and critical values to judge significance

A chi-square test is a test of difference or association. For example, a researcher might want to investigate the differences between males and females in terms of their willingness to use mental health services. The chi-square test is used when the data level is nominal, there is an independent measures design and when you are looking for a difference between two groups. There must be a minimum of 5 scores in each category, to carry out a chi-squared test.

The experimental or alternative hypothesis should state that there will be a difference between the two groups. An example of a one tailed (directional) hypothesis is: More females will be willing to use mental health services than males.

The null hypothesis should state that there is difference between the groups e.g. There will be no difference between males and females in their willingness to use mental health services.

For a chi-square test, if the observed value is greater than the critical value shown in a table, then the null hypothesis can be rejected and the result is viewed as significant. The critical value can be found in a critical values table.

The formula for the chi-squared test is:

$$\chi^2 = \sum \frac{(O - E)^2}{E}$$

O = the frequencies observed

E = the frequencies expected

$\sum$ *= the 'sum of'*

Table to show the willingness of males and females to use mental health services:

	Male	Female	Totals
No	19	10	29
Yes	6	15	21
Totals	25	25	50

First work out the degrees of freedom (df) for this contingency table:

df= (rows-1) x (columns-1)= (2-1) x (2-1) = 1 x1= 1

A table can then be used to help in the process of working out the chi-square value:

O	E	O-E	$(O-E)^2$	$(O-E)^2/E$
19	14.5	4.5	20.25	1.40
10	14.5	-4.5	20.25	1.40
6	10.5	-4.5	20.25	1.93
15	10.5	4.5	20.25	1.93

=6.65

The calculated value of chi-square is 6.65. This is called the observed value because it has been obtained from the data observed by the researcher.

Note:
O= observed frequencies. This refers to the data collected.
E=expected frequencies. This refers to what the researcher might expect to see if there is no association between gender and willingness to use mental health services. For example, if there were 29 'No' answers. You would expect half of them to be given by females and half of them to be given by males. 29/2=14.5. Therefore the expected frequency is 14.5.

In order to find out if the observed value of 6.65 is significant or not, it must be compared to the critical value. You need to find the correct critical value in a critical values table for chi-square. Make sure you look for the critical value that corresponds for df=1 and p ≤ 0.05 for a one-tailed hypothesis. This is 2.71.

As observed value of 6.65 is bigger than the critical value of 2.71, we would say that the result is significant and more females are willing to use mental health services than males.

You need to be able to use the Spearman's Rho test

For example, a researcher might want to investigate whether there is a relationship between male brain score and aggression score.

The table below shows some example data and how d^2 can be calculated by ranking the data.

Participant number	Male brain score (A)	Aggression score (B)	Rank A	Rank B	d=Rank A- Rank B	d^2
1	56	66	9	4	5	25
2	75	70	3	2	1	1
3	45	40	10	10	0	0
4	71	60	4	7	3	9
5	62	65	6	5	1	1
6	64	56	5	9	4	16
7	58	59	8	8	0	0
8	80	77	1	1	0	0
9	76	67	2	3	1	1
10	61	63	7	6	1	1

d=the difference between the ranks
d^2= the difference between the ranks squared

The formula for Spearman's rho is:

$$r_s = 1 - \frac{6 \sum d^2}{n(n^2 - 1)}$$

Step 1: Work out the sum of d^2. Note the symbol, $\sum$, means 'sum of'.

$\sum d^2 = 25+1+9+1+16+1+1=54$

Step 2: We then substitute this into the main equation with the other information. Remember n=10 as there were 10 participants.
$r_s = 1 - 6 \sum d_i^2/n (n^2-1)$
$r_s = 1 - 6 \times 54/10(10^2 - 1)$
$r_s = 1 - (324/990)$
$r_s = 1 - 0.33$
$r_s = 0.67$
The r_s value of 0.67 indicates a strong positive relationship between the male brain score and aggression. That is, the higher you ranked for male brain score, the higher you ranked in aggression.
Note: The Spearman correlation coefficient, r_s, can take values from +1 to -1. A r_s of +1 indicates a perfect positive correlation, a r_s of zero indicates no relationship and a r_s of -1 indicates a perfect negative correlation. The closer r_s is to zero, the weaker the relationship between the co-variables.

You need to be able to compare the observed value of r_s with the critical value. To find the critical value in a critical values table, you need to look for n=10 as there were 10 participants and $p \leq 0.05$. For Spearman's rho, the observed value of r_s need to be bigger than the critical value for the result to be significant.

You need to be able to use the Wilcoxon Signed Rank test

You use a Wilcoxon Signed Rank test when you have a repeated measures design, ordinal data and you are investigating whether there is a significant difference between two conditions. For example, a researcher wants to see whether there is a differences between two treatments for anorexics. In order to do this, they ask seven anorexic patients who have been receiving two different treatments to rate them out of 10.

Table to show rankings for therapy A and therapy B given by the same patients:

Patient	Therapy A	Therapy B
1	7	4
2	9	3
3	8	4
4	7	7
5	8	3
6	5	6
7	9	5

Step 1: Calculate the differences between two scores by taking one from the other. Then rank the differences giving the smallest difference Rank 1.

Patient	Therapy A	Therapy B	Difference between ranks (d)	Ranked differences
1	4	7	-3	2
2	9	3	6	6
3	8	4	4	3.5
4	7	7	0	ignore
5	8	3	5	5
6	5	6	-1	1
7	9	5	4	3.5

Note that the lowest rank is given to the smallest difference score (-1), ignoring whether it is a positive or negative difference.

If two or more difference scores are the same, then these scores get the average of the ranks that those scores would have obtained, had they been different from each other. Here there are two difference scores of 4. Therefore we work out the mean rank that these scores *would* have had, if they had been different from each other (the ranks of 3 and 4). The mean rank is (3+4)/2=3.5 so this is the rank that the two difference scores of 4 are given.

You do not rank any differences of 0 and when adding the number of scores, do not count those with a difference of 0.

Step 2: Add up the ranks for positive differences.

6+3.5+5+3.5=18

Step 3: Add up the ranks for negative difference.

1+2=3

Step 4: Whatever is the smallest value from step 2 and 3 is the value of T. This is your observed value.

Here T=3

Step 5: N is the number of differences, ignoring 0 differences.

There are 6 differences here.

Step 6: Look at the table of critical values for a Wilcoxon Signed Rank test. With an N of 6 for a two-tailed test at 0.05 significance, the critical value is 0.

For a Wilcoxon Signed Rank test, T has to be less than or equal to the critical value for the result to be significant. In this example, T=3 so the observed value is bigger than the critical value and the result is not significant. The null hypothesis must be accepted and so there was no significant difference between therapy A and therapy B for anorexic patients.

Note: When you are looking up critical values in a table, you need to know: whether the hypothesis was one-tailed or two-tailed; the number of participants who had a difference between their scores (shown as 'N' on the table) and the significance level. The values in the Wilcoxon Signed Rank test are termed 'T' and unlike the Spearman-rank and Chi-squared Tests the observed value has to be equal to or less than the critical value for the results to be significant (i.e. to accept the experimental hypothesis and reject the null hypothesis).

You need to be able to use the Mann-Whitney test

You use a Mann-Whitney U test when you have an independent groups design, ordinal data and you are testing for a difference between two groups.

Mann-Whitney U test formulae

$$U_a = n_a n_b + \frac{n_a(n_a+1)}{2} - \sum R_a$$

$$U_b = n_a n_b + \frac{n_b(n_b+1)}{2} - \sum R_b$$

(U is the smaller of U_a and U_b)

n_a is the number of participants rating in group A
n_b is the number of participants in group B
$\sum R_a$ is the sum of the ranks for group A's data
$\sum R_b$ is the sum of the ranks for group B's data

For example, a researcher might ask two groups of schizophrenic patients receiving different therapies to rate their treatment out of 10. There are two conditions, with each participant taking part in only one of the conditions so it is an independent groups design. The data are ratings (ordinal data) and so the Mann-Whitney U test is appropriate.

Table to show rankings for therapy A versus therapy B:

Participants	Therapy A	Participant	Therapy B
1	3	1	9
2	4	2	7
3	2	3	5
4	6	4	10
5	2	5	6
6	5	6	8

Step 1: Rank all the scores together.

Note: For a Mann-Whitney U test, the data from both groups are ranked together. If participants have the same score, they are given the same rank. This way of ranking is different to how data is ranked for the Spearman's rho test.

Participant	Therapy A Rating	Rank	Participant	Therapy B Rating	Rank
1	3	3	1	9	11
2	4	4	2	7	9
3	2	1.5	3	5	5.5
4	6	7.5	4	10	12
5	2	1.5	5	6	7.5
6	5	5.5	6	8	10

Step 2: Calculate Ua by first adding up all the ranks for therapy A to calculate $\sum R_a$:

$\sum R_a = 3 + 4 + 1.5 + 7.5 + 1.5 + 5.5 = 23$

Step 3: Multiply the number of participants in group A (n_a) by the number of participants in group B (n_b)

Note: $n_a n_b$ means n_a multiplied by n_b

$n_a \times n_b = 6 \times 6 = 36$

Step 4: Calculate $n_a (n_a+1)$

$n_a+1 = 6+1 = 7$
Multiply n_a+1 by n_a
As $n_a+1 = 7$ and $n_a = 6$
$n_a (n_a+1) = 7 \times 6 = 42$

Step 5: Calculate $n_a (n_a+1)/2$
Divide $n_a (n_a+1)$ by 2
$42/2 = 21$

Step 6: Calculate $U_a = n_a n_b + n_a (n_a+1)/2 - \sum R_a$

$n_a n_b = 36$
$n_a (n_a+1)/2 = 21$
$\sum R_a = 23$

So $U_a = 21 + 36 - 23 = 34$

Step 7: Calculate Ub by first adding up the ranks for therapy B to calculate $\sum R_b$:

$\sum R_b$ = 11 + 9 + 5.5 + 12 + 7.5 + 10 = 55

Step 8: You already know that $n_a n_b$ =36 from step 3
You already know $n_b(n_b+1)/2=21$ from step 5 as there are the same number of participants in group B as in group A.
You know from step 7 that $\sum R_b=55$
So $U_b = n_a n_b + n_b (n_b+1)/2 - \sum R_b = 36+21-55=2$

Step 9: U is the smaller of U_a and U_b.
So as U_b is the smallest value, U_b is the value of U.
Therefore, U=2

Step 10: Look up the critical values in a critical values table for n_a=6 and n_b=6. This is the number of participants in each group.

To be significant, U has to be equal to or less than the critical value. The critical value for a two-tailed test at 0.05 significance level = 5 and the critical value for a two tailed test at 0 .01 significance level = 2 So, U is less than the critical value of U for a 0.05 significance level. It is also equal to the critical value of U for a 0.01 significance level.

This means that there is a highly significant difference between therapy A and therapy B.

Note: When you are looking up critical values in a table, you need to know: whether the hypothesis was one-tailed or two-tailed; the number of participants in each condition (shown as 'N' on the table) and the significance level. The values in the Mann-Whitney Test are termed 'U' and unlike the Spearman-rank and Chi-squared Tests the observed value has to be equal to or less than the critical value for the results to be significant (i.e. to accept the experimental hypothesis and reject the null hypothesis).

You need to be able to analyse qualitative data using thematic analysis.

A thematic analysis can be used to analyse different types of data, from media articles to transcripts of focus groups or interviews. It is suitable for analysing people's experiences, opinions and perceptions. It can also be used to look at how different issues and concepts are constructed or represented. The types of research questions in clinical psychology that might lead to a thematic analysis of the data are: 'How is mental illness portrayed in the media?' and 'What are women's experiences of dealing with depression?'
There are a number of stages in carrying out a thematic analysis: 1) The researcher familiarises themselves with the data by reading it several times; 2) Codes are generated for important features of the data; 3) The researcher looks for themes by examining the codes and collated data to identify broader patterns of meaning (potential themes); 4) The themes are reviewed by checking them against what people have said. At this stage, themes may be refined or discarded; 5) Themes are named and a detailed analysis of each theme is carried out; 6) Finally, the themes

are written up with quotes from the data collected. The analysis is linked to existing theories.

Evaluation:

A thematic analysis can be used for a wide range of research questions. Rich, detailed data can be obtained, which can lead to a deeper insight into people's experiences, opinions and representations. However, thematic analyses are open to interpretation and hence subjective. They can be hard to replicate and so they have problems with reliability.

You need to be able to analyse qualitative data using grounded theory.

Grounded theory uses an inductive method to develop theories. This is different to the scientific method of generating hypotheses first and testing them. Grounded theory involves the researcher collecting data from a specific area of interest and over time advancing theories. For example, a researcher might investigate how families respond to mental illness by interviewing them. They will then look for codes and categories that emerge from the data. Finally, the researcher might suggest some ideas about how families respond to mental illness.

When analysing qualitative data, the researcher initially assigns codes to every unit of information, for example, each sentence, argument or observation. For example, when Rose et al. (2002) looked at how families responded to mental illness, one family member said, 'We can't and shouldn't do it all.' This could be given the code of 'accepting limitations'. The codes should be specific and not too broad.

Once the researcher has decided which codes are most important or prevalent, they will apply these codes to other data from interviews, articles and observation. This is called focused coding and the aim is to refine, modify and understand the codes in more detail.

The next stage is to identify categories. For example, codes such as 'accepting limitations' and 'inability of the person with the mental illness to look after themselves' might be related to the broader category of 'resolving questions of responsibility'.
The researcher will also write memos as they go along, which are their personal ideas and thoughts that emerge as they reflect on the coding process. This helps the researcher to clarify their ideas. Memos about codes and categories are integrated and refined.
Eventually, the researcher will develop their own theories. For example, Rose et al. (2002) concluded from their research that the families pursued normalcy. This means that the families of people with mental disorder engage in an effort to help the patient be normal.

Evaluation:

Grounded theory has been criticised for being unscientific and subjective. Researchers may interpret the evidence in a biased way especially if they are trying to fit the data with their emerging theories. Another researcher might interpret the evidence in a different way and so the research can lack reliability. A further issue with grounded theory as a method is that it can take a long time to gather and analyse the information. However, if the theory is 'grounded' in evidence then it should have good validity.

You need to be able to describe and evaluate the classic study: Rosenhan (1973) On being sane in insane places

Description:

Aim: To see whether the sane can be distinguished from the insane using the DSM classification system. Rosenhan wanted to see whether clinicians would be able to tell the difference between a patient suffering from a real mental disorder and a healthy 'pseudopatient.'

Procedure: Rosenhan and seven volunteers arrived at a range of hospitals reporting a single symptom, hearing voices saying 'empty', 'hollow' and 'thud.' They gave real information about themselves such as details about their families and childhood. However, they gave false names and those in the medical profession gave a false occupation. As soon as the eight pseudopatients were in hospital, they started behaving normally.

Results: All the pseudopatients were admitted and none were detected as being sane. It was an average of 19 days before any of them were released. Even when they were released all but one were given the diagnosis of schizophrenia in remission. In no case did any of the doctors and nurses notice that there was nothing wrong with them.

Conclusion: Rosenhan concluded that staff in psychiatric hospitals were unable to distinguish those who were sane from those who were insane and that DSM is not a valid measurement of mental illness.

Evaluation:

Generalisability-The study was carried out in 1973 so the findings of the study may not apply to the present day. The DSM had been revised many times since 1973 to improve its validity. Furthermore, doctor-patient relationships have changed.
The pseudo-patients had insisted on being admitted to the hospital themselves so the psychiatrists may have been more cautious about releasing them. Not all people diagnosed with schizophrenia ask to be admitted to a hospital so the treatment of the pseudo-patients may not be representative of how other patients would be treated. The psychiatrists would have also been careful about releasing an individual who had only recently been admitted too fast. However, a wide range of hospitals were used so the results can be generalised to other psychiatric hospitals at the time.

Reliability-The study was conducted in the field so extraneous variables were hard to control and so the study would be difficult to repeat.

Application to real life-The study highlighted problems with DSM and how psychiatric patients are treated in hospital.

Ecological validity-The study had ecological validity as it was carried out the doctors' and nurses' normal working environment (psychiatric hospitals) so they would have behaved naturally.

Experimental validity-The doctors and nurses in the psychiatric hospital were unaware the patients were fake so they would not have displayed any demand characteristics. Therefore, the study has good experimental validity. However, the fact that the pseudopatients were released with the diagnosis of 'schizophrenia in remission' shows that the psychiatrists did recognise something different about them as this is a rare diagnosis for real patients.

Ethics-There are a number of ethical issues with the study. The hospital staff were deceived about the pseudopatients' symptoms and they did not know they were in a study so they were unable to give consent. However, Rosenhan did protect the anonymity of the staff and hospitals afterwards.

You need to be able to describe and evaluate one contemporary study on schizophrenia. Carlsson et al. (1999) Network interactions in schizophrenia – therapeutic implications.

Description:

Aim-To review research on the effects of the neurotransmitters dopamine and glutamate on the symptoms of schizophrenia.

Procedure-The researchers looked at a number of different studies to assess whether high levels of dopamine (hyperdopaminergia) and/or low levels of glutamate (hypoglutamatergia) are linked to schizophrenia.

Results-There is evidence to support the hyperdopaminergia and hypoglutamatergia models of schizophrenia. Clozapine which blocks the activity of dopamine and serotonin has been found to be a more effective treatment for schizophrenia than drugs that block the activity of dopamine alone. This may be because levels of serotonin have an effect on levels of glutamate.

Conclusion: As neurotransmitters such as glutamate and serotonin are linked to the symptoms of schizophrenia, developing drugs that work on these neurotransmitters as well as dopamine is important. Newer drugs may be able to avoid the side effects related to anti-psychotic drugs that work on dopamine alone.

Evaluation:

Generalisability-The review looked at a number of different studies. The use of many studies makes the findings more generalisable to the wider population.

Reliability- Not all studies used in the review may have been equally reliable. However, the studies used in the review were scientific such as PET scans and this makes the review more reliable.

173

Application to real life-The review suggests that new drugs that act on different neurotransmitters should be developed for schizophrenia.

Validity-Not all the studies used in the review may have been equally valid, which could distort the overall findings. However, using evidence from a large number of studies can give more valid conclusions about the effect of different neurotransmitters on the symptoms of schizophrenia.

Ethics-As secondary data was used, there are no ethical issues with this study.

You need to be able to describe and evaluate one contemporary study on anorexia. For example, Guardia et al. (2012) Imagining One's Own and Someone Else's Body Actions: Dissociation in Anorexia Nervosa.

Description:

Background: Previous research has shown that patients with anorexia nervosa overestimate their own body size.

Aim- To see whether anorexic patients make incorrect judgements about their own body only or whether they also had a distorted perception of other people's bodies too.

Procedure-50 young female participants were used: 25 anorexic participants and 25 control participants. The two groups were matched for age and educational level. 51 different door-like apertures (varying from 30 cm to 80 cm in width) were projected onto a wall so that it looked like a realistic 2m high doorway.
The participants had to judge whether or not the doorway was wide enough for them to pass through (i.e. first-person perspective) without turning sideways. They then had to judge whether the doorway was big enough for another person present in the testing room to pass through (i.e. third-person perspective).

Results-Anorexic patients showed a distorted view of their own body size and would frequently say that they couldn't fit through a doorway that was considerably bigger than them. However, when the anorexic patients were asked to judge whether another person could go through a doorway, they were more accurate. The control group showed no significant difference when judging whether they or someone else could pass through a doorway.

Conclusion- Anorexic patients overestimate their own body size but not other people's. The researchers suggest that anorexic patients' perception of their body size does not change even when they have lost weight because their brain has not updated their body size quickly enough.

Evaluation:

Generalisability-The sample was small so it is hard to generalise to all anorexic patients. The participants were all young females so the findings can't be generalised to male anorexic patients or older anorexic patients. However, most anorexic patients are young females so the using a young female sample is representative of the majority of anorexic patients.

Reliability-The study followed a standardised procedure which makes it easy to replicate and test for reliability.

Application to real life-The study suggests that therapists should help change anorexic patients' perceptions and thoughts about their body size.

Validity-In the third-person perspective condition, when participants had to estimate another person's ability to pass through the doorway, the control group were closer in size to the other person than the anorexic patients. This may have been why the anorexic patients made more errors about the other person's ability to pass through the doorway.

Ethics-Some of the participants were under 18 and were particularly vulnerable. It would have been important to make sure the results were discussed in a sensitive way.

You need to be able to describe one key question of relevance to today's society, discussed as a contemporary issue for society rather than an academic argument and apply concepts, theories and research to it. For example, 'How are mental health issues portrayed in the media?'

The media has a powerful influence on how people perceive mental health issues. If television programmes, films, magazines and newspapers portray those with mental health problems in a negative way then this can have an impact on whether people with mental health issues seek help and how people respond to those with mental health problem.

Philo et al. (1994) analysed media coverage of mental health issues and found that it perpetuated negative stereotypes of people with mental disorders. Pirkis and Francis (2012) looked at how newspapers reported mental illness in Australia and found that the most common theme related to 'disorder, crisis and risk'. Dietrich et al. (2006) found that students who read a negative article about mental illness felt more negative attitudes toward people with mental illness. They also found that those students who watched more TV were more wary of those with mental health issues. Wahl et al. (2007) found that many children's TV programmes depicted characters with mental illness as aggressive and threatening.

Rosenhan's study found that when the pseudopatients were admitted to hospital and began to behave normally, it was difficult for them to escape the label they had been given. They were released with the diagnosis of schizophrenia in remission rather than not having schizophrenia at all and their normal behaviour was interpreted as being related to schizophrenia. People with mental health issues may be worried about being labelled especially if there are negative stereotypes in the media.

On the other hand, there has been some positive media coverage of mental health issues. Some celebrities such as Stephen Fry have talked about their mental health issues publicly. This helps to reduce the stigma about having a mental health problem and combats negative stereotypes.

'Time to change' is a mental health campaign that aims to raise awareness and understanding of mental health issues. Surveys have shown that the 'Time to

Change' campaign has improved attitudes towards people with mental illness. In 2013, 64% of people acknowledged that they knew someone with a mental health problem compared to 58% in 2009.

You need to be able to describe one practical research exercise to gather data relevant to topics covered in clinical psychology. This practical research exercise must adhere to ethical principles in both content and intention. Example practical: A content analysis that explores attitudes to mental health

Aim: To investigate how mental illness is portrayed in the media. To undertake a content analysis of two newspaper articles discussing mental health issues.

How was the data gathered and analysed?

The content analysis involved looking for articles on the internet about mental illness. The phrases 'mental health issues and 'mental illness' were put into the google search bar. The articles were chosen because they were from newspapers with different political and ideological agendas. The Guardian is a left-wing newspaper and The Daily Telegraph is a right-wing newspaper.

How was the data analysed?

Positive and negative comments in each article were tallied and mean number of positive and negative comments calculated for each article. The articles were then compared in terms of mean number of positive and negative comments to see whether there was any agreement between the articles.

Results: The Telegraph had fewer positive comments and more negative comments about mental health.

	Mean no. of positive comments	Mean no. of negative comments
The Guardian	3.3	2.4
The Telegraph	2.1	3.1

Conclusion: Both articles had negative stereotypes about mental illness. The political ideology of the media articles was reflected in how positive or negative they were about mental health issues.

You need to be able to discuss ethical issues in clinical psychology

There are ethical issues with working with people with mental health issues as they are more vulnerable. It is particularly important that they are not caused any psychological distress. As part of a clinical trial assessing the effectiveness of a treatment, some patients may be put in a control group who receive a placebo treatment or a less effective treatment. From an ethical standpoint, these patients should be given the best possible treatment as soon as the trial has ended.

You need to be able to discuss practical issues in the design and implementation of research

Qualitative data collected from interviews, observations or case studies of patients is less reliable than quantitative data. However, such data is more valid as it takes into account the patient's opinion and experiences about their illness or treatment.

You need to be able to discuss reductionism

Many treatments in clinical psychology are reductionist because they focus on only one cause of mental disorder. For example, drug therapy is reductionist because it only looks at biological factors in mental disorder not social or psychological. Cognitive behavioural therapy is reductionist because it sees the causes of mental disorder as being related to to irrational beliefs and does not take into account biological or social factors.

You need to be able to compare different factors/themes used to explain mental disorder

There are many different explanations of schizophrenia. One biological factor that can lead someone to develop schizophrenia is high levels of the chemical dopamine in the brain. However, there is evidence that cognitive factors are involved in schizophrenia too. For example, people with schizophrenia have problems with processing information. In contrast, a psychodynamic perspective would argue that poor communication in families causes schizophrenia.

You need to be able to discuss clinical psychology as a science

Biological treatments such as drug therapy are considered more scientific than talking therapies such as family systems therapy. Biological explanations of mental disorder such as the dopamine hypothesis for schizophrenia are more scientific than psychodynamic explanations as they are based on scientific evidence such as brain scans.

You need to be able to discuss cultural issues in clinical psychology

Cultural issues such as country of origin, race, gender and religion can affect the way people report mental health symptoms. These cultural effects can lead to different diagnoses. DSM V takes into account cultural issues in diagnosis.

You need to be able to discuss the nature-nurture debate in clinical psychology

Nature refers to how our genes and biology affect our development. For example, the extent to which mental illness is related to our genes, brain structure and neurotransmitters.

Nurture refers to how our environment affects our development. For example, the extent to which mental illness is based on our family environment and experiences.

The stress-diathesis model suggests that genes may predispose us to mental illness but we also need stressors in our environment in order to trigger the illness. Most psychologists agree that both biological and environmental factors are involved in the development of mental health issues.

You need to be able to understand how psychological knowledge has developed over time in clinical psychology

Each version of DSM has tightened up the criteria for diagnosis and included more mental disorders. DSM V has taken into account cultural issues in diagnosis. One of the main changes is that diagnosis of Asperger's syndrome has been removed from the DSM-5 and is now part of one umbrella term Autistic Spectrum Disorder (ASD). This is to recognise that those previously diagnosed with Asperger's syndrome and autism showed similar traits. Treatments also change over time. For example, newer drugs for schizophrenia have fewer side effects.

You need to be able to discuss issues of social control in clinical psychology

Treatments can be used to control people so that they conform to society's norms. For example, when drugs such as Ritalin are used to treat children with ADHD, this could be regarded as social control as the drugs are used to 'normalise' their behaviour. Some argue that as increasing numbers of younger and younger children are being diagnosed with ADHD, it is not a problem with the children but with society.

You need to be able to discuss the use of psychological knowledge in society

Research in clinical psychology has led to the development of many treatments. Drug therapy combined with talking therapies enable people with mental health issues to live in the community without being institutionalised. Understanding the causes of mental disorder has also contributed to wider acceptance of those who suffer from mental health problems.

You need to be able to discuss socially sensitive research

Sieber and Stanley define socially sensitive research as: 'Studies in which there are potential consequences or implications, either directly for the participants in the research or for the class of individuals represented by the research'. Research looking at the incidence of particular mental disorders in certain races, cultures or genders could be classed as socially sensitive research as it could lead to labelling of certain groups in society.

Student answer to exemplar exam question in Clinical Psychology:

Describe one treatment for schizophrenia from the Biological Approach. Evaluate this treatment using research evidence. (12 marks)

Note: The question asks for one treatment only and how it can be used to treat one mental disorder only.

Student answer:

Drug therapy can be used by the psychiatrist to treat schizophrenia. Anti-psychotic drugs are used with schizophrenics to block the effects of dopamine. The neurotransmitter dopamine is involved in cognitive functions such as attention and problem-solving. Dopamine in the frontal lobes of the brain controls the flow of information from other areas of the brain. Therefore, by reducing the availability of dopamine in the brain, anti-psychotic drugs can reduce symptoms related to information processing such as thought disorders. It is thought that both typical and atypical anti-psychotics work by inhibiting dopamine at the receptor level. Typical anti-psychotics such as chlorpromazine could reduce the symptoms of schizophrenia but cause severe side effects. Atypical antipsychotics (newer drugs) reduce the symptoms of schizophrenia but with fewer side effects. Clozapine is an example of a new generation anti-psychotic drug.

Anti-psychotic drugs can help schizophrenics to manage their symptoms and to live in the community. They tend to act quickly and can stabilise a patient so that they can access other treatments such as cognitive behavioural therapy. However, a problem with anti-psychotic drugs is that they can have unpleasant side effects, which can cause schizophrenics to stop taking the drugs. Patients can develop a tolerance to the drugs so that they need higher doses for the drugs to work. There is also the criticism that anti-psychotics only sedate patients rather than really cure them. Atypical anti-psychotic drugs have fewer side effects but are more expensive than typical anti-psychotic drugs. Anti-psychotic drugs do not work on all schizophrenics.

Level 4 answer: 10 out of 12 marks

Commentary:

This student describes how anti-psychotics can be used to treat schizophrenia well. However, there could also have been some discussion of practical considerations. For example, they could have discussed how psychiatrists prescribing anti-psychotic drugs need to carefully monitor how a patient is responding to them. The psychiatrist may then need to adjust the dosage or even try out a different type of anti-psychotic.

This student could also have used some studies to support their evaluation. Kane (1992) found that chlorpromazine was effective with 75% of schizophrenics. Emsley (2008) found that injecting risperidone could reduce both positive and negative symptoms of schizophrenia and led to high remission rates. The effectiveness of atypical anti-psychotics for schizophrenia in terms of number of re-hospitalisations is similar to that of typical anti-psychotics. Stargardt et al. (2008) found that atypical anti-psychotics were only cost-effective in severe cases as it was only in these cases that the atypical anti-psychotics reduced re-hospitalisations.

Chapter 6-Criminological Psychology

Criminological psychology investigates explanations and treatments for criminal and anti-social behaviour. It also looks at issues related to the justice system and the way criminals are convicted including problems with eyewitness testimony and how jury and defendant characteristics affect sentencing.

A Crime: is when someone commits an act against the law, for example, stealing a car.

Anti-social behaviour: refers to behaviour that causes problems for other people but is not necessarily against the law. An example of anti-social behaviour is when teenagers gather together outside a shop and behave in a rude way to passing customers.

Recidivism: is when a person commits a crime they have already been punished for. An example of recidivism is when a criminal goes to prison for stealing and then steals again on release.

Stereotyping: is judging an individual based on their membership of group when there is limited experience of the group. Based on these stereotypes people are **labelled**. For example, a boy in a hoodie may be labelled as a troublemaker based on his appearance.

You need to be able to describe and evaluate brain injury as a biological explanation of criminal behaviour

Description:

A brain injury caused by an accident, illness or long-term substance misuse may lead to criminal or aggressive behaviour. Brain injury can lead to changes in personality dependent on the area of the brain that has been damaged. For example, Phineas Gage, a railway worker became much more aggressive after his frontal lobe was damaged in a railway accident.

Evaluation:

Studies-Williams et al. (2010) investigated the incidence of brain injury amongst prisoners and found that 60% of them had suffered some kind of brain injury. This suggests that having a brain injury can affect aggression levels, impulse control and judgement, leading to a higher likelihood of engaging in criminal behaviour. Explanation-It is difficult to establish a cause and effect relationship between brain injury and criminal or aggressive behaviour as there may be other factors involved. For example, those who have a brain injury due to alcohol or drug abuse may be more likely to engage in criminal or aggressive behaviour due to the substance misuse rather than the brain injury. Furthermore, people who engage in substance misuse may have other issues that affect their behaviour such as poor family relationships or personality disorders.

You need to be able to describe and evaluate the amygdala as a biological explanation of aggressive behaviour

Description:

The amygdala is a part of the brain involved in regulating emotions. Therefore, damage to this part of the brain can lead to problems with how people express emotion. For example, they may behave in an overly emotional way or show a lack of emotion. Having a smaller amygdala is linked with a lack of empathy for others and aggression. Research shows that psychopaths tend to have smaller amygdalae.

Evaluation:

Studies-Bard (1940) lesioned the brains of cats and found that the hypothalamus and amygdala were responsible for aggression. However, there are problems with generalising animal research to humans as humans are more complex. For example, the prefrontal cortex in animals is smaller than in humans.

Swantje et al. (2012) found that women with smaller amygdalas were more likely to have higher aggression scores. This supports the idea that the amygdala plays an important role in aggression.
Raine et al. compared the brains of murderers and non-murderers and found that differences in the functioning of the amygdala.

Explanation-Having a smaller amygdala does not mean that you will necessarily engage in criminal or aggressive acts. Humans have the ability to control their behaviour and environmental influences affect behaviour too.

You need to be able to describe and evaluate XYY syndrome as a biological explanation of criminal and anti-social behaviour

Description:

Males have the sex chromosomes XY and are more governed by androgens (such as testosterone). Females have the sex chromosomes XX and are more governed by oestrogens. XYY syndrome is when some males are born with an extra Y chromosome. About 1 in 1000 males will have an extra Y chromosome. It has been suggested that males with XYY genes have lower IQs and are more aggressive.

Evaluation:

Studies-Thielgaard (1984) found that men with XYY chromosomes had lower IQs. She suggested that it was these men's learning difficulties that made them more likely to engage in criminal or anti-social behaviour. The study also showed that only a small proportion of criminals had the XYY syndrome.
Explanation-As most of the prison population is made up of men and women without XYY chromosomes, the syndrome cannot explain criminal behaviour in these groups.

You need to be able to describe and evaluate labelling and the self-fulfilling prophecy as a social explanation of criminal and anti-social behaviour

Description:

The self-fulfilling prophecy (SFP) is a prediction that comes true because it has been made. For example, when people become what others expect them to become. The self-fulfilling prophecy explains criminal or anti-social behaviour as arising due to other people's expectations. A person may be labelled as a criminal or a troublemaker due to stereotypes and they may be treated differently as a result. The person may find it difficult to escape this label and so they internalise it and it becomes part of their self-concept. Once a criminal or anti-social label becomes part of the person's self-concept, they may behave according to the label and carry out criminal or anti-social acts. For example, a young person dressed in a hooded top may be stereotyped as anti-social. People may be more wary of them and avoid them in the street. The antisocial label may then become part of their identity and they may actually go on to behave in an anti-social way.

Evaluation:

Studies-Jahoda's (1954) study supports the self-fulfilling prophecy. The Ashanti tribe of West Africa believe that boys born on a Wednesday are more aggressive and boys born on a Monday are calm. Jahoda (1954) examined police records and found that males born on Wednesday had higher arrest rates than those born on Monday suggesting that the tribe's expectations did affect their behaviour. Madon (2004) questioned parents about how much alcohol they expected their children to drink in the next year and found that if parents expected their children to drink too much alcohol, they did. This study can be viewed as support for the self-fulfilling prophecy. However, it may be that parents who drink a lot themselves expect their children to drink more too. Their children may just be copying their behaviour rather than there being a self-fulfilling prophecy. Madon and Jahoda's studies are correlational and therefore cannot establish a causal link between expectations and later behaviour. Rosenthal and Jacobsen (1968) carried out an experiment which supports the self-fulfilling prophecy. They found that when teachers believed certain children in their class were more intelligent, their IQ scores rose. A similar process may occur if children are labelled as naughty or troublemakers.

Explanation-A limitation of the self-fulfilling prophecy is that people with a strong self-image are unlikely to be affected by other people's negative expectations. There are many other reasons for criminal and anti-social behaviour that the self-fulfilling prophecy does not take into account such as observing criminal or anti-social role models (social learning theory), genes, high levels of testosterone, poverty, status and culture.

You need to be able to describe and evaluate the cognitive interview

Description:

If police officers use leading questions during interviews with witnesses, this can lead to inaccuracies later. Therefore, the cognitive interview has been developed to improve witnesses' recall of events. During a cognitive interview, witnesses are asked to freely recall as much information as they can remember and to describe everything they could see, hear, smell or touch. Witnesses are also asked to recall events in different orders and from different perspectives. Open ended questions are used rather than leading ones e.g. What happened next? The cognitive interview is based on Tulving's encoding specificity principle, which suggests that recall is better if a person has the same cues at retrieval as they had when they encoded the information. By getting witnesses, to mentally reinstate the context of an incident using cues such as sight, sound, smell and touch, they should be able to recall the incident better.

Evaluation:

Stein and Memon (2006) and Geiselman (1986) found that the cognitive interviews increases both the quality and quantity of information recalled by witnesses. Research has also shown that people questioned using cognitive interviews are less likely to be influenced by leading questions.
On the other hand, Milne (1997) found that the cognitive interview did not lead to better recall than normal interviewing techniques.
However, the effectiveness of cognitive interviews may be affected by the fact that police officers do not always use all the elements of the cognitive interview properly as it is very time-consuming.

You need to be able to describe ethical interview techniques

In the past, the police used psychological manipulation in order to gain confessions or supporting evidence for a conviction. As a result, some innocent people were convicted of crimes they did not commit. Nowadays, the police are advised to use interview practices which improve the truthfulness of the information given. For example, the police are trained to avoid asking witnesses leading questions and to use techniques which improve memory.

You need to be able to describe and evaluate the use of psychological formulation to understand the function of offending behaviour in the individual

Psychologists may be asked to come up with a psychological formulation for a why an offender committed a crime. The psychological formulation may consist of biological reasons, social circumstances, relationships and life events that might have led to the person committing the crime. Formulations usually take into account different psychological theories for explaining behaviour. For example, an individual may get into a fight in pub and end up killing another person. A psychological formulation might take into account the individual's high testosterone levels, the breakdown of a romantic relationship and their family history of domestic violence.

Evaluation:

It is helpful to understand what caused an offender's behaviour in order to provide the best rehabilitation. For example, if a person's violence stems from anger, then they may be offered anger management as a treatment.

Psychological formulations can be presented in a diagram, which is easy for professionals working with an offender to digest.

A limitation of psychological formulations is that the psychologist may not have access to all the information about an individual. For example, the offender might not know that they have a brain injury from childhood unless a brain scan is done.

You need to be able to describe and evaluate one cognitive behavioural technique for treating offenders. For example, anger management.

Description:

Anger management is a cognitive-behavioural technique. Anger management programmes are based on the idea that individuals can learn to control their aggression by changing their thought patterns. There are three steps to anger management 1) Cognitive preparation-Offenders are taught to identify situations which trigger anger and thought patterns are challenged 2) Skills acquisition-Offenders are taught skills to control their feelings of anger such as counting to ten and relaxation techniques to calm themselves down 3) Application practice-Offenders are given anger-provoking scenarios such as someone swearing at them so that they can practice how to deal with difficult situations. Anger management programmes can be used in prisons or with people on probation. The courses are usually conducted in small groups and last for around ten sessions.

Evaluation:

Directive-Anger management can be viewed a directive treatment as the therapist has a lot of power and tells the offenders that their thinking is wrong and that they need to change it.

Effectiveness- Dowden, Blanchette and Serin (1999) investigated the effectiveness of an anger management programme in Canada. They found that it was effective at reducing recidivism with high risk offenders over a 3 year period. Goldstein et al. (1989) also found that anger management combined with social skills training could reduce recidivism. However, Watt and Howells (1999) found no difference between offenders who had been through an anger management programme and offenders who had not been treated yet using a range of measures including anger experience, anger expression, prison misconduct and observations of aggressive behaviour. They suggested that the anger management programme had not worked because of the offenders' poor motivation and the limited opportunities to practice the skills learnt. Prisoners may say the programmes are useful simply because they enjoy the break from routine.

Side effects- Anger management programmes do not include a discussion of morality or understanding from a victim's point of view, which has been said to limit their success. Men convicted of domestic violence may become less physically violent after attending an anger management programme but may be more verbally and emotionally abusive.

Expense- Anger management is expensive as it requires highly trained professionals to deliver the programme. It also requires time and commitment from both the prison service and the prisoners as the course requires a number of sessions.

Reasons-Anger management does not uncover any underlying reasons behind the offender's aggression such as childhood issues. It only tries to change present thinking.

Types of people- Anger management works better with offenders who have reactive aggression. It does not work well on offenders whose aggression does not stem from anger. Some offenders use aggression to manipulate others. Watts and Howells (1999) study found that anger management programmes were ineffective but this may be because the offenders were not assessed to see if their aggression was related to anger. Loza and Loza-Fanous (1999) found no link between anger and violent offences.

You need to be able to describe and evaluate one biological treatment for offenders. For example, diet.

Description:

Offenders may suffer from a deficiency in certain vitamins, minerals or essential fatty acids, which leads to increased aggression. This may be because diet can affect hormone levels. Low blood sugar levels have been linked with irritability and this may also lead to aggressive behaviour. Offenders can be given vitamins supplements to address any deficiencies in their diet. They can also be given advice by a dietician about how to eat healthily and how to avoid low blood sugar levels.

Evaluation:

Directive-Offenders may feel under pressure to follow a certain diet.

Effectiveness- Gesch et al. (2002) compared young offenders who were given a dietary supplement to a group of young offenders who were given a placebo. The young offenders who were receiving a supplement showed a 35% reduction in bad behaviour compared to only a 7% reduction amongst the offenders given the placebo. This study supports the idea that a good diet can reduce anti-social behaviour.

Side effects- There are usually no side effects from taking a dietary supplement.

Expense- Employing a dietician or other professional to improve prisoner's diets can be costly.

Reasons-Changing an offender's diet does not address other reasons for the offender's behaviour such as relationship issues.

Types of people- Dietary supplements can be used with most people. Care needs to be taken with pregnant offenders or those with medical issues.

You need to be able to discuss factors influencing eye-witness testimony, (including post-event information and weapon focus).

Post-event information can influence eye-witness testimony. Memory is not like a DVD-recording but instead it is an imaginative reconstruction of events. If there are gaps in our memory, we use schemas to fill in the gaps so that events make sense to us. Leading questions can influence eyewitness memory and produce errors in recall. Loftus and Palmer (1974) found that they could affect participants' recall by changing the way a question was worded. Participants were asked how fast a car was going when it 'hit', 'smashed', 'collided' or 'bumped'. Participants gave a higher estimate of speed if the word was 'smashed' rather than 'collided', they were also more likely to report seeing broken glass in the 'smashed' condition when asked back a week later.

Anxiety levels can also affect recall. Valentine and Mesout (2009) found that participants with high anxiety levels had poorer recall of an actor who stepped in front of them in the London Dungeon.

Studies show that when a weapon is used by a criminal, witnesses focus on the weapon rather than the criminal's face or their environment, probably because a weapon is a major threat. This is called the weapon focus effect. Loftus et al. (1987) showed half of their participants a film with a customer in a restaurant holding a cheque, and the other half were shown a film with a customer holding a gun. They found that participants had worse recall for the customer's face when they were holding a weapon.

If there is a long period of time between recall and the incident, eye-witnesses are likely to forget details.

Stereotypes can affect eyewitness memory. People's views on what type of person commits a crime can affect recall. People are less likely to believe that a man in a suit committed a crime compared to someone who is scruffily dressed.

The memory conformity effect can affect witnesses' memory for events. For example, if witnesses discuss a crime incident together, their memory for events becomes more similar. Wright et al. (2000) placed people in pairs to investigate the memory conformity effect under controlled conditions. One of the pair saw pictures of a man entering with the thief; the other saw pictures without the man. They were then asked to recount the story together but fill out questionnaires separately. About half of the participants who had not seen the picture with the man agreed to their partner's account and said that there was a man entering with a thief.

You need to be able to discuss factors influencing jury decision-making, including characteristics of the defendant and pre-trial publicity. You need to be able to refer to studies.

There are a number of factors that affect jury decision making:

Characteristics of the defendant-Jurors may have stereotyped views about a defendant which influences their reactions. Research suggests that the race and accent of the defendant can affect a jury's decision making. Mahoney and Dixon (1997) found that defendant's with 'Brummie' accents were judged as guiltier than those with standard British accents. In a meta-analysis of 80 studies using mock juries, Mazzella and Feingold (1994) found it was an advantage for a defendant to be physically attractive.

Pre-trial publicity-Jurors may be influenced by media coverage of a high profile case. Fein et al. (1997) used cuttings from the O.J. Simpson case with a mock jury. They found that those who had access to pre-trial publicity were more likely to find the accused guilty.

The foreperson chosen-The foreperson speaks most and is more likely to be white, male and middle aged. Males tend to have less liberal attitudes than women on average. Kerr et al. (1982) found that a disproportionate number of jury forepersons are male and in mixed sex groups, men tend to dominate conversations.

Conformity-One person who is not in agreement with the others is likely to go along with the majority view. Conformity can occur through normative influence, which is the desire to fit in with other members of the group. If a minority of jurors disagree with the majority, they are likely to be presented with a set of persuasive arguments to move them towards the majority view. Group polarisation is when the majority favours one side at the start of a discussion and by the end of it, the majority view is held more strongly. Hastie et al. (1983) found that if at the outset, the majority favoured a guilty verdict, in 90% of cases that was the final outcome.

The size of the jury- In Britain, juries always consist of 12 individuals but in the US juries can be smaller than this. However, evidence suggests larger juries are more effective.

You need to be able to discuss individual differences in criminal and anti-social behaviour including personality as a factor in criminal/anti-social behaviour and individual differences affecting whether a self-fulfilling prophecy occurs.

Individual differences in personality may make people more likely to engage in criminal and anti-social behaviour. Eysenck suggested that high scores for psychoticism, extraversion and neuroticism are linked with criminal and anti-social behaviour. Rushton and Chrisjohn (1981) found a relationship between high extraversion and psychoticism scores and delinquency. Personality disorders are also related to criminal and anti-social behaviour. May violent offenders have anti-social and paranoid personality disorders.

People with low self-esteem are more likely to be affected by other people's negative labels and expectations. Therefore, a self-fulfilling prophecy is more likely to occur with such individuals, which makes them likely to engage in criminal and anti-social behaviour.

You need to be able to discuss social learning theory as a theory of human development that can account for criminal/anti-social behaviour.

Social learning theory suggests people commit crimes because they are exposed to criminal role models. They may look up to a criminal and pay attention to their behaviour. They may remember how the crime is committed and if they are able to carry out the crime themselves (reproduction) and they are motivated to do so, they may commit the same or similar crime themselves (modelling). For example, a boy may observe an older boy stealing cars, he may pay attention to how to do it and be capable of reproducing the behaviour, finally if he identifies with the boy and looks up to him as a role model, he may be motivated to copy the behaviour. Anti-social behaviour can be explained through observation of anti-social role models. The most powerful role models are the same-sex, high status and a similar age to the observer.

If a model is rewarded, a behaviour is more likely to be copied. This is called vicarious reinforcement. For example, if a criminal is successful and becomes rich from their crimes, their behaviour is more likely to be imitated. A criminal such as gang leader may also be rewarded in terms of approval from peers and this also makes their behaviour more likely to be imitated.

However, if the model is punished the behaviour is less likely to be copied. For example, a criminal may be caught and sent to prison for their crimes.

Evaluation of theory:

Use SE to evaluate a theory that has already been applied to criminological psychology.

Studies-What studies support or contradict the theory?

Explanation-What are the problems and limitations of the theory? What alternative explanations are there?

Studies- Bandura, Ross and Ross' (1961) study found that children would copy aggressive behaviour shown by a model so this supports social learning theory. However, this study only looked at whether the children copied the aggressive behaviours soon after rather than whether the children were affected in the long-term. Huesmann and Eron (1986) followed people's viewing habits over 22 years and found that the more violence people watched on TV, the more likely they were to have committed a criminal act by the age of 30. However, correlational studies such as this cannot show a causal relationship as people with a tendency to be antisocial or aggressive may seek out aggressive media. On the other hand, field experiments such as Parke et al. do show a causal link between observed aggression and actual aggression. They carried out a field experiment on boys in an institution for juvenile offenders. One group of boys watched violent TV programmes and one group watched programmes without violence over 5 days. They found that viewing violent

TV programmes led to an increase in aggressive behaviour. However, juvenile offenders are not representative of the wider population and may be more prone to aggressive behaviour.

Explanation-It is difficult to establish a causal link between observing criminal or anti-social behaviour and carrying out such behaviour due to the time lapse. Social learning theory does not take into account biological factors in criminal behaviour such as genes, hormones or structural differences in the brain. Another limitation of social learning theory is that it does not consider how social factors such as unemployment and poverty can affect criminality. It also does not explain why many offenders have mental health issues and learning difficulties.

Exam tip: If you use a study to support or contradict a theory, then briefly say what it found and how it supports the theory. You do not need to give a full description of a study in this context, only enough detail so it is recognisable. The examiner only wants to know how the study supports/contradicts the theory. You can make one evaluative point per study used.

Exam tip 2: Do not spend too much time discussing alternative theories. There is often only one mark for this. Instead focus on the limitations and problems of the theory you are evaluating.

You need to be able to discuss biological causes for criminal/anti-social behaviour in relation to development.

Males are most likely to be involved in violent crime between 15 and 25 years old. This may be related to a surge in testosterone levels during this developmental period.

You need to be able to describe and evaluate laboratory experiments in terms of assessing eye-witness effectiveness.

Description:

In a laboratory experiment assessing eye-witness effective, an independent variable such as weapon focus effect or leading questions is manipulated and a dependent variable such as eye-witness recall is measured. For example, in the Loftus and Palmer's (1974) experiment, the independent variable was the verb in the question 'how fast was the car going when it 'hit'/ bumped'/ 'collided'/'smashed.' The dependent variable was participants' estimates of the speed of the car. Laboratory experiments control extraneous variables so that a cause and effect relationship can be established.

Evaluation:

Laboratory experiments are easily replicable as there are good controls over extraneous variables and a standardised procedure is used. In Loftus and Palmer's study, all participants watched the same seven video clips of different traffic accidents and were given the same questionnaire. Loftus and Palmer's study has been replicated several times with the same results, increasing its reliability.

Researchers have carried out many laboratory experiments investigating eyewitness effectiveness and have come up with similar findings, which show that the studies are reliable.

Laboratory experiments lack ecological validity as they take place in an artificial setting. For example, Loftus and Palmer's study lacks ecological validity because watching film clips of traffic accidents does not have the same impact or lead to the same emotions as seeing a real-life accident and the interview stage would not seem as important as it would if the incident were real. Loftus and Palmer said that the study avoided demand characteristics as the critical questions were randomly hidden amongst others, so participants couldn't guess the aim of the study. However, the participants may have felt that they had to give a higher speed estimate when the verb 'smashed' was used so that they didn't come into conflict with the experimenter (experimenter effects).

Laboratory experiments investigating eye-witness recall are likely to require some level of deceit, because the independent variable has to be kept secret so that participants do not deliberately change their behaviour. For example, in the Loftus and Palmer (1974) experiment, the participants might have changed their speed estimates if they knew the researchers were investigating leading questions. As there is some level of deceit required when investigating eyewitness testimony, there is unlikely to be fully informed consent.

You need to be able to describe and evaluate field experiments in terms of assessing eye-witness effectiveness.

Description:

Field experiments take place in participants' natural environment and involve manipulating an independent variable. For example, in Yarmey's study a woman approached participants in a public place (a natural environment). A number of independent variables were manipulated such as whether the participants were asked to recall the target immediately or 4 hours later and whether the target wore a disguise or not. In a field experiment, a dependent variable is measured. In Yarmey's study, the researchers measured how many details participants could correctly remember about the woman, whether participants could correctly identify her amongst a set of photos when she was present and whether participants could correctly point out that she was not there in a set of photos where she was absent. As field experiments take place in a natural environment, extraneous variables are not easily controlled although the researcher tries to control as many aspects of the situation as they can.

Maass and Kohnken (1989) carried out a field experiment in which participants were approached by a woman holding either a pen or a syringe. Participants in the 'pen' condition were able to supply more accurate descriptions of the woman. However, this could be due the syringe being an unusual object in the situation rather than because it is a threat. Mitchell et al. (1998) investigated whether people's recall would be affected if someone was holding a celery stick (an unusual object) and they found that it was.

Evaluation:

Field experiments take place in the participants' natural environment. This means that not all the extraneous variables can be controlled and the findings may not be reliable. However, as field experiments have carefully controlled and planned procedures, they often give the same results when repeated. This means that they can be as reliable as laboratory experiments.

Field experiments are carried out in the participants' natural environment so they have ecological validity in terms of setting. However, the independent variable is still carefully manipulated to see the effect on the dependent variable, and therefore, the procedure may not be valid. On the other hand, researchers try to make the procedure as realistic as possible to enhance validity.

Field experiments are often less ethical than laboratory experiments because the participants are approached in public places and often do not know beforehand that they are in a study at all. In field experiments, participants can be asked for their consent afterwards. In Yarmey's study, participants did not know initially that they were part of a study so they did not give consent. The participants were also deceived as the target lied to them about needing help. However, they were told about the study 2 minutes after they met the target. BPS guidelines advise that participants should not be caused distress and that they should leave a study in the same emotional state they started in. Field experiments are more likely to cause a participant distress because the participants do not initially know they are in a study. For example, in the Maass and Kohnken (1989) study, some of the participants were approached in the field by a woman with a syringe. This may have caused the participants distress.

You need to be able to describe and evaluate case studies in terms of assessing eye-witness effectiveness.

Description:

A case study can be carried out if a unique incident or event occurs naturally that might be of interest to the researcher. For example, a natural event could be a real crime and the researchers might want to investigate witnesses' recall of the incident later. For example, in the Yuille and Cutshall study, witnesses observed a real gun shooting and then asked details about the incident later on. Dependent variables can be measured e.g. the number of details recalled accurately about the incident.

Evaluation:

Case studies often take advantage of a naturally occurring incident so they have less ethical issues that field experiments and greater validity. However, they may still involve deception and asking participants to recall a traumatic incident can cause distress. For example, in Yuille and Cutshall's case study participants were deceived about the leading questions. The study could have also caused distress as the participants were asked to recall a gun shooting. On the other hand, participants were given the choice about whether to take part or not.

As case studies often involve a unique incident, they are not replicable and cannot be tested for reliability.

You need to be able to describe and evaluate the classic study: Loftus and Palmer (1974) Reconstruction of automobile destruction: An example of the interaction between language and memory.

Description:

Aim-To see if leading questions affect participants' speed estimates.

Procedure for experiment 1-45 students were put into groups. They watched 7 films of traffic accidents, ranging in duration from 5 to 30 seconds, which were presented in random order to each group. After the film, the participants had to fill in a questionnaire. First they were required to given an account of the accident and then to answer specific questions. The critical question was the one asking about the speed of the vehicles. Nine participants were asked 'about how fast were the cars going when they hit each other?' and equal numbers were asked the same question, but with the word 'hit' being replaced by 'smashed', 'collided' 'bumped' and 'contacted.

Results for experiment 1-They found that if a different verb is used to indicate the speed of a car, such as 'hit', 'smashed', 'collided' or 'bumped', then participants gave a different speed estimate. The highest mean speed estimate was when the verb 'smashed' was used and the lowest mean speed estimate was when the verb 'contacted' was used in the question. There was a 9 mph difference between the speed estimates when the verb 'smashed' was used and when the verb 'contacted' was used.

Conclusion for experiment 1-The wording of a question can affect participants' responses.

Procedure for experiment 2-There were 150 participants involved in this experiment. A 1 minute film with a multiple car accident lasting 4 seconds was shown. After the film, the participants had to give a general account of what they had seen and then answer more specific questions about the accident. 50 participants were asked 'about how fast were the cars going when they hit each other?', another 50 'about how fast were the cars going when they smashed each other?' and another 50 acted as control group who were not asked the question at all. One week later, participants were asked to answer ten questions, one of which was the critical question 'did you see any broken glass? Yes or no?' even though there was no broken glass in the film.

Results for experiment 2-The verb 'smashed' increased the estimate of speed and the likelihood of seeing broken glass even though there was no broken glass. 16/50 participants in the group where the word 'smashed' had been used said they had seen broken glass compared to 7/50 when the word 'hit' had been used and 6/50 in the control group.

Overall conclusion-This study suggests that leading questions can affect recall and lead to distorted memory.

The study questions the reliability of eyewitness testimony and shows that care must be taken when questioning witnesses.

Evaluation:

Generalisability- The study lacks generalisability as all the participants were students who are not representative of the wider population. Students tend to be less experienced drivers and so may have been more easily influenced by the verbs smashed/collided/ contacted etc. in giving their speed estimates.

Reliability-The study had a standardised procedure and good controls. For example, all the participants in experiment 1 watched the same 7 film clips under controlled conditions. This makes the study replicable, and therefore, reliable.

Application to real life- This study suggests that the police should be careful to avoid leading questions when interviewing witnesses. The justice system should also be careful about trusting eyewitness testimony unless it is supported by other corroborating evidence.

Validity-The study lacks ecological validity because the participants lacked the emotional involvement of real eyewitnesses. The participants may have felt correct recall was not as important compared to witnesses of a real crime. The study also used questionnaires, which is nothing like a real police interview.
It could be argued that the study has experimental validity as the critical (leading) questions were all randomly hidden amongst other distractor questions so the participants were not able to guess the aim of the study and so the study avoided demand characteristics. However, others have criticised the study for suffering from experimenter effects as the participants may have felt they had to give a higher speed estimate when the word 'smashed' was used so that they did not come into conflict with the experimenter.
The researchers gathered quantitative data in the form of estimates of speed, which makes the study more objective.

Evidence-Yuille and Cutshall (1986) reported a case of real eyewitness testimony and found that leading questions had little effect on the accuracy of recall even five months after viewing a gun shop robbery. This study contradicts Loftus and Palmer's study.

You need to be able to describe and evaluate one contemporary study in criminological psychology. For example, Valentine T and Mesout J (2009) Eyewitness identification under stress in the London Dungeon.

Description:

Aim-To see whether a situation that causes anxiety and high levels of stress affects eyewitness recall and identification.

Procedure-Visitors to the London Dungeon were offered a reduction in the admission price if they agreed to complete some questionnaires after their visit. 29 female and 27 male volunteers were recruited. Participants were asked to wear a heart rate monitor during their visit. The Horror Labyrinth is the first exhibit in the tour of the London Dungeon and it is designed to scare visitors. During their tour of this section, an actor dressed in a dark robe and wearing theatrical make-up stepped out in front of each participant and blocked their path to prevent them passing. The participant's heart rate was measured using the monitor. At the end of the tour, participants were asked to fill in a questionnaire to measure their state anxiety (how they felt at that moment) and their trait anxiety (their normal level of anxiety). They were also asked to complete a second questionnaire designed to record free recall and cued recall of the scary person. The participants were shown a nine-person photographic line-up and asked to identify the scary person. They were told that the person might or might not be in the line-up. They were then asked to rate their confidence in the decision from 0-100%.

Results-The mean state anxiety score was 49.0. State anxiety was higher for females than for males (52.8 vs. 45.3 respectively). There was no difference in trait anxiety between males and females (36.3 vs. 37.3). People who reported higher state anxiety recalled fewer correct details.
In order to see the effect of state anxiety further, the participants were divided into high and low state anxiety groups based on the median score of 51.5. Participants who reported high state anxiety were less likely to correctly identify the person in the labyrinth. Only 17% of eyewitness who scored above the median on the state anxiety scale correctly identified the person they saw from a nine-person culprit-present photograph line-up. In contrast 75% of eyewitnesses who scored below the median correctly identified the 'culprit'.

Conclusion-Eyewitness identification was dramatically impaired by high state anxiety. Female witnesses may be particularly vulnerable to the effects of stress. The study suggests that the emotional state of witnesses at the time of an incident should be taken into account when considering their testimony.

Evaluation:

Generalisability-All the participants had chosen to visit the London Dungeon. People who choose to visit such a place may be more or less affected by scary situations than average. This means that the sample may not be generalisable to the wider population.

Reliability-The study had good controls and a standardised procedure. All the participants were approached by a scary person at the same point on the tour of the London Dungeon and in the same manner. This makes the study replicable and reliable.

Application to real life-The study suggests that the police and courts should take into account the anxiety level of witnesses when considering the accuracy of their testimony.

Validity- The study has ecological validity as measuring participants' recall of a scary person in the London Dungeon relates to real life witness recall as it was a natural situation. The questionnaires used in to measure state and trait anxiety had previously been shown to be valid.

Ethics-Although the participants were deliberately scared in the study, they had chosen to go to the London Dungeon to experience a scary situation. The participants were told at the end of the tour the purpose of the experiment and given the right to withdraw.

You need to be able to discuss one key question of relevance to today's society, discussed as a contemporary issue for society rather than as an academic argument and apply concepts, theories and/or research to it. For example, 'Is eye-witness testimony too unreliable to trust?'

Eyewitness testimony refers to the recalled memory of a witness to a crime or incident. People have been convicted on the basis of eyewitness testimony alone and have later been found innocent using DNA evidence. Cases like this call into question the reliability of eyewitness testimony. This is an issue as juries place a lot of trust in eyewitness testimony. The police can also distort witnesses' memories by the way they ask questions. Bartlett suggests that people reconstruct their memories so witnesses may fill in the gaps in their memory of an incident using schemas (packets of information about the world). However, witnesses to real life incidents may have a better memory of events due to the strong emotions involved.

Eyewitness Testimony is unreliable because:

Leading questions can influence eyewitness memory and produce errors in recall. Loftus and Palmer (1974) found that they could affect participants' recall by changing the way a question is worded. Participants were asked how fast a car was going when it 'hit', 'smashed', 'collided' or 'bumped'. Participants gave a higher estimate of speed if the word was 'smashed' rather than 'collided', they were also more likely to report seeing broken glass in the 'smashed' condition when asked back a week later.

Anxiety level can affect recall. Valentine and Mesout (2009) found that participants with high anxiety levels had poorer recall of an actor who stepped in front of them in the London Dungeon.

Weapon focus effect: Studies show that when a weapon is used by a criminal, witnesses focus on the weapon rather than the criminal's face or their environment, probably because a weapon is a major threat. Loftus et al. (1987) showed half of their participants a film with a customer in a restaurant holding a cheque, and the other half were shown a film with a customer holding a gun. They found that participants had worse recall for the customer's face when they were holding a weapon.

Yarmey's (2004) study supports the view that jurors should question the reliability of witness identification from line-ups. The found that when participants had actually spoken to a female target, only 49% of them could identify her in a photo line-up when she was present and when she was not present 38% of them identified someone in the photo line-up who was completely different.

Poor line-up procedures may lead to misidentification of a suspect. Simultaneous line-ups (where all the people are presented together in the line-up) may lead to witnesses using a relative judgement strategy (choosing a person who looks most like the perpetrator of the crime rather than really looking at the person's individual characteristics to see whether they match up).

Meissner and Brigham (2001) found that people are less able to recognise people from a different ethnic background to them so this can lead to problems in eyewitness identification.

Buckout (1974) highlighted that photo line-ups can be biased if the suspect's photo is physically different from the fillers.

Busey and Loftus (2006) pointed out that lack of double-blind procedures can mislead witnesses. They gave the example of a police officer who knew who the suspect was in a line-up and when a witness identified the suspect, the police officer said sign here as if to confirm their identification was correct.

Wells and Bradfield (1998) found that if participants were told that their identification of a criminal was correct, they became more confident about their identification. Therefore, by the time a case gets to court, if a witness has had their identification confirmed by a police officer, they may be overly confident even if they are wrong.

If there is a long period of time between recall and the incident, people are likely to forget details.

Stereotypes can affect eyewitness memory. People's views on what type of person commits a crime can affect recall. People are less likely to believe that a man in a suit committed a crime compared to someone who is scruffily dressed.

The memory conformity effect can affect witnesses' memory for events. For example, if witnesses discuss a crime incident together, their memory for events becomes more similar. Wright et al. (2000) placed people in pairs to investigate the memory conformity effect under controlled conditions. One of the pair saw pictures of a man entering with the thief; the other saw pictures without the man. They were then asked to recount the story together but fill out questionnaires separately. About half of the participants who had not seen the picture with the man agreed to their partner's account and said that there was a man entering with a thief.

Eyewitness Testimony is reliable because:

Yuille and Cutshall (1986) examined the recall of witnesses to a real life gun shooting in Canada. 21 witnesses saw a man try to rob a gun shop and then shoot the shop owner. The shop owner shot back and killed the thief. After the witnesses had been interviewed by police, the researcher used the opportunity to ask them whether they would like to take part in the research into eyewitness testimony. 13 of the 21 witnesses agreed to take part in their research 5 months later. They found that even 5 months after the incident, witnesses had good recall of events and were not affected by the leading questions asked. This study suggests that eyewitness memory in real life is not as likely to be distorted as laboratory experiments suggest.

Riniolo et al. (2003) questioned 20 survivors of the shipwrecked Titanic shipwreck and found that 15 of the 20 witnesses were able to recall details accurately many years later despite inaccurate media coverage.

Cognitive interviews can improve eyewitness testimony: this involves getting the witness to freely describe events without the risk of leading questions. Eyewitnesses are asked to not leave out any detail even if they think it is unimportant and they may be asked to recall the incident in reverse order. Questions can be asked at the end in order for information to be un-altered.

Flashbulb memory may lead witnesses to recall crime incidents very clearly as they are likely to have strong emotions related to the incident and may replay events in their mind.

You need to be able to describe and evaluate one practical investigation you have carried out in criminological psychology. Example practical: The effect of leading questions on participant's responses.

Aim-To investigate whether the wording of a question can affect participant's answers

Background research-Loftus and Palmer(1974) carried out a study into the effects of leading questions. The aim of the experiment was to see how recall is affected by the verb used in a question. The procedure involved five groups of students being shown film clips of traffic accidents. Once they had watched the film clips each group was asked the question, 'How fast were the cars travelling when they ....?
The last word varied, each group had a different word from the list: contacted, hit, bumped or smashed. The results showed that the group with the verb 'contacted' gave a much lower mean speed estimate of 32 miles per hour compared to 41 miles per hour in the 'smashed' group. This allowed Loftus and Palmer to conclude that simply changing a single word in a sentence can greatly affect the recall of participants or something more important like a witness in court.
Another study looking into leading questions is that of Harris (1973). Participants were shown some basketball players. Some participants were asked 'How tall is the basketball player?' and some were asked, 'How short is the basketball player?'. The results found that when asked 'how short...?' the average answer was 69 inches compared to the 79 inches estimated when asked 'how tall...?

Directional hypothesis- Participants who are asked the question 'How long is this piece of string?' will give a longer estimate compared to participants who are asked the question 'How short is this piece of string?'

Null hypothesis- There will be no difference in participants' estimates of the length of string whether they are asked the question 'How long is this piece of string?' or 'How short is this piece of string?'

Research Method-A laboratory experiment was used so a cause an effect relationship could be established. The independent variable was the question 'How short is this piece of string?'/'How long is this piece of string?' The dependent variable was the estimated length of the string. Extraneous variables were kept the same (the piece of string, the environment).

Design-An independent group design was used so that each participant only experienced one condition (one of the two questions). This was to avoid demand characteristics.

Sample-An opportunity sample of 24 participants was recruited from friends and family. There were an equal number of males and females and their age ranged from 18 to 80 years old.

Procedure-Participants were approached individually and asked to take part in an experiment on eyewitness testimony. They were briefed on the experiment and what it would involve. They were shown the piece of string and the first twelve participants were asked, 'How short is this piece of string?'. The second twelve participants were asked, 'How long is this piece of string?' Their answers were noted down in a notepad. Participants were debriefed afterwards and given the right to withdraw.
A table to show the difference in recall when asked 'How long is this piece of string?' compared to the recall when asked 'How short is this piece of string?'

	RECALL WHEN ASKED HOW LONG? (CM)	RECALL WHEN ASKED HOW SHORT? (CM)
MODE	43	31
MEAN	43.6	31.8
MEDIAN	44	31
RANGE	7	8

Results-There was a significant difference between the sets of results. The group asked 'How long is this piece of string?' estimated a mean length of 43.6cm while the group asked 'How short is this piece of string?' estimated a mean length of 31.8cm. This is a difference of 11.8cm. This is a significant enough difference to allow me to accept my directional hypothesis (that those asked 'How long...?' will give a longer estimate).

Conclusion-People are affected by leading questions. There was a significant difference in participants' length estimates when asked 'How long is this piece of string?' compared to 'How short is this piece of string?'

Evaluation-As this experiment is a laboratory experiment, it lacks ecological validity as people are not usually asked to estimate the length of string in real life. It is not the same as being asked questions about a witnessed incident by the police or in court.
An opportunity sample was used, which makes it difficult for somebody else to get the same type of sample and makes the study less reliable. However, there was good control over extraneous variables which makes the study easier to replicate and increases the reliability.

It is hard to generalise from an opportunity sample to the wider population. However, a large age range was used, which makes the study more generalisable.

You need to be able to describe ethical issues in criminological psychology

Psychologists need to be careful that they do not cause distress to participants when investigating eyewitness effectiveness and jury decision-making as these can involve mock trials and fake crime incidents. Experiments looking at factors affecting eyewitness testimony can involve deception so it is important that participants are protected from psychological harm and thoroughly debriefed at the end. Field experiments where participants do not know that they are part of an experiment initially need to be particularly careful to avoid causing harm.

You need to know practical issues in the design and implementation of research

Field experiments take place in participants' natural environment so they have good ecological validity. They are a useful research method as the participants' behaviour will be more like real witnesses compared to participants in laboratory experiments, who are engaged in artificial tasks in an artificial setting. In a field experiment, participants often do not know initially that they are part of a study, so their attention to the environment will be similar to real witnesses. For example, in Yarmey's study the participants did not pay particular attention to a target woman when she approached them asking for directions or help finding a lost piece of jewellery. In contrast, laboratory experiments involve asking witnesses to focus their attention on a film clip or slides of an incident. Therefore, laboratory experiments lack ecological validity. A weakness of field experiments is a lack control over the extraneous variables, which makes them less reliable than laboratory experiments. On the other hand, this lack of control over the extraneous variables makes field experiments more like a real incident.

You need to be able to discuss reductionism in criminological psychology

Criminological psychologists often reduce criminal behaviour down to single factors such as genes, relationships or environment in order to explain it. When psychologists consider only one influence on criminal behaviour at a time, then this is reductionist as it does not take into account all the factors that affect criminality.

You need to be able to compare different ways of explaining criminal behaviour

Both social learning theory and the self-fulfilling prophecy suggest that criminality is affected by other people's behaviour. However, social learning theory suggests that criminal behaviour occurs through observing others whereas the self-fulfilling prophecy proposes that it occurs as a result of other people's expectations. Social learning theory would say criminal behaviour runs in families due to the role models provided by parents whereas the biological approach would explain it as a result of genes.

You need to be able to discuss whether criminological psychology is a science

Laboratory experiments in criminological psychology such as Loftus and Palmer's study on leading questions are scientific because they control extraneous variables and establish cause and effect relationships. Field experiments have less control over extraneous variables and are therefore less scientific. However, both types of experiment collect quantitative data, which is objective and can be statistically analysed.

When interviews or case studies are used, the data is more subjective and less scientific.

You need to be able to discuss cultural issues in criminological psychology

Stereotypes can influence eyewitnesses and juries. The legal system needs to be aware of how cultural factors affect witness recall and jury decision making. For example, accent can influence whether someone is found guilty and race can affect witness recall of an incident.

You need to be able to discuss gender in criminological psychology

Most research in criminological psychology focuses on male offenders. Therefore, findings from such research cannot be generalised to female offenders.

You need to be able to discuss the nature-nurture debate in criminological psychology

The nature side of the debate would argue that criminal behaviour is caused by biological factors such as genes, hormones and brain structure. The nurture side of the debate would argue that criminal behaviour is affected by environmental factors such as family background and role models. Twin studies show that MZ twins have a higher concordance rate for anti-social behaviour than DZ twins. However, as the concordance is not 100%, this suggests that environmental factors influence anti-social behaviour too.

You need to be able to discuss how psychological understanding has developed over time in criminological psychology

James Cattell carried out the first research into eyewitness testimony in 1893. He found that although people might be confident in their answers they weren't always correct. His research led to a wealth of research into the inaccuracy of eyewitness testimony. Psychologists started to be used as experts in court to explain the problems with witnesses' memories. More recently, brain scans have been used to understand differences in the brain functioning of criminals.

You need to be able to discuss how psychological knowledge has been used in criminological psychology

Research on eyewitness testimony has led to reforms in the way witnesses are questioned. For example, the cognitive interview technique has been developed to improve eyewitness testimony and there have been changes in the way line-ups are conducted. Studies looking at jury decision-making have led to a better understanding of how race, accent and social class affect jurors' judgements.

You need to discuss issues related to socially sensitive research in criminological psychology

Research looking at how genes and brain structure affect criminal behaviour can be considered socially sensitive as it could identify individuals who are more likely to commit a crime. It also has implications for society in terms of whether offenders are responsible for their actions.

You need to be able to discuss issues of social control in criminological psychology

Treatments used with offenders can be seen as a form of social control. For example, Token Economy Programmes (TEPs) are used in prisons to control behaviour but research suggests that they don't change behaviour long-term. Other treatments such as anger management are more likely to prevent re-offending once a person leaves the prison environment.

Exemplar exam question: Using psychological research, explain whether courts should rely on eyewitness testimony. You must evaluate eyewitness testimony research in you answer. (12 marks)

Student answer:

Some studies suggest that eyewitness testimony is unreliable. Loftus and Palmer found that when they used a verb that had more force behind it (i.e. smashed compared with bumped) participants gave higher speed estimates. These results from this study suggest that courts should be careful with eyewitness testimony as it isn't completely reliable.

Other studies such as Yuille and Cutshall found that participants who were real life participants weren't affected by leading questions or by the time lapse of five months after the incident had happened. This study suggests that eyewitness testimony is not completely unreliable and shouldn't be disregarded.

The two studies above create a small problem as they contradict each other. However, Yuille and Cutshall's study used real life witnesses whereas Loftus and Palmer used students from a university who watched video clips. There is a big difference as participants watching the video clips may feel that their statements won't matter as much as it isn't real life; compared to real life witnesses who have been affected by the incident and their statement can affect another person's life. Bartlett's theory of reconstructive memory is crucial to understanding eyewitness testimony. He suggests that recall is subject to personal interpretation that is dependent on our culture, values and the way we make sense of the world. When we store things in our memory, we do so in the way that makes most sense to us using schemas. Therefore, memories can be distorted and courts should be cautious about the accuracy of eyewitness testimony.

There are other factors that can affect a person's memory of an incident, for example the media has a major influence. If the incident is covered in the media, eyewitnesses may pay attention to the story and find themselves believing the story given.

In the past, there have been cases where people are convicted due to eyewitness evidence given in court but later found innocent. The research suggests that some other evidence (i.e. forensic or physical) other than eyewitness testimony should be present to convict a person of a crime.

Laboratory experiments are easily replicable as there is a standardised procedure and good controls over extraneous variables. Therefore, laboratory experiments investigating eyewitness testimony are reliable. However, laboratory experiments can lack ecological validity. Getting participants to watch film clips or slides of an incident does not lead to the same emotions as watching a real life incident. Therefore, participants may not respond in the same way as real witnesses. Participants in a laboratory experiment may also not place the same importance as real witnesses on recalling events accurately.

Field experiments are less reliable than laboratory experiments as not all the extraneous variables can be controlled. However, researchers do try to control the extraneous variables as much as possible so field experiments into eyewitness testimony can be reliable. Field experiments often have greater ecological validity as they are carried out in participants' natural environment. For example, if participants see a fake robbery in a public place, they are likely to experience the same emotions as real witnesses.

8/12 marks

Commentary:

This answer does not refer to enough psychological research. More studies should be given related to whether eyewitness testimony is accurate or not. You should know at least three studies related to eyewitness testimony in detail but it is better to know more in order to answer this type of question.

The second part of the question is asking for an evaluation of eyewitness testimony research more generally. This student makes a good attempt at discussing the validity and reliability of both laboratory and field experiments as used to investigate eyewitness testimony. They could have highlighted that the independent variable(s) is still carefully manipulated in a field experiment and so the procedure can lack validity. There could also have been some discussion of ethical issues. Field experiments have more ethical issues than laboratory experiments because setting up fake crimes in the field or fake car crashes can be more distressing than watching film clips or slides of an incident as is often the case in laboratory experiments.

Chapter 7-Child Psychology

Child psychology studies how biological factors and childhood experiences affect children's development. It covers topics such as attachment, deprivation, privation, autism and the issue of day care.

You need to be able to describe and evaluate Bowlby's work on attachment

Bowlby's theory of attachment consists of many different elements.

Exam tip: You may be asked to describe and evaluate only one element of Bowlby's theory of attachment so be prepared.

1) The evolutionary basis of attachment

Bowlby's evolutionary theory of attachment is the idea that attachment, which leads to children maintaining close proximity to their carers is instinctive and adaptive i.e. attachment increases the chances of a child's survival. Mothers are also genetically pre-programmed to respond to their baby's needs. Babies encourage their carers to stay close, by crying when left and smiling when their carers pays attention to them (proximity-seeking behaviours). Bowlby used ethology (the study of animals) as the basis for his evolutionary theory of attachment. He noted that animals have evolved to stay close to their mothers when young to aid their survival and he extended this behaviour to humans. Bowlby also thought there was a critical period within which attachment needs to occur.

Bowlby suggested that there are three phases in the development of attachment:

Phase 1-When a baby is first born it shows no preference for a particular adult, but it will make eye contact and grasp to encourage adults to stay close. It uses social releasers, which are innate mechanisms, such as smiling and crying to encourage their caregivers to stay close.

Phase 2-Around 3 to 6 months old, the baby will show a preference for their primary caregiver. They will smile and interact with them more than other adults.

Phase 3-Around 6 months, the baby will demonstrate a strong attachment for their primary caregiver. They become distressed when separated from their caregiver (separation anxiety) and they seek comfort from their caregiver if they feel vulnerable.

Evaluation:

The evolutionary basis of attachment has face validity. Babies do demonstrate social releasers (behaviours such as smiling, sucking or crying) that lead to instinctive parenting responses. Tronick et al. (1978) found that if mothers remained expressionless for a short time in a face-to-face interaction with their babies, the babies became distressed very quickly, which suggests it is instinctive for mothers and babies to interact with each other. It also makes sense that babies are genetically programmed to stay close to their primary caregiver to improve their chances of survival. Lorenz found that geese imprinted very quickly on the closest moving object, which supports the idea that there is a critical period for attachment. Animals are also quicker to imprint in stressful environments and this supports the idea that attachment aids survival.

2) Monotropy

Bowlby thought that children form a particularly strong attachment to a single primary caregiver out of instinct. The idea of a single caregiver is called monotropy.

Evaluation:

Bowlby's idea of a single caregiver has been criticised because children can form multiple attachments with fathers, grandparents and siblings. Bowlby's theory of attachment suggests that a child should not be separated from their primary caregiver when young at all. However, it could be argued the quality of interaction with the primary caregiver is more important than the amount of time they have with them.

3) The Internal Working Model

Bowlby said that infants develop an internal working model, which is a mental representation of themselves and their caregivers. This model of relationships is stored like a schema and allows them to predict how other people will behave towards them in the future. A child with a secure attachment will have an internal working model where they view themselves as deserving of love; they believe that other people will accept them as they are, and they find it easy to make friends. Children with secure attachments are often socially competent and popular. As adults, they can form long-lasting romantic relationships and are usually good parents. A child with an insecure attachment is likely to have worse quality friendships and is more likely to be bullied or bully. As adults, they may either avoid intimacy in relationships (insecure-avoidant attachment) or need constant reassurance in a relationship due to fears of abandonment (insecure-resistant attachment). People with insecure attachments find it harder to bond with their children and are less sensitive parents.

Evaluation:

Hazan and Shaver 's (1987) study supports the theory that a positive internal working model is linked to secure attachment. They placed a 'Love Quiz' in a newspaper. The 'quiz' questioned people about their current relationships, attitudes to love and their attachment history. They found that people with secure attachments reported happier and longer-lasting relationships than those with insecure attachments. The people with secure attachments also had positive internal working models.

4) Safe Base

Bowlby believed that infants gain comfort from their caregivers' touch and close proximity and it is this physical comfort that leads to a strong emotional bond between an infant and their caregiver. Infants not only use their caregiver for comfort but also as a safe base from which to explore. For example, infants will return to their caregiver when they are scared or in a strange environment.

Evaluation:

Harlow and Zimmerman's (1959) study provides support for the idea that infants use their mothers as a safe base. They took baby rhesus monkeys and raised them in a laboratory away from other monkeys. The baby monkeys were given a wire monkey with a bottle to feed from and a cloth monkey to get comfort from and hold. The monkeys spent far more time on the cloth monkey than the wire monkey, which suggests they were using it for comfort. When the monkeys were scared they immediately clung on to the cloth monkey and used it as a safe base. The monkeys showed long-term emotional and social problems. This supports Bowlby's view that children get comfort from their primary caregiver and that disruption of this bond has long-term consequences for development.

5) Maternal deprivation hypothesis

Bowlby's maternal deprivation hypothesis states that a child requires the continuous presence of a primary carer throughout a sensitive period lasting until a child is 18-months to 2-years-old. Bowlby thought that there is a critical period to form an attachment and if this critical period is missed, then no attachment will form. Bowlby identified two serious consequences of failure to form an attachment: Affectionless psychopathy (the inability to experience guilt or deep feelings for others) and developmental retardation (very low intelligence).

Evaluation:

Bowlby's forty-four juvenile thieves study provides support for the maternal deprivation hypothesis because it found a link between separation from the mother in the first two years of life and affectionless psychopathy. However, Bowlby has been criticised for failing to distinguish between privation and deprivation.

Bowlby's research has been influential: Hospitals now allow parents to stay in hospital with their child over night to prevent separation anxiety; day care providers are encouraged to assign every child a keyworker who provides more tailored support and care; childcare ratios are set by the government to ensure children receive more individualised care and maternity leave has been increased to allow mothers to have more time to bond with their babies.

However, Bowlby's work has led to working mothers feeling guilty about leaving their children as it suggests there are long-term consequences to disruption of the mother-child bond.

You need to be able to describe and evaluate Ainsworth's work on attachment, including types of attachment and the 'Strange Situation'.

The Strange Situation was developed by Ainsworth and Wittig (1969) to classify attachment. It consists of eight episodes lasting 3 minutes each.

Aim: To measure attachment type by observing how 12- to 18-month-old children respond to their parents after being left with a stranger.

Procedure: The observation involved recording children's behaviour through a one-way mirror during eight 3-minute episodes. Each parent-child pair were observed at different times. Episode 1 involved the parent and child being introduced to the experimental room. During episode 2, the parent and child were left alone, and the parent was told to let the child explore the room. Episode 3 involved a stranger entering the room and talking to the parent for a short time whilst approaching the child. The parent was then asked to leave quietly. During episode 4, the child was left alone with the stranger who tried to interact with them. Episode 5 involved the parent coming back and trying to comfort their child, before leaving again. During episode 6, the child was left alone in the room completely. The stranger then came back into the room in Episode 7 and tried to approach the child. The final part of the observation, episode 8, involved the parent entering the room, greeting their child and picking them up. The stranger then left quietly.

Observers behind a one-way mirror rated the child's separation anxiety (how distressed the child was at being left by their parent). Children with secure attachments will become distressed at being left alone by a stranger but they will not be inconsolable. The observers also looked at the child's willingness to explore and proximity to their parent. A securely attached child will feel confident to move further away from their parent and explore. The third aspect of behaviour that was observed was stranger anxiety. Children who are more securely attached show greater stranger anxiety. The fourth type of behaviour observed was how the children behaved on being reunited with their parent. Securely attached children show happiness and relief at being reunited with their parent whereas insecurely attached children will ignore or show anger on reunion with their parent.

Results: 70% of the children had a Secure Attachment (type B). They did show distress at being parted from their parent, but they were easily consoled when their parent returned. 20% of the children had an insecure/avoidant attachment (type A). They showed indifference to their parent when they left and did not show any stranger anxiety. They also avoided contact with their parent when they were reunited. The parent tended to ignore their child when they were playing. 10% of the children had an insecure/resistant attachment (type C). These children became very distressed when their parent left and were inconsolable. When they were reunited with their parents they showed their anger by seeking comfort from their parents and then rejecting it. The parent tended to be over-sensitive or angry and rejecting.

Conclusion: Secure attachments (type B) are the most common.

Evaluation:

Generalisability- This study was conducted in the USA and so the findings may not be generalisable to other cultures. However, the strange situation has been used to assess attachment type in other cultures and secure attachments (type B) have been found to be the most common.

Reliability- The observation had a standardised procedure, which makes it easy to repeat and so the study is reliable. Waters (1978) found 90% reliability when infants were tested and retested using the strange situation between the ages of 12 and 18 months.

Application to real life-Parents with insecurely attached children can be given training to help them be more sensitive to their children.

Validity-The study lacks ecological validity because it was an artificial situation. The children's behaviour may have been more affected by how well they adjusted to the unfamiliar setting rather than their parent leaving. Children who are used to being left in day care are less likely to be affected by their parents leaving the room, so the strange situation may be measuring how familiar the children are with being left rather than attachment type. This calls into question the validity of the strange situation for measuring attachment.

Children's temperament rather than attachment type may also affect their behaviour during the observation. Children who are born with a more irritable temperament may be inconsolable after being left by their parent, but this may not be because they are insecurely attached. However, Sroufe et al. (1999) found that children who had been assessed as securely attached using the Strange Situation at 12-months-old, were more popular, more empathic and had greater self-confidence and leadership skills in adolescence. This study suggests the strange situation is a valid way of measuring attachment type as it can predict future behaviour. One problem with this study is that it does not take into account children who have atypical attachments. It is now recognised that some children have disorganised attachments (type D), which are related to abusive parenting.

Ethics-The study did not protect the children from psychological harm as many of the children became very distressed. However, it could be argued, that the children were only left for short periods of time as might happen in everyday life.

Note: Mothers of securely attached infants are more responsive to their needs, provide more social stimulation (talking to and playing with the infant) and express more affection. This is called sensitive responsiveness or maternal sensitivity. Looking at the two classifications of insecure attachment, resistant behaviour appears to be related to maternal unresponsiveness and general lack of emotional involvement with the baby, while avoidant behaviour is related to maternal hostility and rejection.

Note: You need to be able to explain the type of attachment a child has based on its behaviour in different scenarios. For example, a securely attached child likes to maintain close proximity to their caregiver and will be upset if they are separated but

211

they can be consoled. They are also willing to explore a strange environment, whilst using their mother as a safe base. In contrast, a child with an insecure-avoidant attachment (type A) will not be upset when their caregiver leaves and will not seek closeness on their return. They will explore a room independently without concern for their caregiver. A child with an insecure-resistant attachment (type C) will be very distressed if their caregiver leaves and will not easily be consoled. They are clingy and will not readily explore a new environment. They are also likely to cry and show signs of anger when their caregiver returns after even a short absence.

You need to be able to discuss cross-cultural issues with the strange situation

Ainsworth's classification of different attachment types has been criticised for being culturally biased. Different cultures may view attachment differently and the judgement of attachment type is subjective (open to bias).

Cross-cultural research has been carried out to compare attachment types using the strange situation across different cultures. Research has found that type B (secure) attachments are the most common across all cultures. This suggests that the strange situation procedure is not culturally biased.

Cross-cultural studies:

Sagi et al. (1985) found that Israeli children raised on a kitbbutzim have a higher proportion of type C (resistant) attachments. This may be because children in Kibbutz are brought up by different caregivers within the collective community and they have little contact with their parents.

Grossman et al. (1985) found that German infants have a higher proportion of type A (avoidant) attachments. They found that German mothers were less responsive to their babies, but this may be because they want their babies to be independent at an earlier age.

Miyake et al. (1985) found that Japanese infants have a higher proportion of type C (resistant) attachments, which may be due to Japanese mothers rarely leaving their children with anyone else and encouraging dependency.

You need to be able to describe and evaluate the classic study: Van Ijzendoorn amd Kroonenberg (1988) 'Cross cultural patterns of attachment: A meta-analysis of the Strange Situation'.

Description:

Aim-To look at similarities and differences in attachment type in different countries.

Procedure-A meta-analysis of 32 studies using the Strange Situation as a measure of attachment type was carried out. The studies were from eight different countries so that cross-cultural comparisons could be made. Any studies that had overlapping samples or children over 24 months were excluded from the meta-analysis.

Results-They found that there were differences in the proportions of different attachment types in different cultures. Type B (secure) attachments were the most common type of attachment in all the studies from different cultures, with the exception of one study from Germany. Interestingly, there were more differences in attachment types within a culture compared to between cultures.

Conclusion-Secure attachment must be important for normal development as it is the most common attachment type in all countries. Variations in attachment type may be due to cultural factors, poor education or country-specific issues.

Evaluation:

Generalisability-Most of the studies used were from individualistic cultures such as the US and very few were from collectivist cultures. 18 studies were from the US and only 1 study was from China. This means that the meta-analysis was not representative of all cultures across the world.

Reliability-As the meta-analysis involved looking at the results of studies that had already been conducted and it followed a careful procedure, the study can be replicated and is reliable.

Application to real life-The study suggests that secure attachment is important for healthy social and emotional development. At risk parents can be given advice on how to interact with their infants in order to ensure secure attachments are formed.

Validity- Van Ijzendoorn and Kroonenberg increased the validity of their meta-analysis by excluding certain studies, for example, those which had overlapping samples.
However, they only used studies that used the Strange Situation to measure attachment. As the Strange Situation procedure was developed in the US and is based on observations of American children, it may not be a valid measure of attachment in other cultures. For example, Japanese children are rarely left by their mothers and so are likely to be more distressed in the Strange Situation than American children.

Ethics-The study used data from studies that had already been carried out so does not have any ethical issues. You do not need to mention this in the exam.

You need to be able to discuss nature-nurture issues when explaining attachment types across different cultures

Bowlby suggests that children maintain close proximity to their caregivers because it is adaptive i.e. attachment increases the chances of a child's survival. Mothers are also genetically pre-programmed to respond to their baby's needs. Cross-cultural research shows that children form close emotional bonds with their mothers in all cultures. This suggests that attachment is instinctive and supports the nature side of the debate. However, the type of attachment formed seems to depend on cultural views about parenting. How children respond to strangers and separation is affected by how their parents have cared for them. This suggests that attachment is related to nurture.

Note: The strange situation has been used to measure attachment type in different cultures. However, it may not be a valid measure of attachment type in other cultures as it was developed in the US and may only reflect attachment types there.

You need to be able to describe the short-term effects of deprivation: protest, despair, detachment

Deprivation is when an infant has formed an attachment but is then deprived of their attachment figure for a period of time.

Hospitalisation is an example of short-term deprivation. When children are separated from their attachment figure during hospitalisation they can become quite distressed.

Robertson and Bowlby filmed several children in hospital and based on their observations, they proposed three stages children go through when experiencing this type of separation:
Stage 1-Protest: Children at first are panic-stricken and upset. They cry frequently and try to stop their parents leaving (clinging behaviour). They express feelings of anger.
Stage 2-Despair: After a time, children show signs of apathy/depression. They actively ignore others and any attempts to play with them.
Stage 3-Detachment: Children show detachment by superficial interaction with others and when their attachment figure returns, they ignore them.

You need to be able to describe and evaluate research that looks at the effects of hospitalisation as a form of short-term deprivation

Bowlby and Robertson (1953) filmed Laura, age 2 years and 6 months during an eight day stay in hospital to have a minor operation. They found that Laura cried frequently for her mother but would also sometimes be quiet and apathetic. Her behaviour in hospital supports the protest-despair-detachment model. When Laura went home, she could be quite anxious, clingy and aggressive.

Robertson and Robertson (1968) filmed John, a 17-month-old boy, who was staying a residential nursery while his mother had a second child. John's behaviour followed the protest-despair-detachment model.

Evaluation:

The factors surrounding a period of short-term deprivation may affect how distressed a child becomes. Kirkby and Whelan (1996) reviewed research into the effects of hospitalisation on children and found that factors such as length of hospital stay, and medical condition affected how negative the consequences were of hospitalisation.

However, other research suggests that separation from the mother is the key cause of distress in short-term deprivation irrespective of other factors such as familiarity of the surroundings and carers.

You need to be able to describe the effects of day care as a form of short-term deprivation

Children in day care may react in the same way as hospitalised children, following the protest-despair-detachment model.
There is debate about the long-term effects of day care on children's emotional, cognitive and social development.

You need to be able to describe and evaluate research into day care including advantages and disadvantages for the child.

Studies on the advantages of day care

A study that supports the use of day care is the EPPE project (Effective Provision of Pre – school Education) Sylva et al. (2004)

Description:

It was a longitudinal study into the effectiveness of pre-school care for over 3000 children in the UK.

Aim-The aim was to look at the impact of preschool provision on a children's cognitive and social development.

Procedure-It compared children's cognitive and social development between the ages of 3 and 7 for those attending nurseries, playgroups or pre-school classes with those cared for at home. It used SATs results and reports from pre-school staff, parents and schoolteachers to assess development. The children were also observed and interviews were carried out with parents and teachers. The sample included 3000 children from a wide range of backgrounds.

Results-It found positive effects for day care in terms of social and cognitive development particularly if they started before the age of 3. Children who had been in daycare longer were more sociable and had better attention spans. Children from disadvantaged backgrounds showed the most progress.

Conclusion-Daycare can improve children's social and cognitive development.

Evaluation:

Generalisability-The study had a large sample of over 3000 children from a wide variety of backgrounds, which makes the study generalisable. However, as the study was only conducted in the UK, it is cannot be generalised to other cultures. The study mainly looked at children in day care from 3-years-old onwards so the findings can't be applied to using day care at an earlier age. The study focused on social and cognitive development and did not look at emotional development.

Reliability-The study was carried out in the children's natural environment so there are many extraneous variables that cannot be controlled. The interviews that were carried out with parents are also difficult to replicate and may have been open to interpretation. However, it would be easy to replicate some features of the study such as results from the SATs.

Application to real life-The study implies that the government should provide funding for children, especially those from deprived backgrounds, to attend preschool at an early age.

Validity-A range of measures were used to assess the children's development e.g. SATs, reports and interviews with parents. This makes the study more valid. The study took into account other factors that could have affected the children's development such as parental occupation and qualifications and social background. It was a longitudinal study, which meant that the same children were followed throughout and their development over time could be assessed.

Ethics-The study obtained fully informed consent from parents. However, there may have been issues of confidentiality as school reports and SATs results were used.

Another study that supports the use of day care is **Andersson (1996)**. This study followed up 126 Swedish children who had been in day-care in early childhood, and assessed them on their intellectual and social-emotional development at 13-years-old. Their development was compared with a control group who had not experienced any daycare when young. They found that children who had spent time in day care scored higher for academic achievement and social skills.

Studies on the disadvantages of day care

NICHD (National Institute for Child Health and Human Development) study-USA (1991)

Description:

Aim-To investigate the effect of childcare on children.

Procedure-Participants for the study were recruited from designated hospitals at ten different locations in the USA. Recruitment began in January 1991 and was completed in November 1991. A total of 1,364 families with full-term, healthy newborns were enrolled. Participants were selected to ensure that the recruited families included: a) mothers who planned to work or go to school, either full time (60%) or part time (20%), and mothers who planned to stay at home with the child (20%) in his or her first year and b) reflected the demographic diversity (economic, educational, and ethnic) of the sites. Both two-parent and single-parent families were included. The longitudinal study involved gathering data from many different methods, including observations, interviews and surveys. The study took into account many variables, including characteristics of the child care and the family environment. Researchers measured many facets of the children's development (e.g., social, emotional, intellectual, and language development; behavioural problems and adjustment; and physical health).   Data collection started when participating children were one month old, and continued (in Phases I and II) through to when they started school in first grade. 1,226 children of the original 1,364 children remained in the study to this point. Over this nearly seven-year period, research assistants saw each child at home, in child care (if used), in elementary (primary) school, and in a laboratory playroom. The assistants also completed telephone updates every three months to four months, ending when the child was 54 months (4½ years) of age, with a six-month phone follow-up within a month of the child's 5th birthday. Researchers assessed the child, the parent(s), and the social and physical characteristics of the home, of the child-care (and after-school) environments, and the elementary (primary) school.

Findings-The children who attended day care had more behavioural problems when in school compared to those looked after at home. However, children in high quality day care had better cognitive development, language comprehension and production and a higher level of school readiness. Children from economically deprived backgrounds benefited most from day care, perhaps because they received more stimulation and education in day care than at home. The quality of daycare is important for children. High quality daycare (with responsive staff and a stimulating environment) improved cognitive (intellectual) development but poor quality daycare could have negative effects on emotional and social development. Children who were put into daycare at an early age and who spent continuous and intensive time in daycare were more likely to have behavioural problems later on compared to children who started daycare later, and for shorter periods of time.

Evaluation:

Generalisability-The study recruited participants from a variety of socioeconomic and ethnic backgrounds, which makes this study more representative of the wider population. However, there were fewer low-income families in the sample, which makes the sample biased. 10 different locations were used in the USA, which gives the study population validity. However, the study may not be representative of the effects of childcare in other cultures.

Reliability- A number of different research methods were used, so the data from each method could be used to check for reliability. What constituted aggression was not used consistently throughout the observations, which makes the study hard to replicate and affects reliability. Furthermore, studies into day care cannot control all the variables that are significant to a child development, such as temperament, economic background, parenting styles, etc. all at the same time.

Application to real life-The study suggests that long periods of time in day care can have detrimental effects on children's behaviour. However, no weight was given to the economic and psychological benefits day care provides by allowing both parents to work. In particular, the researchers statistically erased the potential positive effects of increased family income by matching families in the control group with families of comparable incomes in the experimental groups.

Validity-It was a longitudinal study, which makes it more valid as it assessed the long-term effects of day care on child development. More than one research method was used before drawing conclusions, which increases the validity of the research. However, childcare is such a wide area and so many factors affect child development such as temperament and parenting styles that it is hard to draw meaningful conclusions.

Ethics-Parents gave consent for their children to take part in the study, but the children were too young to give consent themselves and may have been distressed by some of the observations and tests.

Another study that looks at the disadvantages of day care is Belsky and Rovine (1998)

Description:

Aim-To look at the effects of day care on children's attachment type in the first year of life.

Procedure-Evidence from two American longitudinal studies were combined and examined to assess the effects of day care. The sample consisted of 90 male and 59 female firstborn infants. All the families were intact and from a middle-class background. Interviews were carried out when the infants were 3-months-old, 9-months-old and 12-months- old to find out about the children's day care arrangements and parents' employment.

The strange situation task was carried out on all 149 infants at twelve months old using the mothers and again at thirteen months using the fathers (only 130 infants took part when the father was used). Videos of each of the procedures were shown to different observers. The observers had 90% inter-rater reliability and rated the attachments using Ainsworth's attachment types A, B and C.

Results-The children in full-time day care were more likely to be insecurely attached, compared to infants who spent less time in day care. 47% of infants in full-time day care (more than 35 hours) were insecurely attached, 35% of infants experiencing extensive part-time care (20-35 hours). Insecure attachments were much lower amongst children experiencing 10-20 hours of part-time care (21%) and those experiencing little or no care (25%). 50% of boys whose mothers worked full-time had insecure attachments to their fathers. More boys had insecure attachments than girls.

Conclusion-Belsky and Rovine concluded that infants who are left in day care for long periods of time are more likely to be insecurely attached to their mothers.

Evaluation:

Generalisability-The study was carried out in America so the results cannot be generalised to other countries. All the families were intact and from middle class backgrounds, so they were not representative of the wider population.

Reliability-The strange situation was used which is easy to replicate and so the study has reliability. The children were also categorised by the number of hours they spent in day care, which is easy to replicate. Barglow et al.'s (1987) study supports the findings that more than twenty hours a week of day care under 12 months old is linked to insecure attachments.

Application to real life-The study implies that mothers should be offered one year's paid maternity leave so that children do not have to experience prolonged day care in their first year of life.

Validity-The strange situation, has been criticised for lacking ecological validity as the children may be responding to the artificial situation. Children who have experienced day care are less likely to be upset by being left with a stranger compared to children who are usually cared for by their parents. Therefore, the strange situation may not be a valid method for comparing attachment types in children who have experienced day care versus those who have not. Furthermore, the children's temperament may have affected their responses to the strange situation rather than their attachment type.

Ethics-The children may have been caused unnecessary distress by the strange situation in the study.

Another study that looks at the negative effects of day care is **Baydar and Brooks-Gunn (1991)**. They surveyed 1000 mothers by telephone, asking questions about their use of day-care and their children's behaviour and academic progress. They found that children whose mothers had returned to work in their first year had a higher incidence of behaviour difficulties and poor cognitive development.

You need to be able to describe good quality day-care in terms of cognitive, social and emotional development

Good quality day care involves well trained staff. There also needs to be consistency of care with prolonged contact with the same carers, a low staff turnover, appropriate staff-child ratios and a key worker for each child. Staff should be able to devote sufficient time to the child meaning fewer insecure attachments.

You need to be able to explain how to reduce the negative effects of short-term deprivation

Children should not spend too long in day care. According to Belsky and Rovine, children who spend more than 20 hours a week in day care are more likely to be insecurely attached and those who spend more than 10 hours per week are more likely to be aggressive.

Parents should wait until a child has formed an attachment before putting them in day care. The younger the child the more negative the effects of day care. There is almost no evidence that day care in older children has negative effects.

Nurseries and pre-schools should assign a keyworker for each child so that they have an attachment figure when their parents are not there.

Nurseries and pre-schools should have high staff to child ratios so that children can receive more individual attention and care.

Parents should be encouraged to stay with children during hospitalisation and this reduces the negative effects of short term deprivation. Many hospitals now offer camp beds for parents to stay with their children overnight.

You need to be able to describe the problems of researching day care

There are several factors that influence whether day care has positive or negative effects including the mother's happiness with her own situation, the age at which a child enters day care, the amount of time the child spends in day care and the quality of day care.

You need to be able to describe and evaluate one contemporary study in child psychology. For example, Li et al. (2013). Timing of High-Quality Child Care and Cognitive, Language and Preacademic Development

Description:

Aim-To see whether high quality infant-toddler care (care up to 24 months) and high quality preschool care (care up to 54 months) improves cognitive, language and pre-academic development. To see if having high quality care at both stages improves outcomes for children compared to having low quality at any of the stages. To see if the benefits of high quality care during the infant-toddler period are lost after low quality care in the preschool period.

Procedure-1364 families with full-term healthy babies were recruited for the study from hospitals in the USA. The sample included a range of families with different socioeconomic status and ethnicity. The child's race, gender, birth order, temperament, maternal attitudes about raising children, maternal age, maternal educational level and paternal educational level were recorded. The child's health, maternal separation anxiety, maternal depression, maternal employment status, whether the mother's partner was present in the household and the family income-to-needs ration were also measured at 1 month and 24 months of age.

The researchers carried out observations, interviews, questionnaires and child assessments from 1 month after the children's birth. The Observational Record of the Caregiving Environment (ORCE) was used to measure the quality of care the children were receiving at 6, 15, 24, 36 and 54 months whether they were being cared for at home by a relative or in a day care setting such as a nursery. Quality of care was rated on 4-point scales. Scores higher than 3.0 indicated higher quality care. At 24 months, the children were assessed using the Bayley Mental Development index, which is linked to IQ. At 54 months, outcomes were measured using the Woodcock-Johnson Cognitive and Achievement Batteries and the Preschool Language Scale (PLS), which measured memory, language development and intelligence.

The children were split into four groups. Children who had received high quality care in the infant-toddler period and preschool period were classed as high-high. Those who had experienced low quality care in both periods were classed as low-low. Those who had low followed by high quality care were classed as low-high and those who had received high followed low quality care were classed as high-low.

Results-High quality care during both the infant-toddler period and preschool period led to the best outcomes at 54 months for memory, language development and intelligence. Low quality care during both periods led to the worst outcomes. The high-low and low-high groups were close together in terms of outcomes. High quality care during the infant-toddler period led to better memory development for children who experienced low quality care during the preschool period. High quality care during the preschool period led to improved reading and maths ability for children who had experienced low quality care during the infant-toddler period.

Conclusion-High-quality care during the infant-toddler period and preschool period leads to the best outcomes for children. Children who receive high-quality care before 24 months have better memory development and children who receive high-quality care during the preschool period have improved academic skills.

Evaluation:

Generalisability-Only around 50% of participants responded at the six-month interview. This led to a biased sample with a disproportionate number of economically advantaged white families who are not representative of the wider population. As the study was conducted in the USA, it is hard to generalise the findings to other cultures.

Reliability-The study used the Observational Record of the Caregiving Environment (ORCE) to measure the quality of care and 4-point scales. Standardised tests such as the Bayley Mental Development index, the Woodcock-Johnson Cognitive and Achievement Batteries and the Preschool Language Scale (PLS) were used to measure outcomes, which makes the study easier to replicate and more reliable.

Application to real life-The study suggests that investment in good quality child care should be distributed across the early childhood periods as both periods are important for cognitive development. However, if there is only enough money for one of the time periods, then high quality care should be offered during the preschool period as it costs less.

Validity-It was a longitudinal study, which makes it more valid as it assessed the long-term effects of high or low-quality day care on child development. However, the study did not take into account the quantity or types of childcare received when assessing quality of childcare, so this reduces the validity of the findings.

Ethics-Parents gave consent for their children to take part in the study, but the children were too young to give consent themselves and may have been distressed by some of the observations and tests.

You need to be able to describe and evaluate research into long-term deprivation

Bowlby's 44 Juvenile Thieves

Description:

Aim-Bowlby looked at 44 young offenders to see whether those who displayed a lack of empathy for other people and lack of guilt for their actions (affectionless psychopathy) had experienced an early separation from their mothers (maternal deprivation).

Procedure-Bowlby chose 44 young offenders who had been referred to a child guidance clinic. He assessed them to see whether they had affectionless psychopathy and interviewed their relatives to see whether there had been a prolonged separation from the mother in the first two years of life. The children also completed IQ assessments and psychiatric assessments.

Results-Bowlby found that 14 out of the 44 children had affectionless psychopathy and that 12 of these 14 children had been deprived of their mother in the first two years of their life. In contrast, only 5 of the 30 children not classified as affectionless psychopaths had experienced a prolonged separation from their mother when young.

Conclusion-Children who experience prolonged separation from their mothers in the first two years of life are more likely to become affectionless psychopaths than those who do not experience such a separation. This supports Bowlby's maternal deprivation hypothesis.

Evaluation:

Generalisability-Young offenders are not representative of the wider population so the study is not generalisable. 75% of the children were boys so the study has a gender bias.

Reliability-It would be hard to repeat the study and get the same results as unstructured interviews were used and on a different day, participants may have answered questions differently. IQ tests and psychiatric assessments were conducted, which are more reliable.

Application to real life-The study suggests that children should not be separated from their mother for a prolonged period of time in the first two years of life.

Validity-Information about the early separation was collected retrospectively during interviews. This relies on the participants' accuracy of recall and their honesty. Bowlby carried out both the interviews and the psychiatric assessments himself, so he may have biased because he knew what he wanted to find.
However, Bowlby did use triangulation to establish validity (triangulation involves bringing together data from different research methods and looking for agreement/trends). For example, he carried out psychiatric assessments on the

children and interviewed their families. He also compared the young offenders to a control group of non-delinquent children to see how frequently maternal deprivation occurs in the wider population.

Bowlby found a relationship/correlation between affectionless psychopathy and prolonged separation from the mother in the first two years of life, but this does not establish cause and effect. There may be a third factor such as a child's difficult temperament or domestic violence that caused both the maternal separation and the child's maladjustment.

Ethical issues-The study interviewed the children's relatives about childhood experiences of separation and the children's relationships. This may have caused psychological distress. The children were emotional disturbed and vulnerable, and the tests and interviews may have put pressure on them.

Cockett and Tripp (1994)

Description:

Aim-To look at the effects of parental separation on children in comparison to living with parental conflict.

Procedure-The study consisted of 152 children divided into three groups matched on age, gender, socio-economic status and maternal education. One group consisted of children from reordered families where the parents had divorced or separated. One group consisted of children from families where there was serious parental conflict and the final group consisted of children from harmonious families. The children were asked to complete questionnaires and take part in interviews to assess their performance at school, behaviour and self-esteem. They also interviewed the children from the reordered families about their experiences.

Results-The children from the reordered families performed worse at school, had more behavioural issues and poorer self-esteem than the children from the families where the parents were still together even when there was parental conflict. As expected, the harmonious families had the fewest problems. Very few of the children from divorced or separated families had been prepared for it and less than half had regular contact with their non-custodial parent. Children who had experienced more family reorderings fared the worst and had less contact with their extended family.

Conclusion-Parental separation and divorce are more harmful than parental discord.

Evaluation:

Generalisability-The study used a large sample of children who were matched on age, gender, socio-economic status and maternal education. This makes the study generalizable to the wider population.

Reliability-The study would be hard to replicate as it used in-depth interviews, which would be hard to replicate. On a different day, the children might offer different responses about their lives.

Application to real life-The study suggests that parents who are separating should prepare their children better for the changes and that more effort should be made to keep in contact with the absent parent and the extended family.

Validity-The study collected in-depth detailed data about the children's experiences from interviews and questionnaires, which is likely to be valid. However, the children may not have been entirely truthful about all their experiences and given socially desirable answers.

Ethics-Interviewing and questioning children about their experiences of parental separation and divorce or parental conflict may have caused the children distress.

Other studies on long-term deprivation:

Richards (1995) found that parental separation due to divorce or family break-up could lead to lower levels of academic attainment at school, higher rates of behavioural problems and worse outcomes as an adult in terms of relationships and socio-economic status. This study suggests that there can be long-term consequences for children who experience parental separation.

Bilfuco et al. (1991) found that women who had experienced the death of their mother before 6-years-old had higher rates of depression.

Rutter (1981) found that children who experienced death of a parent had better outcomes than children who had experienced a high conflict divorce.

Saler and Skolnick (1992) found that the effects of the death of a parent can be lessened by allowing a child to fully express their feelings openly and letting them be part of the mourning process.

You need to be able to describe how to reduce the effects of long-term deprivation

How to reduce the negative effects of separation or divorce:

Parents can prepare their children for the separation and discuss new living arrangements.
The non-custodial parent should be allowed contact with the child.
Parents should try to avoid high levels of conflict especially in front of the children.
Adequate arrangements should be made to keep in contact with the extended family, for example, grandparents and cousins.

How to reduce the negative effects of death of a parent.

Following death of a parent, a child should be allowed to mourn openly and to take part in the mourning process.
Children should be encouraged to express their feelings of anger and sadness but not forced to.
They may also want to share their memories of their parent and visit places that remind them of their parent.

You need to be able to define privation

Privation occurs when children never have the opportunity to form an attachment to a primary carer, or when any attachment they do form is disrupted due to abuse. Privation can produce serious social-emotional and intellectual problems. An important debate is whether the effects of privation are reversible.

You need to be able to describe and evaluate research into privation

Curtiss' (1997) case study of Genie

Description:

Aim- To investigate whether a child can form attachments later on despite privation and whether there is a critical period for language development. Curtiss also wanted to help Genie overcome her extreme privation.
Background-In 1977, Genie was found and taken into care aged 13-years-old. She had spent most of her life alone with a potty chair, a cot where she was chained to at night and some cotton reels to play with. Genie's father believed she was mentally retarded and so locked her in a room and neglected her. She was beaten by her father if she made noises and rarely met anyone outside her immediate family. Genie's father committed suicide before he could be prosecuted for Genie's abuse.
Procedure-After Genie was found by the authorities, she was fostered by the Los Angeles Children's hospital. Initially, Genie could not dress herself or use the toilet properly. However, Genie was taught to dress herself and use the bathroom quickly. She was also given intensive speech therapy to help develop her speech. The hospital carried out many tests and observations on Genie to assess her abilities and to monitor her progress.
Genie's mother who was blind was interviewed by researchers. However, the data was not used as it was thought it could not be trusted.

Results-Initially, Genie showed many signs of distress such as crying, biting and scratching. However, she showed signs of attachment to the researchers. Genie was given some neurological tests and the results suggested that there was some mental retardation. Genie's speech did get better with therapy but she was not able to use correct grammar. When the funding for Curtiss' study ran out, Genie's mother was reappointed her legal guardian.

Conclusion-The study suggests that the effects of privation are irreversible. Genie made a small amount of progress but did not acquire language fully or develop 'normally'. There is a critical period for language development.

Evaluation:

Generalisability-Genie was a unique case of extreme privation and she may have had brain damage from birth, so she is not representative of other children who have experienced privation.

Reliability-It would be impossible to replicate the Genie study as it was a unique case.

Application to real life-The study suggests that a child who has experienced privation can form attachments. However, it may not be possible for a child to develop language normally once they have gone past a 'critical' period of language development.

Validity-This case study has ecological validity as it collected rich, detailed information about Genie using a number of different techniques.

Ethics-It has been said that the researchers put the research ahead of Genie and cared more about the results than her welfare. Genie was very vulnerable given her background and extreme privation but she was subjected to endless tests, observations and questions. Some argue that the researchers did not consider what would happen to Genie after the study finished. Genie's mother was appointed her legal guardian at the end of the study even though she was involved in Genie's neglect.
However, Genie was given intensive therapy and care, which would not have been possible if she had not been part of a study. The constant scans and tests that were run helped the researchers understand her condition better and adapt their treatment methods. Genie's true name was kept a secret from the media but her photograph was published.

The Czech twins Koluchova (1972, 1991)

Description:

Koluchova' reported the case of two identical twin boys 'the Czech twins' whose mother died soon after their birth. At first they were placed in institutionalised care and then they were cared for by their aunt up until 18 months old. When their father remarried, they were returned to their father and their new stepmother. The stepmother kept the boys locked in a dark, cold closet most of the time and they were beaten regularly until they were rescued at the age of seven and fostered. By the age of 14, they showed no social-emotional or intellectual deficits and by 20 they both showed average intelligence, were working and experiencing successful romantic relationships. The study suggests that the effects of privation are reversible.

Evaluation:

The twins formed an attachment with each other, so this may not be case of true privation. They also had reasonably good care up to the age of 18 months.

Hodges and Tizard (1989)

Description:

Hodges and Tizard (1989) wanted to see whether being raised in an institution (a residential nursery) from only a few months old can lead to behaviour problems and insecure attachments. It was a longitudinal study that followed children from age 4-

to 16-years-old. The policy of the nursery was to discourage the formation of close relationships with care-givers and this was compounded by very high staff turnover. By age 4, some of the children had been adopted, some returned to their parents (restored) and some stayed in the residential nursery. There was also a control group of children who lived with their own families. They found that at age four, none of the institutionalised children had formed attachments. However, by age eight, the adopted children had formed good attachments and at age sixteen there was little difference between them and the control group. The restored children and the children, who stayed in the institution, had more insecure attachments and more behavioural problems. All the children who had been institutionalised when young had worse peer relationships.

Evaluation:

Hodges and Tizard used interviews and questionnaires to assess the social and emotional competence of the children. However, the children, parents and teachers involved may have given socially desirable answers. Some of the families dropped out of the study later on and this may have biased the results. Furthermore, there the children who remained in the institution may have been less socially and emotionally competent in the beginning, which is why they were not adopted.

Rutter and Sonuga-Barke (2010) English and Romanian Adoptee (ERA) Study

Description:

Aim-To investigate the effects of privation on social, cognitive and physical development.

Procedure-Rutter and Sonuga-Barke (2010) carried out a longitudinal study following a group of 165 Romanian children who had been left in Romanian orphanages as babies and then later adopted by English families. They compared the social, cognitive and physical progress of these Romanian children with a control group of 52 British children who had been adopted in the UK.

Results-They found that at the time of adoption, the Romanian orphans were behind the British children in terms of social, cognitive and physical development. However, by the age of four the Romanian children who had been adopted before the age of six months had caught up in their development. However, the children who had been in the Romanian orphanages after six months were more likely to have disinhibited attachments, a type of insecure attachment where children show the same level of friendliness and affection to strangers as they would to their own parents. The children who had been adopted later also had more problems with peer relationships.

Conclusion-Children are more likely to recover from the effects of privation if they are adopted before the age of six months and given the opportunity to form attachments. However, children experience privation for longer periods of time find it harder to form secure attachments.

Evaluation:

Generalisability-The conditions in the Romanian orphanages were appalling and the children experienced extreme physical neglect not just emotional neglect. Therefore, it is hard to generalise the findings of the Romanian orphan studies to other instances of privation.

Reliability-The studies used reliable tests to measure the children's development. Application to real life- The studies show how important it is to minimise the effects of institutional care, for example in hospitals or children's homes. Ideally, children should have a dedicated caregiver in institutions and be adopted as early as possible to enable secure attachments to form.

Validity-Rutter and Songua-Barke's study is longitudinal so it is able to look at the children's progress over time. This increases the validity of the study as it has been able to show the long-term effects of privation and how some of the effects have reduced over time.
Some children perhaps because of their temperament are better able to recover from the effects of privation, which means that firm conclusions cannot be drawn.

Ethics-The children in this study were vulnerable and so the psychologists carrying out tests on the children and interviewing their parents and teachers needed to be sensitive and to consider the well-being of the children at all times so that they were protected from psychological harm. There are also issues of consent when using children in a study.

You need to be able to discuss the reversibility of privation

There is a debate about whether the effects of privation are reversible or not. The study of Genie showed that the effects of privation are not reversible. Genie was looked after by psychologists from the age of 13 and made a small amount of progress but did not acquire language fully or develop 'normally'. On the other hand, recent research following Romanian adoptees in the UK suggests that recovery from extreme early privation is possible. The Koluchova study of twins who were privated early in their lives also suggests that privation is reversible. When the twins were found, the twins had very low IQ scores and could not walk or use language normally for their age. They were fostered into an extremely caring environment and developed average intelligence and formed successful romantic relationships as adults.
The Hodges and Tizard study looked at the development of children who had experienced institutional care at a very young age. The compared the behaviour of these children with a control group of children who lived with their families. They found that the children who had been adopted by 4-years-old formed good attachments and were similar to the control group at 16-years-old despite their early privation. This suggests that the effects of privation can be overcome if children are subsequently brought up in a loving environment. However, these adopted children had more difficulty in peer relationships than the control group. The children who were restored to their natural parents or who stayed in the institution had poorer outcomes. They had more insecure attachments, more behavioural problems, were more attention-seeking and had poorer peer relationships.

228

One of the main difficulties with research into privation is that it is difficult to assess whether a child has formed any attachments along the way. For example, in the Koluchova study, the twins were able to bond with each other, so they may not have been truly privated. Therefore, the study cannot conclusively say that privation is reversible.

In contrast, the case study of Genie suggests that privation is irreversible. However, we cannot be sure that Genie did not have a problem with development from the start. Neurological studies on Genie showed that she had brain activity similar to a child that had suffered brain damage. Therefore, Genie may not have fully recovered from her privation due to brain damage rather than the fact that privation is irreversible.

You need to be able to describe the features of autism

Autism affects about 1% of the population and boys are five times more likely to be diagnosed than girls. It is classed as a spectrum disorder as all people with autism share certain difficulties, but it can affect them in different ways.

Autism is related to a triad of impairments. Autistic children have: 1) Difficulties with social interaction. For example, they find it hard to make friends. 2) Problems with verbal and non-verbal communication. For example, they have difficulty expressing their emotions or understanding other people's emotions. They also find it hard to read people's facial expressions. 3) Difficulties with imaginative play. For example, they might find it hard to pretend that a wooden block is a train or a rocket. Children with autism may not engage with other people or share their interests and achievements. They can also be quite sensitive to stimuli in their environment such as loud noises. There can be speech and language difficulties in children with autism but not always. Examples of speech and language difficulties are: not speaking by 16 months, repeating words and phrases over and over again, repeating questions rather than answering them, not being able to communicate their desires and not understanding humour.

Other characteristics of autism are lack of eye contact, sensitivity to environmental stimuli and repetitive behaviour.

Children with autism can be quite inflexible, for example, they do not cope well with changes in routine. Other signs of inflexibility are: attachments to strange objects such as wires or keys, lining up toys or spending long periods of time staring at moving objects such as a wheel spinning on a car. Some children with autism can show an amazing memory for facts such as train schedules.

Autism may lead a child to feel emotionally isolated. This may lead to anxiety and unhappiness. Many autistic people have certain routines that help them deal with their anxieties e.g. wearing the same clothes, eating the same foods and repeating the same movements (hand flapping, finger flicking).

Note:

The new versions of the diagnostic manuals such as DSM-V refer to both autism and Asperger syndrome as autism spectrum disorder (ASD). This is to reflect that people with ASD have similar communication and social issues but there is not always a delay in language or cognitive development.

You need to be able to describe and evaluate one biological explanation for autism. For example, the genetic explanation for autism.

Description:

The genetic explanation states that genes can predispose someone to develop autism. Yuen et al. (2017) identified 18 candidate genes that are linked to autism. They also found insertions and deletions in the DNA sequences of individuals with autism. Furthermore, in some individuals they found copy number variations and chromosomal abnormalities. Herring et al. (2017) found eight mutations in a small area of the TRIO gene that are associated with autism. Whole genome sequencing, a technique that provides a patient's complete genetic information suggests that autistic individuals have genetic changes that alter gene function and protein production. There are areas of the genome that do not contain genes but are responsible for turning genes on and these may not be functioning fully in those with autism. Genetic abnormalities may lead to damage to neural pathways (nerve cells carrying messages) in the brain. Behaviour that is controlled by these neural pathways may then be abnormal.

Note:

Candidate genes are genes that are linked to a particular characteristic or disorder.

Copy number variation (CNV) relates to when sections of the genome are repeated. The number of repeats can vary between people.

The genome refers to all our genetic material, including the genes that code for particular characteristics and the non-coding DNA.

Whole genome sequencing refers to reading and understanding the genetic information found in the DNA of any organism.

Evaluation:

Studies-Bailey et al. (1995) found a 60% concordance rate for autism in monozygotic (MZ) twins compared to 0% in dizygotic (DZ) twins. When they looked at other abnormalities such as communication and social disorders, they found 92% concordance in the MZ twins compared to 0% concordance in the DZ twins. This study suggests that genes play an important role in the development of autism and autism-related behaviours.

Hallymayer et al. (2011) found higher concordance rates amongst both female MZ twins and male MZ twins compared DZ twins. This supports the view that genes contribute to the development of autism.

Sandin et al. (2017) carried out a family study which included 37,570 twin pairs, 2,642,064 full sibling pairs, and 432,281 maternal and 445,531 paternal half-sibling pairs. 14,516 children were diagnosed with autism, and the heritability for autism was estimated as 83 per cent, while the non-shared environmental influence was estimated as 17 per cent. This study supports the view that genes play a significant role in the development of autism.

Yuen et al. (2017) found 18 candidate genes for autistic spectrum disorder (ASD) and other genetic variations in families with ASD.

Explanation-There are a variety of gene mutations that are linked to autism but as no single gene has been found so it is hard to pin down a genetic cause. Autism may be caused by the interaction of multiple genes or abnormalities in gene functioning. Environmental factors must also play a role in the development of autism as the concordance rate is not 100% in MZ twins. Being born prematurely (before 35 weeks) and exposure to sodium valproate in the womb is linked to autism. High levels of testosterone in the womb may also lead autism. Auyeung et al. (2009) found that pregnant women who had high levels of testosterone in the amniotic fluid were more likely to have children who had autistic traits at age eight, such as a lack of sociability and poor verbal skills.

You need to be able to describe and evaluate one other explanation for autism. For example, lack of theory of mind.

Description:

Theory of mind is the ability to read others' intentions and to understand other people's feelings. Baron-Cohen said that theory of mind gives us a number of abilities in social situations including being able to persuade and deceive others and to pretend. Baron-Cohen suggests that people with autism lack theory of mind and that they have 'mind-blindness', the inability to understand other people's feeling and intentions.

Evaluation:

Studies- Baron-Cohen et al. (1985) developed the Sally-Anne task to test for autism. They compared children with no developmental disability, children with autism and children with Down's syndrome. In the Sally-Anne task, a child is presented with two dolls called Sally and Anne. The child watches while Sally places a marble in her basket. The experimenter then says that Sally is going out of the room. While Sally is away, Anne hides the marble in a different place. Sally is then brought back to the room. The child is then asked, 'Where will Sally look for the marble?' Children over 4 years older who do not have ASD should be able to understand that Sally thinks the marble is still in the original place. However, children with ASD tend to think that Sally will know the new hiding place for the marble. This is because children with ASD have difficulty understanding that other people have different thoughts and feelings to them. Baron-Cohen et al. found that 85% of the 'normal' children and the children with Downs Syndrome gave the correct response to the question, 'Where will Sally look for the marble?'. However only 20% of children with autism gave the correct answer. This study supports the view that autistic children lack theory of mind.

Explanation-Lack of theory of mind is not a causal explanation of autism. It describes the problems that children with autism have but it does not explain why children develop it. The genetic explanation is better at explaining why children might develop autism. Furthermore, lack of theory of mind does not explain why some children with autism have problems with language.

You need to be able to describe and evaluate therapies for helping children with autism.

Applied Behaviour Analysis (ABA)

Description:

One therapy that has been found to be effective for autism is Applied Behaviour Analysis (ABA). ABA involves teaching children with autism the skills to communicate effectively and interact with others. Once the children have been shown how to interact with others, they are rewarded for appropriate behaviours such as waiting for their turn in a game. Therapists systematically observe the children's behaviour and identify what behaviours need to change. The therapist then adapts what they are teaching based on the children's behaviour and sets up opportunities for the children to improve their skills further.

Evaluation:

Directiveness-The therapy is directive as the therapists tell children how to improve their behaviour and how to interact more effectively with others. The therapist has power over the therapy.

Effectiveness-Lovaas (1987) compared autistic children who had received 40 hours of ABA per week for two years to a control group who hadn't received ABA. They found that 9 out of 19 children in the ABA group had normal cognitive development and were able to perform in school with minimal support compared to only 1 of 40 children in the control group. This study supports ABA as a therapy for improving the cognitive development of children with autism.
Cohen et al. (2006) replicated Lovaas' study. They compared 21 children who received 35 to 40 hours of ABA per week to a control group of 21 age- and IQ-matched children. The ABA group obtained significantly higher IQ and adaptive behaviour scores than control group. 6 of 21 ABA children were fully included in regular education without assistance at year 3, and 11 others were included with support compared to only 1 of 21 in the control group. This study suggests that ABA is an effective therapy for autism and can help improve behaviour and IQ.
Peters-Scheffer et al. (2011) carried out a meta-analysis of 11 studies with 344 children with autism and found that the experimental groups who had received ABA performed better than the control group in terms of IQ, language and behaviour. This study strongly supports the use of ABA to improve behaviour and cognitive development in children with autism.

Side effects-Children with autism may feel that they aren't accepted for who they are as their behaviour is classed as abnormal and needing improvement. Some adults have said they have been traumatised by the treatment they received as a child. Expense-The therapy is expensive as it is intensive and requires trained professionals to deliver it. The therapist needs to make sure that rewards are given consistently for desired behaviour in order for ABA to be effective.

Reasons-The therapy has been criticised for only changing behaviour at a surface level. Children with autism can be taught how to communicate in a socially acceptable way to make them appear 'normal' but they may not understand why they are performing the behaviours they have been taught.

Types of people-The therapy can be used with autistic children with a range of behaviours as it can be adapted to the individual.

Cognitive Behavioural Therapy

Description:

Cognitive behavioural therapy (CBT) can be used to address any anxious thoughts that a child with autism might be experiencing. The cognitive part of the cognitive behavioural therapy (CBT) involves questioning and changing the child's irrational thoughts and replacing them with more realistic ones. For example, the therapist might question the child's beliefs about a situation that they find stressful such as going to a new place. The behaviour part of the therapy involves teaching the child the skills to deal with the situation such as touching a toy in their pocket to reduce the anxiety felt.

Children with autism find it difficult to recognise their emotions so the therapist will work with them to help them distinguish between their thoughts, feelings and behaviours. They may also use pictures to help them identify how they are feeling.

Evaluation:

Directiveness-CBT is supposed to be a collaborative process where the therapist and child work together to address irrational thoughts. However, as the therapist tells the child which thoughts are irrational and challenges their thinking, the therapy can be viewed as directive as there is a power imbalance between the child and therapist.

Effectiveness- Sofronoff et al. (2005) looked at the effectiveness of CBT on children who had autism and were exhibiting anxiety symptoms. They found that CBT reduced the children's anxiety symptoms compared to the control group who were on a waiting list for the treatment. Active parent involvement improved the effectiveness.

Wood et al. (2009) found that CBT reduced anxiety symptoms in 78.5% of children with autism. This study supports the effectiveness of CBT for reducing anxiety in autistic children.

Side effects-None

Expense-CBT is expensive as it requires a trained therapist to deliver the treatment. However, it can reduce anxiety in autistic children in just 16 sessions (Wood et al., 2009).

Reasons-CBT does not confront the causes of anxiety. It just challenges present thinking.

Types of people-The treatment works better with autistic children who have reasonable language skills and can express their thoughts or those who can at least respond to pictures. Some children with autism cannot use language and so CBT would not be suitable for them.

You need to be able to describe a key question: What issues should parents take into account when deciding about day care for their child?

Exam tip: Use studies looking at the advantages and disadvantages of day care.

According to Belsky and Rovine, more than 20 hours of childcare per week for a child under the age of 1-year-old is associated with insecure attachments. A US study of more than 17,000 children found that there is a relationship between number of hours in non-parental care and behaviour (Early Childhood Longitudinal Study, Ritter & Turner, 2003). This research suggests that mothers should not go back to work too early or for long hours. However, many mothers find caring for a baby or toddler tiring and stressful. They may not want to stay at home looking after their child. Obviously, if a mother is very stressed and unhappy this will affect the baby and in such situations, it would be better for the mother to return to work. Brown and Harris (1978) found that women who don't work and have several young children to care for are more likely to be depressed. There is no sense in a mother staying at home if she is depressed and unhappy. The child is more likely to become securely attached if the mother is happy but around less. Ultimately, it is hard for a mother to meet her child's needs and at the same time meet her own needs, but a mother must be happy for her child to be happy.

The Institute of Education in London studied 17,000 children born to American and British mothers in the 1990s, 1970s and 1980s (Joshi, 2002). They did not find any major impact on children from mothers returning to work in the preschool years and the increased income from mothers working would have improved the children's standard of living. However, children whose mothers returned to work after their first year and who worked only part-time were slightly less anxious than children whose mothers had gone back to work full-time before they turned one.

Baydar and Brooks-Gunn (1991) surveyed 1000 mothers by telephone, asking questions about their use of daycare and their children's behaviour and academic progress. They found that children whose mothers had returned to work in their first year had a higher incidence of behaviour difficulties and poor intellectual development.

Vandell and Corasantini (1990) studied children who experienced daycare from when they were small babies. These children were rated as having poor peer relationships and poor emotional health.

Belsky (2002) examined aggression and defiance in pre-school children in relation to time spent in day care in the first, second, third and fourth sixth-month periods of children's lives. The more time children spent in day care, in particular during the first year, the higher the levels of aggression and defiance. Belsky concludes that it is long hours in early infancy spent in day care that can have negative effects

However, Harr (1999) measured emotional adjustment and academic attainment in 628 children and found very few differences between children of mothers who did not work and those who worked full-time. However, once children reached school age, those children whose mother worked part-time were better adjusted than those of full-time employed mothers. Interestingly, children's emotional adjustment and academic progress were positively associated with mothers' satisfaction with their parent/worker status. This supports the common-sense view that it is happy mother rather than working or non-working mothers who are the most successful parents.

Another study that supports the use of day care is Andersson (1996). This study followed up 126 Swedish children who had been in day-care in early childhood, and assessed them on their intellectual and social-emotional development at 13-years-old. Their development was compared with that of a control group who had had full-time maternal care in their early childhood. The children who had spent time in day care scored higher for academic achievement and social skills.

Parents need to be careful about choosing day care. Good quality day care is important and too many hours in day care can have detrimental effects.

Good quality day care involves well trained staff. Research shows that the more experienced the staff the better the quality of day care given. When staff had high level qualifications such as NVQs in childcare, they provided better care. Therefore, parents should look at the qualifications of the people offering day care before making a decision on where to place their child.

Children also need stability. They need to be able to form strong emotional bonds to their carers and this is only possible if they have access to the same carer regularly and consistently. High staff turnover can lead to problems with children forming attachments. If parents are going to use a nursery or preschool for day care, they should question the nursery about staff turnover. Alternatively, they may choose to use a nanny or a childminder instead as this may provide more consistent care.

Parents also need to consider how much attention their child will receive in the day care setting they are considering. Nurseries should have a high staff to child ratio so that children get enough attention and care. However, a nanny may be able to provide more one-to-one care but is more expensive.

Children in a nursery or preschool should be assigned a key worker who they can go to if they are upset or require help. The key worker can also look out for signs of distress in their assigned children and help them with certain tasks.

Adults who are sensitive, empathic and attuned to a child's feelings have been found to be better carers. Good carers enable infants and young children to feel confident, encourage them to communicate and talk, to think and have ideas, and to learn and discover. Parents should look for these qualities when choosing a day care provider.

Stimulation is very important for children's intellectual and language development. Nurseries, preschools and childminders should have lots of books, dressing up outfits and colourful toys that encourage children to learn through play. Parents should look for stimulating environments for their child. Carers also need to ask children questions and to respond to the children's vocalisations or talk.

You need to be able to describe factors that contribute to good quality childcare in nurseries

Good quality childcare involves well trained staff. Research shows that the more experienced the staff the better the quality of childcare given. When staff had high level qualifications such as NVQs in childcare, they provided better care.
Children also need stability. They need to be able to form strong emotional bonds to their carers and this is only possible if they have access to the same carer regularly and consistently. High staff turnover can lead to problems with children forming attachments.
Nurseries should have a high staff to child ratios so that children get enough attention and care.
Children should also be assigned a key worker who they can go to if they are upset or require help. The key worker can also look out for signs of distress in the particular children they are assigned to and can help them with certain tasks.
Adults who are sensitive, empathic and attuned to a child's feelings have been found to be better carers. Good carers enable infants and young children to feel confident, encourage them to communicate and talk, to think and have ideas, and to learn and discover.
Stimulation is very important for children's intellectual and language development. Nurseries should have lots of books, dressing up outfits and colourful toys that encourage children to learn through play. Caregivers need to ask children questions and to respond to the children's vocalisations or talk.

You need to be able to describe and evaluate observations as a research method in child psychology

Description:

In child psychology, observations are used to watch and record children's behaviour in a variety of settings such as at home, at school or in a nursery.

Structured laboratory observations involve careful controls and a set-up situation that can be repeated. The strange situation is an example of a structured observation as there are certain set stages in the observation and the behaviour of the child is recorded when their mother leaves them alone and when they are with a stranger.

Naturalistic observations involved observing children in their natural setting. For example, children might be observed playing with each other in a nursery or at home with their parents.

Observations often have more than one observer to ensure inter-observer reliability. If a number of observers agree about what they have observed, this increases the reliability of the findings. This is because an individual observer can be biased.

Observations can be overt or covert. Covert observations involve observing a child or group of children without their knowledge, for example, through a one-way mirror. This ensures that the researchers' presence does not affect the children's behaviour. However, a parent or legal guardian must give consent for the observation to take place. Overt observations involve observing a child or group of children with their knowledge.

Observations can also be participant or non-participant. A participant observation involves the researcher getting actively involved with the child or children that are being observed. For example, during a participant observation, the researcher may play with a child. A non-participant observation involves the researcher observing behaviour from a distance without getting involved. For example, observing children's aggressive behaviour in the playground.

An observation can be carried out by counting the frequency of certain behaviours during a fixed period of time.
Event sampling-when you record every time an event such as a kick occurs
Time sampling-when you record what is happening every set amount of time e.g. every 5 minutes.
Point sampling- The behaviour of just one individual in the group is recorded.

Evaluation:

The presence of the observer might influence behaviour (social desirability). It may be difficult to record all the behaviour although event sampling, time sampling and point sampling help. Video recordings allow an observation to be played back later so that nothing is missed. However, it may be difficult to analyse or interpret all the data collected. Observers have to be specially trained to categorise and record behaviour quickly without bias. Having more than one observer can reduce the problem of researcher bias and establish inter-observer reliability.

Participant observations allow researchers to experience the same environment as their participants. However, the researcher's involvement can affect the behaviour of participants. In contrast, non-participant observations allow researchers to observe participants' behaviour more objectively as they are not directly involved in the action. However, if participants are aware they are being observed, they may still change their behaviour.

Covert observations enable researchers to observe participants behave naturally as the participants do not know they are being observed. However, there are ethical issues with observing participants without their consent. They do not have the right to withdraw, they have not given informed consent and there also issues of confidentiality especially if their behaviour has been video-recorded. The British Psychological Society advises that it is only suitable to conduct a covert observation in a place where people might reasonably be expected to be observed by other people such as a shopping centre or other public place. Overt observations do not have as many ethical issues as covert observations. However, when participants know they are being observed they may change their behaviour so that it appears socially desirable. Therefore, overt observations can be less valid. However, very young children are often unaware of being observed so they are less likely to change their behaviour due to the researcher's presence. Therefore, demand characteristics may not be a problem with young children.

Naturalistic observations have high ecological validity as the children are in their natural environment and are more likely to behave naturally compared to a laboratory observation. However, it can be difficult to control all the extraneous variables when children are observed in their natural environment. For example, the presence of a certain teacher may affect what type of aggression is observed in a playground. Therefore, it can be difficult to replicate the findings of a naturalistic observation. Researchers do not normally have to get consent to observe adults in public places but they do have to get parental consent when observing children.

Structured observations are replicable and reliable as they have a standardised procedure and control over extraneous variables. For example, the strange situation follows a carefully controlled procedure.

You need to be able to describe and evaluate case studies as a research method in child psychology

Description:

A case study is an in-depth study of one person or one group of people. A number of different techniques are used to gather data. For example, the researcher may observe, interview and carry out a number of experiments on the same person. In child psychology, case studies can be used to look at unique cases of privation, such as Genie. The researchers who studied Genie, carried out experiments, observations and interviews to assess whether her privation had affected her social, emotional and cognitive development. Triangulation is used to pool data together from the different types of research method and to draw conclusions.

Evaluation:

Case studies are not generalisable as they are carried out on only one person or one group of people who are often unique and not representative of the wider population. It is also difficult to replicate case studies because they involve unique individuals and the interpretation of the observations and interviews is subject to bias. Therefore, it is hard to establish reliability in case studies. However, triangulation is used to draw conclusions about the same concept, so this improves the reliability of the findings. An advantage of case studies is that they gather rich, detailed information about the individuals using a number of different techniques, so this increases their validity.

There can be ethical issues with case studies. Often they involve studying unique individuals who are more vulnerable than normal. Therefore, researchers have to be careful to protect them from psychological distress.

To be able to describe and evaluate longitudinal studies in child psychology

Description:

Longitudinal studies involve studying the same person or group of people over a long period of time. In child psychology, longitudinal studies are used to look at children's development over time. For example, how attachment, deprivation and privation affect children over time. In the EPPE study, the researchers looked at the long-term effects of day care on children's social, cognitive and emotional development.

Evaluation:

An advantage of longitudinal studies is that they allow researchers to follow the development and progress of children over time. There are also less likely to be participant variables compared to cross-sectional studies as the same children are used throughout. However, longitudinal studies can be expensive. Furthermore, erosion of the sample (children dropping out of the study) may cause bias. For example, if the researchers are looking at the effects of preschool education in a deprived area over time and some children leave the study to move to a more affluent area, then that can bias the results. It is also difficult to replicate a longitudinal study and establish reliability.

You need to be able to describe and evaluate cross-sectional studies in child psychology

Description:

Cross-sectional studies involve comparing different groups of children to each other. Charlton et al.'s St. Helena study used a cross-sectional design. They observed children's behaviour in two school playgrounds before TV was introduced and then five years later to see if there were any differences. The children in the playgrounds were different due to the time difference. Cross-sectional studies can also compare children of different ages or in different settings at the same time.

Evaluation:

Cross-sectional studies are less time-consuming than longitudinal studies and they allow researchers to compare children in different settings or of different ages at the same time.
An issue with cross-sectional studies is that there are participant variables. As the children are not the same, there may be differences between them that affect results.

You need to be able to describe and evaluate cross-cultural research in child psychology and the use of the meta-analysis

Description:

Cross-cultural research involves comparing studies carried out in different cultures. In child psychology, cross-cultural research may be used to compare attachment types, language development and the play of children in different cultures. For example, Van Ijzendoorn and Kroonenberg carried out a meta-analysis to compare attachment type (measured using the strange situation) in different cultures. A meta-analysis involves looking at the findings of a numbers of studies and drawing conclusions.

Evaluation:

Cross-cultural research can help us understand to what extent behaviour is nature or nurture. Behaviour that is similar across cultures is likely to be due to biology. Behaviour that is different across cultures is likely to be due to environment. However, a problem with cross-cultural research is that researchers may interpret the findings of the studies in terms of their own cultural beliefs (ethnocentrism). An issue with meta-analyses is that not all the studies used may be equally valid and reliable.

Ethical issues when researching with children, including children's rights and the UNCRC (1989), and issues around participation and protection

Researchers should try to fully inform children about what a study involves if they are old enough to understand. They should also obtain their consent where possible. However, even if children do give consent, they may not fully understand what a study entails. Therefore, parental consent should also be gained. Researchers should not try to bribe children to take part with treats. Children should also be encouraged to ask questions and given the right to withdraw if they seem distressed or are experiencing difficulties. The children's anonymity should be protected. As with adults, children should be protected from psychological and physical harm. The UN convention on the Rights of the Child (UNCRC) sets forth guidelines that countries should follow to ensure that children are protected, have their views listened to, are treated fairly, grow up healthy and can learn at school. Researchers conducting research need to make sure they respect these guidelines.

The benefits versus the costs of the research on children should also be considered. Costs can include anxiety about taking part, time taken and intrusion of privacy. Children can also benefit from taking part in research in terms of having their views listened to and increased confidence from participating in research. Carrying out research on children can also lead to improvements in how children are treated.

You need to be able to describe a practical you carried out in child psychology. Exemplar practical. A questionnaire investigating whether day care can provide positive experiences for young children

Aim-To see if parents' have more positive views about their children's experience of nursery versus preschool.

Non-directional hypothesis-There will be a difference in how positive parents feel about their children's experiences of nursery versus preschool.

Null hypothesis-There will no difference in how positive parents feel about their children's experiences of nursery versus preschool.

Sample-Opportunity sample of family and friends who were parents of three-year old children attending preschool or nursery. Five parents had children who were attending nursery and five parents had children who were attending preschool.

Ethics-The participants were briefed before the questionnaire was administered and fully informed consent was obtained. Participants were then emailed the link to the questionnaire on Survey Monkey. They were given the right to withdraw during and after the questionnaire. They were also debriefed at the end of the questionnaire. Participants were assured that their responses would be kept anonymous and confidential as they were answering questions about their children's experiences of day care.

Procedure-A structured questionnaire was designed with nine closed questions to find out about parents' beliefs about their children's experiences of day care. There were three questions on social development, three questions on emotional development and three questions on cognitive development. The questions were on a Likert scale so that quantitative data could be obtained. A total score of 45 was possible. The questionnaire was set up on Survey Monkey so that it could be emailed to parents. It included a clear briefing and debriefing of the purposes of the research. Five parents of three-year-old children attending preschool and five parents of three-year-old children attending nursery were used. Parents completed the questionnaire in private and results were collated on Survey Monkey.

Results-

Table to show parents' overall scores for preschool and nursery care

Preschool care (Total score/45)	Nursery care (Total/45)
41	42
42	39
36	34
45	41
38	32

A Mann-Whitney U test was used to analyse the data as it was testing for a difference, it was an independent groups design and ordinal data was collected.

Mann-Whitney U test formulae

$$U_a = n_a n_b + \frac{n_a(n_a+1)}{2} - \sum R_a$$

$$U_b = n_a n_b + \frac{n_b(n_b+1)}{2} - \sum R_b \qquad \text{(U is the smaller of } U_a \text{ and } U_b\text{)}$$

241

n_a is the number of participants rating in group A
n_b is the number of participants in group B
$\sum R_a$ is the sum of the ranks for group A's data
$\sum R_b$ is the sum of the ranks for group B's data

Step 1: Rank all the scores together.

Note: For a Mann-Whitney U test, the data from both groups are ranked together. If participants have the same score, they are given the same rank. This way of ranking is different to how data is ranked for the Spearman's rho test.

Preschool care (Total score/45)	Nursery care (Total/45)	A-Rank for preschool care	B-Rank for nursery care
41	42	6.5	8.5
42	39	8.5	5
36	34	3	2
45	41	10	6.5
38	32	4	1
	Sum total of ranks	32	23

Step 2: Calculate Ua by first adding up all the ranks for preschool care (A) to calculate $\sum R_a$:

$\sum R_a = 6.5 + 8.5 + 3 + 10 + 4 = 32$

Step 3: Multiply the number of participants in group A (n_a) by the number of participants in group B (n_b)

Note: $n_a n_b$ means n_a multiplied by n_b

$n_a \times n_b = 5 \times 5 = 25$

Step 4: Calculate $n_a (n_a+1)$

$n_a+1 = 5+1 = 6$
Multiply n_a+1 by n_a
As $n_a+1 = 6$ and $n_a = 5$
$n_a (n_a+1) = 6 \times 5 = 30$

Step 5: Calculate $n_a (n_a+1)/2$
Divide $n_a (n_a+1)$ by 2
$30/2 = 15$

Step 6: Calculate $U_a = n_a n_b + n_a (n_a+1)/2 - \sum R_a$

$n_a n_b = 25$

$n_a (n_a+1)/2=15$
$\sum R_a=32$

So $U_a=25+15-32=8$

Step 7: Calculate U_b by first adding up the ranks for nursery care-B to calculate $\sum R_b$:

$\sum R_b = 8.5 + 5 + 2 + 6.5 + 1 = 23$

Step 8: You already know that $n_a n_b = 36$ from step 3

$n_b(n_b+1)/2=15$ from step 5 as there are the same number of participants in group B as in group A.
You know from step 7 that $\sum R_b = 23$
So $U_b = n_a n_b + n_b (n_b+1)/2 - \sum R_b = 36 + 15 - 23 = 28$

Step 9: U is the smaller of U_a and U_b.
So as U_a is the smallest value, U_a is the value of U.
Therefore, U=8

Step 10: Look up the critical values in a critical values table for $n_a=5$ and $n_b=5$. This is the number of participants in each group.

To be significant, U must be equal to or less than the critical value. The critical value for a directional (two-tailed) test at 0.05 significance level is 2. As, U is more than the critical value of U for a 0.05 significance level, this means that there is no significant difference in the positive experiences of children in preschool care and nursery care.

Note: When you are looking up critical values in a table, you need to know: whether the hypothesis was one-tailed or two-tailed; the number of participants in each condition (shown as 'N' on the table) and the significance level. The values in the Mann-Whitney Test are termed 'U' and unlike the Spearman-rank and Chi-squared Tests the observed value must be equal to or less than the critical value for the results to be significant (i.e. to accept the experimental hypothesis and reject the null hypothesis).

Discussion-The results suggest there is no difference between the positive experiences of children attending preschool compared to those attending nursery. This may be because the government sets standards of care in both settings.

Evaluation:

Participants may have given socially desirable answers on the questionnaire. Parents may want to believe that their children are receiving positive experiences in day care and are unlikely to report negative experiences as it reflects on their own decision to place their children in day care. This affects the validity of the result. There can be problems with the Likert scale in collecting data on beliefs as participants can be inclined to give answers towards the middle of the scale rather than at the extremes, which could have affected overall scores. A small opportunity sample was used so the sample may be unrepresentative of the wider population.

A strength of the research is that participants answered the questions in private, so they would have been less influenced by researcher effects than if an interview had been carried out. As set questions were used, the study is easy to replicate, which makes it more reliable. Ethical guidelines were followed, and participants were fully informed of the purpose of the research. They were also given the right to withdraw and fully debriefed.

Suggestions for improvement-The questionnaire could have included open questions to allow participants to expand on their views. This would have improved the validity of the results. A larger, random sample could have been obtained to improve the generalisability of the findings. For example, a wide range of nurseries and preschools could be approached to take part in the study, and the children could be randomly chosen to take part using a computer. Parents could then be contacted to obtain their agreement.

You need to be able to describe ethical issues in child psychology

Psychologists need to be careful that they do not cause distress to children when carrying out research. Children are particularly vulnerable and may feel coerced into taking part. Researchers need to be sensitive to children's needs and look out for signs of distress even in babies. The strange situation has been criticised for causing distress but others argue that it is only stressful for a short period of time.

You need to know practical issues in the design and implementation of research

In child psychology, observations are used to watch and record children's behaviour in a variety of settings such as at home, at school or in a nursery. Structured laboratory observations involve careful controls and a set-up situation that can be repeated. The strange situation is an example of a structured observation as there are certain set stages in the observation and the behaviour of the child is recorded when their mother leaves them alone and when they are with a stranger. Inter-observer reliability can be established by having more than one observer code behaviour and making sure there is agreement in what has been observed.

Naturalistic observations involved observing children in their natural setting. For example, children might be observed playing with each other in a nursery or at home with their parents.

Interviewing children can pose problems. Children may be intimidated by the researchers or they may give different answers depending on whether a parent is present. This can affect the validity and reliability of the findings.

Longitudinal studies allow researchers to study child development over time. However, longitudinal studies can suffer from attrition and this discourages researchers from carrying out any studies that are longer than 4 or 5 years.

You need to be able to discuss reductionism in child psychology

Research on attachment types using the strange situation can be seen as reductionist as it doesn't take into account how temperament, cultural norms and experiences of day care can affect a child's behaviour.

Bowlby's evolutionary theory of attachment can be seen as reductionist as it reduces attachment behaviour down to a simple survival mechanism.

However, much of the research in child psychology takes into account the many different factors that affect children's behaviour such as family background, parenting style and day care.

You need to be able to compare different ways of explaining child behaviour and attachment

Bowlby's theory of attachment consists of a number of different concepts. He suggests that attachment is related to evolutionary needs and using the mother as a safe base in order to aid survival. Bowlby also draws on cognitive concepts in describing attachment. For example, he suggests that children develop an internal working model of their primary caregiver, which is a mental representation of what to expect from relationships. A further concept is monotropy and the importance of one single caregiver. However, Bowlby has been criticised for not taking into account other attachment figures. Schaffer and Emerson found that at one-year-old most infants have formed multiple attachments. These multiple attachments can be with the father, grandparents and siblings.

Behaviourists argue that a baby forms an attachment to its mother because she provides for its physical needs in the way of food. Attachments form due to classical conditioning and operant conditioning. Classical conditioning explains attachment as a learnt association. For example, a baby may become attached to its mother because it associates her with food. Operant conditioning explains attachment as a learnt behaviour too. For example, when a mother provides food for their baby, the baby feels satisfied and this is rewarding. However, the idea that attachments occur due to the association of the mother with food is flawed as other research suggests comfort is far more important for an attachment (Harlow and Zimmerman). On the other hand, infants may develop attachments through associating their caregiver with responsiveness rather than food or by seeing their caregiver's interactions as rewarding.

You need to be able to discuss whether child psychology is a science

Laboratory observations in child psychology such as the strange situation are scientific because they use standardised procedures, control extraneous variables and establish cause and effect relationships. The strange situation involved careful coding of behaviour and inter-rater reliability was established.

When interviews or case studies are used in child psychology, the data is more subjective and less scientific.

Bowlby's evolutionary theory of attachment is considered less scientific as it is hard to test. However, there are animal studies such as Lorenz's study on geese that suggest that attachment is instinctive.

You need to be able to discuss cultural issues in child psychology

Cultural bias can occur in child psychology if research from one culture suggests that their way of child-rearing is better than other cultures. For example, Miyake et al. (1985) used the strange situation, which was developed in the USA, to measure attachment type in Japanese babies. They found that Japanese infants had fewer secure attachments and a higher proportion of type C (resistant) attachments than American infants. Such research suggests that Japanese methods of child-rearing are worse than American methods. However, the Japanese babies' response to the strange situation may have been due to their mothers rarely leaving them with anyone else and encouraging dependency. This does not mean that their child-rearing style is worse or that it leads to poorer attachments.

You need to be able to discuss gender in child psychology

Most research in child psychology focuses on mother-child bond. The role of the father and other attachment figures has been ignored. The focus on the mother-child bond may put undue pressure mothers. For example, the maternal deprivation hypothesis suggests that separation from the mother in a child's first two years can lead to affectionless psychopathy and development retardation.

You need to be able to discuss the nature-nurture debate in child psychology

Whether attachment is instinctive (nature) or as a result of the way we are brought up (nurture) is an important debate in child psychology. Cross-cultural research can help us understand to what extent attachment is nature or nurture. Behaviour that is similar across cultures is likely to be due to biology. Behaviour that is different across cultures is likely to be due to environment. Cross-cultural research suggests that attachments between children and their caregivers form in all cultures. However, the quality of the attachment varies. This suggests that attachment type is dependent on nurture.

However, a problem with cross-cultural research is that researchers may interpret the findings of the studies in terms of their own cultural beliefs (ethnocentrism). For example, Miyake et al. (1985) found that Japanese infants have a higher proportion of type C (resistant) attachments but this may be due to Japanese mothers rarely leaving their children with anyone else. This means the Japanese babies were much more likely to show distress in the strange situation.

You need to be able to discuss how psychological understanding has developed over time in child psychology

Before Bowlby's work on attachment, the dominant belief was that love originated in a baby's biological needs being met by the mother. Behaviourists believed that babies become attached to their mothers because they associate them with food and find their mothers' responses to their social signals rewarding. Freud had a similar view and suggested that babies form an attachment because their oral pleasures are satisfied through feeding. These views led to rigid child-rearing practices such as regulated feeding schedules and emotionally distant parenting.

Bowlby's theory of attachment argued that babies get comfort from their mother and use them as a safe base. The emotional aspect of the mother-baby bond was emphasised. Bowlby also suggested that if the mother-baby bond was disrupted that this could have negative effects on the child's development and future relationships. His work has led to a better understanding of the importance of the bond between a child and their primary caregiver and his work still influences psychologists today. However, Bowlby over-emphasised the idea of a single caregiver as children benefit from having multiple attachments.

As more mothers are working and leaving their children, there has been an increased interest in the effects of day care. This had led to research that examines the effects of day care on children's social, emotional and cognitive development of the child.

Our understanding of autism has also developed over time. The current diagnostic statistical manual (DSM-V) no longer make a distinction between Asperger's syndrome and autism. Autism is now viewed as a spectrum disorder and is usually referred to as autism spectrum disorder (ASD). More recent research has found candidate genes linked to autism.

You need to be able to discuss how psychological knowledge has been used in child psychology

Research on the effects of deprivation has led to improvements in both day care and hospital care.

Research on the effects of day care suggest that the quality of day care is very important. Nurseries and pre-schools should assign a keyworker for each child, the environment should be stimulating and there should be high staff to child ratios so that children can receive more individual attention and care. Research also suggests that children should not spend too long in day care when they are very young.

In the past hospitals only allowed parents to see their children for a short-time during hospitalisation. Nowadays, due to research on the effects of deprivation, parents are encouraged to stay with children.

Research on autism has led to improvements in people's understanding of the disorder and better treatments.

You need to discuss issues related to socially sensitive research in child psychology

Research suggesting that poor parenting affects attachment type is socially sensitive as it blames parents for any insecure attachment formed. Bowlby's maternal deprivation hypothesis suggests that children who experience separation from their mother in the first two years of life are more likely to develop affectionless psychopathy. This theory could be used to blame mothers for anti-social behaviour in society.

Research into day care is socially sensitive especially if it highlights negative effects as it may lead to parents feeling guilty about going to work and leaving their children in day care.

You need to be able to discuss issues of social control in child psychology

Bowlby's emphasis on the mother-child bond, could lead to women feeling pressurised to stay at home and look after the children. This can be seen as a form of social control.

Applied behaviour analysis (ABA) has been criticised for trying to make children with autism fit into societal norms. Some adults who received ABA as children have said that they were traumatised by the treatment.

Exemplar exam questions:

Describe the characteristics of autism and give one explanation of the disorder. Explain how this explanation can help parents understand the disorder better.
(8 marks)

The characteristics of autism include lack of eye contact, repetitive behaviours, lack of empathy, poor social skills and delayed speech and language development.

One explanation of autism is lack of theory of mind. This means that autistic children cannot see things from another person's point of view or imagine what another person is thinking. This leads to problems with empathy and understanding other people's intentions. Baron-Cohen carried out the Sally-Anne task with autistic children and found that they could not understand that Sally would not think the same thing as them. They thought that Sally would think that the ball was hidden in the same place as they did. If parents understand that their autistic child can't understand things from the other people's viewpoints, then they may be more accepting of their autistic child's lack of empathy and social skills. It can also help them understand why their child can't engage in pretend play.

Level 2 answer: 4 out of 8 marks.

Commentary:

This student gives a list of the characteristics related to autism but has not described any in detail. For example, poor social skills could have been elaborated on. Autistic children can find it hard to make friends as they have difficulties with verbal and non-verbal communication. They can have difficulty expressing their emotions and understanding other people's emotions. They also have problems reading people's facial expressions. The explanations of autism: lack of theory of mind is done well. There is also a good attempt at explaining how the theory can aid parent's understanding of the disorder. A point that could have been made about lack of theory of mind is why autistic children have poor language development. Children with autism may lack the motivation to develop good communication skills because they don't understand that other people have different thoughts to them.

Kelly experienced separation from her mother when she was young and she has a distant relationship with her father. She found it difficult to form friendships at school and now she is finding it hard to have a meaningful romantic relationship as an adult. Evaluate Bowlby's theory of attachment with reference to the context. (16 marks)

Student answer:

Bowlby's internal working model says that we form a mental representation of our primary attachment figure and that this affects our expectations of other relationships. There is supporting evidence for the internal working model. For example, Hazan and Shaver (1987) placed a 'Love Quiz' in a newspaper. The 'quiz' questioned people about their current relationships, attitudes to love and their attachment history. They found that people with secure attachments reported happier and longer-lasting relationships than those with insecure attachments. The people with secure attachments also had positive internal working models. This study supports the view that early attachment affects later relationships. As Kelly was separated from her mother when she was young she may have a negative internal working model. This mental representation of what relationships are like may have affected her friendships at school and her expectations of romantic relationships.

Simpson et al. (2007) followed a group of 78 people from infancy into adulthood. They found that people who had been classed as securely attached at 12 months old were more socially competent as children, had closer friends at age 16 and more intimate romantic relationships in their 20s. This study supports the view that attachment type predicts later relationships.

Infants use their caregivers as a safe base from which to explore. Bowlby used ethology (the study of animals) as the basis for his theory of attachment. He noted that animals have evolved to stay close to their mothers when young to aid their survival and he extended this behaviour to humans. Harlow and Zimmerman (1959) took baby rhesus monkeys and raised them in a laboratory away from other monkeys. He gave the baby monkeys a wire monkey with a bottle to feed from and a cloth monkey to get comfort from and hold. The monkeys showed long-term emotional and social problems. This supports Bowlby's view that children get comfort from their primary caregiver and that this bond has long-term consequences for development. Kelly's separation from her mother when she was young could have affected her emotionally and socially.

Bowlby argued that children form one special bond with a primary caregiver. The idea that children attach to a single caregiver is called monotropy. Kelly may not have been able to form a special bond with her mother as she was separated from her when she was young. As she has a distant relationship from her father, it appears she did not form a bond with him either. Bowlby's concept of monotropy has been criticised because children can form multiple attachments, for example, with fathers, grandparents and siblings. Attachment is also more likely to form with a caregiver who is sensitive to the baby's signals rather than the person who spends the most time with them. This suggests that the focus should be on quality of interaction and not the monotropic bond.

Bowlby's maternal deprivation hypothesis suggests that separation form the mother in the first two years of life can lead to mental retardation and affectionless psychopathy. Bowlby's 44 juvenile thieves study found that children who had been separated from their mothers in the first two years of life were more likely to show affectionless psychopathy and were more likely to have committed an offence than a control group of children. This study supports the idea that separation from a primary caregiver in the first two years of life can have long-lasting effects on a child's development. Kelly may have affectionless psychopathy and be unable to empathise with others, which has affected her relationships.

Bowlby's emphasis on the mother-child bond as being essential for normal development has led to working mothers feeling guilty about going to work. Mothers may experience anxiety about going to work and leaving their children. This can be seen as a form of social control. Bowlby ignored the role of the father in attachment.

Bowlby suggested that there is a critical period for forming an attachment in children. Kelly may have missed the critical period for forming an attachment as she was separated from her mother when she was young. Lorenz's study on geese supports the idea of a critical period for attachment. The geese that hatched in front of Lorenz imprinted on him and followed him around. Lorenz found that there is a critical period of two days in which geese will imprint on a persistently moving object. Attachment in humans is slower than in animals but the characteristics are the same as that of imprinting.

Level 4 answer 16/16 marks

Commentary: This student demonstrates an accurate and thorough knowledge and understanding of the different concepts within Bowlby's theory and applies it to Kelly. They also clearly link their descriptive points to evaluative points.

Assess the usefulness of Bowlby's theory of attachment. (8 marks)

Bowlby's internal working model says that we form a mental representation of our primary attachment figure and that this affects our expectations of other relationships. Hazan and Shaver (1987) placed a 'Love Quiz' and found that people with secure attachments reported happier and longer-lasting relationships than those with insecure attachments. Understanding how negative internal working models can affect later relationships can be used in therapy to improve people's relationships.

Bowlby believed that children use their primary caregiver as a safe base. Harlow and Zimmerman (1959) took baby monkeys and raised them in a laboratory away from other monkeys. He gave the baby monkeys a wire monkey with a bottle to feed from and a cloth monkey to get comfort from and hold. All the monkeys formed strong attachments with the cloth monkey and mainly used the wire monkey for food. Bowlby's theory that children need their primary caregiver for comfort has led to a better understanding of why children become distressed when separated from them. It has useful real-world applications. For example, children who go into hospital should not be separated from their primary caregiver and arrangements should be made to allow their carers to stay close.

Bowlby argued that children form one special bond with a primary caregiver. The idea that children attach to a single caregiver is called monotropy. The idea that the primary caregiver is important to a child's development has led to increased maternity leave, which is a benefit to society. However, it has also led to working mothers feeling guilty about leaving their children. Bowlby over-emphasised the mother-child relationship as children can form multiple attachments with fathers, grandparents and siblings. The importance of a special relationship with a single caregiver has been applied in day care settings. Nurseries and preschools tend to have a single key worker who provides tailored care for a child.

Bowlby's theory has many useful applications. It has changed the way children are looked after in hospitals, nurseries, preschools and other institutions. It has also led to increases in maternity leave and emphasised the importance of the primary caregiver. On the other hand, Bowlby's theory has led to working mother's guilt and been less useful in enabling mothers to work. It has also been less useful at explaining the role of the father and multiple attachments.

Level 4 answer 8/8

Commentary:

Some students make the mistake of evaluating when the question asks them to assess. In this assess question there are 4 marks for demonstrating a knowledge and understanding of the Bowlby's theory and 4 marks for considering whether Bowlby's theory has been useful and making a balanced judgement. This student describes elements of Bowlby's theory in turn and discusses their usefulness. They also come to a balanced judgement at the end.

To what extent are interviews as a research method in child psychology reliable? (4)

Student answer:

Structured interviews in child psychology can be reliable as they use set questions. This means they can easily be replicated. However, they can be seen as unreliable due to the interviewer effect. For example, if the interviewer is intimidating then this might affect children's answers. If a child is interviewed with one of their parents present, this may affect the answers they give as well. Without their parents, a child may give different answers, so this affects the reliability of the results.

3/4 marks

Commentary:

This student has focused on the reliability of interviews rather than discussing validity. A common mistake is to talk about validity when the question is only asking about reliability. They have also applied their knowledge of interviews to children well. To achieve 4 marks, the student should have referred to unstructured and semi-structured interviews as well. Unstructured and semi-structured interviews are less reliable as questions are adapted based on the child's responses.

Chapter 8-Issues and debates

You need to be able to discuss issues and debates in relation to social psychology, cognitive psychology, biological psychology, learning theories, clinical psychology and your option application e.g. criminological psychology.

At the end of chapters 1-6, there is a section on issues and debates related to each topic area.

This section outlines some of the key debates and issues.

Key Debates

The Nature-Nurture Debate

The nature-nurture debate refers to the controversy over whether we are born to think, feel and behave in a certain way or whether we learn it from our environment. The nature side of the argument says that our behaviour is determined from birth. The biological approach is the main supporter of nature side of the debate. It focuses on how our genes, nervous system, brain structure and hormones affect our behaviour. It used research methods such as twin and adoption studies, DNA studies and brain scans to study the effects of genes and brain structure on behaviour. The biological approach promotes treatments such as drug therapy, electroconvulsive therapy and brain surgery because it believes that behaviour is changed only through physical means. Twin and adoption studies have been carried out to demonstrate a genetic basis for behaviour.

The nurture side of the debate suggests that we learn all our behaviour from our environment. The learning approach supports the nurture side of the debate as it says that we learn behaviour through classical conditioning, operant conditioning and social learning. The learning approach has used experiments to show how children can learn behaviours from their environment. For example, Watson and Rayner classically conditioned little Albert to be afraid of a white rat he was originally unafraid of. Bandura, Ross and Ross (1961) found that children would copy aggressive behaviour shown by an adult role model to a plastic bobo doll. Such studies support the idea that we learn behaviour from our environment.

However, behaviour is likely to be a mixture of both nature and nurture. For example, a child may be born with a genetic predisposition to have a high IQ but they will only develop a high IQ if they are exposed to a stimulating environment and have a good education.

The debate over whether psychology a science

There is a debate over whether psychology is a science. This may be because there are different approaches within psychology. Some approaches such as the learning approach and biological approach are more scientific and use well, controlled laboratory experiments to collect objective, quantitative data. They use theories to develop hypotheses, which are then tested to see whether they are supported or not by empirical evidence. These approaches aim to build a body of scientific knowledge from the data collected. In contrast, other approaches in psychology such as the psychodynamic approach are less scientific as they use cases studies and interviews, which are open to interpretation. Some approaches such as the cognitive and the social approach are scientific in some ways but not others. The cognitive approach uses controlled laboratory experiments to investigate memory and forgetting. However, the operationalisation of the variables in experiments may lead to problems with validity. For example, learning and recalling a list of words may not be a valid way of testing memory. The cognitive approach also has concepts that are less scientific such as schema, which are difficult to test. The social approach uses laboratory experiments to investigate obedience and prejudice, which are scientific. However, it also uses interviews and field studies to gather data, which can be subject to bias and are less scientific.

The debate over whether animals should be used in psychological research

It could be argued that animals should be used in research to ease human suffering and that we should have more sympathy for our own species than other species. Another argument is that animals do not have the same feelings or experience the same pain as humans. Therefore, we should use animals in preference to humans for research. There are also strict laws and codes of conduct that protect animals used in research which minimises animal suffering. Less invasive methods are used where possible to study animal behaviour.

A problem with using animals in research is that it is difficult to generalise the findings to humans as we are more complex. The human brain is different to animals, for example, we have consciousness and can imagine what others are thinking. Research shows that animals can suffer distress, pain and anxiety. Therefore, we should not use animals on moral grounds.

Key Issues

Cultural issues in psychological research

Ethnocentrism can occur if we interpret research findings or people's behaviour entirely through the lens of our own culture without taking into account cultural differences. This can lead to cultural bias. For example, researchers may not take into account the beliefs, customs or language of people from a different culture when conducting research and interpreting findings. The vast majority of psychological research has been carried out in the USA by white, middle class, males which can create bias in the interpretation of findings. If the findings of studies conducted in the USA are generalised to all cultures, this can be seen as ethnocentric. For example, views about the signs and symptoms of mental disorders in DSM may be ethnocentric. However, DSM-V tries to overcome cultural issues in diagnosis by describing how people from different cultures talk about mental health issues differently.

Cross-cultural research

Cross-cultural research refers to researchers repeating studies in different countries/cultures to see if a theory is universal and can explain human behavior across all cultures. Cross-cultural research on obedience has been carried out. For example, Milgram's study has been repeated in other countries with similar results. This suggests that people have similar obedience levels in other countries.

There has also been cross-cultural research on attachment types using the Strange Situation. Ainsworth's classification of different attachment types has been criticised for being culturally biased. However, research has found that type B (secure) attachments are the most common across all cultures. This suggests that the strange situation procedure is a useful tool for assessing attachment type across all cultures. Van Ijzendoorn and Kroonenberg (1988) compared the results of 32 cross-cultural studies and found that there were differences in the proportions of different attachment types in different cultures. However, type B (secure) attachments were the most common type of attachment in all the studies from different cultures, with the exception of one study from Germany. Interestingly, there were more differences in attachment types within a culture compared to between cultures.

How can cultural bias be reduced?

By taking into account a culture's customs and norms before interpreting the results of studies. For example, it is important to take Japanese culture into account before deciding that more children in Japan have insecure resistant attachments. Miyake et al. (1985) found that Japanese infants had a higher proportion of resistant attachments but this may be due to Japanese mothers rarely leaving their children with anyone else and encouraging dependency.

Issues related to the use of psychological knowledge as a means of social control

Psychology has been used to get people to conform to the rules and norms of society. This is called social control.

Psychological therapies can be used to control people so that they conform to society's norms. If therapies are being used to control people rather than help them then this raises ethical issues. Furthermore, if professionals delivering therapies have too much power then this is an ethical issue to. Sometimes people who are a danger to themselves or others due to mental health reasons are forcibly brought to a psychiatric institution under the Mental Health Act. Society needs to be careful that the rights of the individual are not infringed in these circumstances. However, it could be argued that we need social control so that people can live in society safely without fear of harm.

Ethical Issues in psychological research with humans

When psychologists carry out research they have two considerations in mind: the benefit to the society and psychological understanding and the costs in terms of possible harm to the participants. This is called an ethical dilemma.

Psychologists need to adhere to the following ethical guidelines when carrying out research:

Distress-Participants should be protected from psychological or physical harm. The risk of harm should be no greater than that found in everyday life.

Informed Consent-Participants should be provided with enough information about the aim of the study and the procedure so that they can make an informed choice about whether to take part or not.

Deception-Participants should not be deceived about the aim of the study or the procedure. If deception is unavoidable, then permission should be sought from the British Psychological Society.

Debriefing-Participants should be fully informed of the purpose and expected outcomes of the study after they have taken part.

Right to withdraw-Participants should be told that they are free to leave the study at any time and they have the right to remove their results at the end, regardless of any payment they have received.

Confidentiality-Participants' should be guaranteed anonymity and their data should be stored securely.

Ethical Issues in animal experiments

Animals are only used in experiments when there is a clear benefit to the research. Bateson's cube can be used to determine whether the research should go ahead. Bateson's cube has 3 edges labelled; quality of research, animal suffering and certainty of medical benefit. These are on a scale high to low. When a research proposal falls into the opaque region, experiment should not be conducted i.e. when quality of research is low, animal suffering is high and certainty of benefit is low.

The following ethical guidelines need to be followed when carrying out research on animals:

Caging and Stress-Experimenters should avoid or minimise stress and suffering for all living animals. The cages the animals are kept in during the experiment should be large enough for the animals to be comfortable.

Number or animals used-Researchers should use as few animals as possible.

Wild Animals-Endangered species should not be used, unless the research has direct benefits for that species e.g. conservation.

Qualified Experimenters-The researchers conducting the experiment should have the necessary qualifications. They should also have a licence from the Home office for that particular experiment.

Look for alternatives-Alternatives to using animals must always be sought, such as using humans or computers.

Exemplar Exam Question: Discuss issues of social control in relation to treatments and therapies (12 marks)

Student Answer:

Psychological therapies can be used to control people so that they conform to society's norms or for other reasons. When therapies are used to control people rather than to help the individual then this raises ethical issues.
It can be argued that society needs social control so that members of society can work and live together in harmony, without aggression and safely. Society benefits by controlling those with mental health problems and those who commit crimes but but it could be said they benefit too if their lives improve.
Drug therapy is a form of social control and is given to people with mental health problems. For example, schizophrenics are given anti-psychotic drugs to control their symptoms. However, some schizophrenics and their families suggest that the drugs only sedate them rather than help them. There are also many side-effects to taking anti-psychotic drugs. It might be claimed that drugs are a medical 'straitjacket' and are used to control people in a way that seems unethical. Another problem with drug therapy is that it does deal with the underlying causes of mental disorder it just suppresses the symptoms. It could be argued that schizophrenics are given drugs so they live and behave by society's rules and expectations rather than to treat their illness. Another example social control is when drugs such as Ritalin are used to treat children with ADHD. Some argue that as increasing numbers of younger and younger children are being diagnosed with ADHD, it is not a problem with the children but with society. It has been said that Ritalin just slows children down so that parents and teachers can cope with behaviour that might actually be quite normal in young children. Perhaps behaviour management techniques should be taught to parents and teachers so that they can control their children rather than giving the children drugs.

Token economy programmes are used in mental health institutions, schools and prisons to control behaviour and these are a form of social control. In mental health institutions, patients are rewarded for more adaptive behaviour. For example, anorexic patients are given tokens if they eat well or gain a certain amount of weight each week and these tokens can be exchanged for leisure time or outings. However, if a TEP is the only therapy used it only serves to control their behaviour rather than change it. TEPs may only change behaviour in the short term and learnt behaviour does not transfer easily to the outside world especially if the underlying causes of the disorder have not been dealt with. Token economy programmes are also used with prisoners and they are rewarded with tokens for desired behaviour such as compliance and non-aggressive behaviour. The prisoners can then spend the tokens they receive in the way they want to as a sort of shop system is operated in prisons. A problem with using TEPs with prisoners is that it is not effective at reducing recidivism once the criminal has left the prison.

10/12 marks

Commentary:

This answer explains issues with social control in relation to drug therapy and token economy programmes well. However, they could have referred to other treatments such as the use of anger management with offenders and cognitive behavioural therapy with mental health patients.

Chapter 9-Research Methods

You need to be able to describe and evaluate different types of research method used in psychology

Laboratory Experiments

Description:
Laboratory experiments involve manipulating an independent variable and measuring a dependent variable. Extraneous variables are controlled so that a cause and effect relationship can be established.

Evaluation:

Laboratory experiments have standardised procedures, which are easy to replicate so that reliability can be tested. Data from laboratory experiments is quantitative and objective. Therefore, such data is considered scientific. However, laboratory experiments lack ecological validity because they take place in artificial environments and often involve artificial tasks.

Field experiments

Description:

Field experiments are carried out in participants' natural environment. An independent variable is manipulated and a dependent variable is measured. Field experiments often involve a clear procedure and researchers try to control extraneous variables as much as possible so that the study can be tested for reliability.

Evaluation:

Field experiments have greater ecological validity than laboratory experiments as they take place in participants' natural environment. They also have carefully controlled and planned procedures so the study can be repeated. This means that they can be as reliable as laboratory experiments. However, as field experiments take place in the participants' natural environment, not all the extraneous variables can be controlled and the findings might not be reliable despite the researchers' efforts. Field experiments may lack validity as the independent and dependent variables are carefully operationalised.

Natural Experiments

Description:

Natural experiments are carried out in real-life settings. The independent variable occurs naturally but a dependent variable is still measured. It is difficult to establish cause and effect due to lack of control over the independent variable.

Evaluation:

Natural experiments are not reliable as the extraneous variables cannot be controlled due to the natural environment. However, natural experiments have good ecological validity as the participants are in a real-life setting.

Questionnaires

Description

Questionnaires involve written questions to find out about people's views and opinions. They are able to collect data from lots of people as everyone is asked the same questions and can answer them in their own time. Questionnaires can be sent by post, filled in on the internet, given face-to-face or left in a public place for people to pick up. The questions can either be closed or open. Closed questions may involve a Likert type scale or yes/no questions. Open questions ask people explain what they think about a certain topic in their own words. If closed questions are used then quantitative data can be obtained. If open questions are used then qualitative data can be obtained.

Evaluation:

Questionnaires allow data to be gathered from large samples without too much cost. If closed questions are used, the quantitative data can be statistically analysed. It is also easy to compare the data from closed questionnaires as everyone answers the same questions. Questionnaires with closed questions can be easy to replicate. Questionnaires with open questions can collect rich, qualitative data. However, a problem with questionnaires is that people may give socially desirable answers because they want the researchers to think well of them. Participants may also misunderstand the questions and interpret the questions differently. Questions asked beforehand could affect later answers. Questionnaires with closed questions can limit participants' responses, which affects validity. Questionnaires with open questions are subject to interpretation.

Observations

Description:

There are structured laboratory observations and naturalistic observations. Structured laboratory observations involve careful controls and a set-up situation that can be repeated. There is often more than one observer and observations tend to be carried out through a one-way mirror to avoid the researchers' presence affecting participants' behaviour. Naturalistic observations involve observing participants in their natural environment. For example, observing children's behaviour in a playground.

Observations can be overt or covert. Covert observations involve observing a person or group of people without their knowledge. Overt observations involve observing a person or group of people with their knowledge.

Observations can also be participant or non-participant. A participant observation involves the researcher interacting with the person or group of people that they are observing. A non-participant observation involves the researcher observing behaviour from a distance without having any influence or getting involved.

An observation can be carried out by counting the frequency of certain behaviours during a fixed period of time.
Event sampling-when you record every time an event such as a kick occurs
Time sampling-when you record what is happening every set amount of time e.g. every 5 minutes.
Point sampling- The behaviour of just one individual in the group at a time is recorded.
Inter-observer reliability-Comparing the ratings of a number of observers as an individual observer may be biased. This would increase the reliability of the data collected if all the observers agree.

Evaluation:

Researchers may find it difficult to record all the behaviours shown, although event sampling, time sampling and point sampling can help. Video recordings can be used to record participants' behaviour and played back later so that all actions can be noted. It may also be difficult to analyse or interpret all the data collected. Observers often have to be specially trained so that they can record behaviours quickly and to avoid bias.

Participant observations allow researchers to experience the same environment as their participants. However, the researcher's involvement can affect the behaviour of participants. In contrast, non-participant observations allow researchers to observe participants' behaviour more objectively as they are not directly involved in the action. However, if participants are aware they are being observed, they may still change their behaviour.

Covert observations enable researchers to observe participants behave naturally as the participants do not know they are being observed. However, there are ethical issues with observing participants without their consent. They do not have the right to withdraw, they have not given informed consent and there also issues of confidentiality especially if their behaviour has been video-recorded. The British Psychological Society advises that it is only suitable to conduct a covert observation in a place where people might reasonably be expected to be observed by other people such as a shopping centre or other public place. Overt observations do not have as many ethical issues as covert observations. However, when participants know they are being observed they may change their behaviour so that it appears socially desirable. Therefore, overt observations can be less valid.

Interviews

Description:

An interview involves the researcher asking the respondent questions. It may form the basis of a case study or as a follow-up to other research methods. Structured interviews produce quantitative data. All participants are asked the same questions in the same order. They are very similar to questionnaires except questions are read out. An unstructured interview involves an informal or in-depth conversation. Little is planned in advance (perhaps the first couple of questions) and this allows the interviewee to explain answers and introduce new issues. Unstructured interviews obtain rich, qualitative data. A semi-structured interview involves some prepared questions but also some opportunities for interviewees to expand on their answers.

Evaluation:

Unstructured interviews tend to be valid because they allow the interviewer to explore issues that the interviewee wishes to discuss. However, interpretation of participants' responses can be subjective and participants may give socially desirable answers. Certain characteristics about the interviewer such as their dress or manner can also affect replies. Structured interviews are more replicable, and therefore, more reliable.

Content analysis

Description:

A content analysis involves changing qualitative data into quantitative data. This often means tallying how many times certain themes occur within a source such as a newspaper article, magazine article, journal article, radio programme or television programme. The source may be coded or broken down into manageable categories, for example, by words, phrases, sentences or themes. The researcher then analyses the presence and meaning of these categories and draws conclusions.

Evaluation:

As the data comes from secondary sources such as newspaper articles or television programmes, it does not change. Therefore, other researchers can check whether any conclusions are correct or not. The quantitative tallying of themes allows the data to be statistically analysed. There are unlikely to be any ethical issues with a content analysis, as it only involves analysing existing sources. However, the categorising and tallying of themes in a content analysis can be subjective.

Case Studies

Description:

A case study is an in-depth study of one person or one group of people. A number of different techniques are used to gather data. For example, the researcher may observe, interview and carry out a number of experiments on the same person. Triangulation is used to pool data together from the different types of research method and to draw conclusions.

Evaluation:

Case studies are not generalisable as they are carried out on only one person or one group of people who are often unique and not representative of the wider population. It is also difficult to replicate case studies because they involve unique individuals and the interpretation of the observations and interviews is subject to bias. Therefore it is hard to establish reliability in case studies. However, triangulation is used to draw conclusions about the same concept so this improves the reliability of the findings. An advantage of case studies is that they gather rich, detailed information about the individuals using a number of different techniques, so this increases their validity. There can be ethical issues with case studies. Often they involve studying unique individuals who are more vulnerable than normal. Therefore, researchers have to be careful to protect them from psychological distress.

Correlational Techniques

Description:

Correlational studies look for a relationship between two variables. For example, it may look for a relationship between number of hours of violent TV watched and levels of aggression. An example of a positive correlation is: the more hours of violent TV watched, the more aggressive people become. An example of a negative correlation is: the more hours of violent computer games played, the less helpful people are.
Adoption and twin studies are types of correlational study. For example, a twin study might see how strong the relationship is between one twin's IQ and the other twin's IQ.

Evaluation:

Correlational studies can demonstrate a relationship between two variables, which was not noticed before. They can also be used to look for relationships between variables that cannot be investigated by other means. For example, researchers can look to see whether there is a relationship between parents having low expectations of their children and the children's later academic performance. Manipulating such variables would be unethical. However, correlational studies cannot establish cause and effect relationships. A third factor may affect both variables under investigation. For example, although a correlational study might show a relationship between the number of hours of violent TV watched and levels of aggression, we cannot be certain that the violent TV programmes led to the aggression. It may be that children who watch violent TV programmes are naturally more aggressive and so seek such programmes out.

Thematic Analysis

Description:

A thematic analysis can be used to analyse different types of data, from media articles to transcripts of focus groups or interviews. It is suitable for analysing people's experiences, opinions and perceptions. It can also be used to look at how different issues and concepts are constructed or represented. There are a number of stages in carrying out a thematic analysis: 1) The researcher familiarises themselves with the data by reading it several times; 2) Codes are generated for important features of the data; 3) The researcher looks for themes by examining the codes and collated data to identify broader patterns of meaning (potential themes); 4) The themes are reviewed by checking them against what people have said. At this stage, themes may be refined or discarded; 5) Themes are named and a detailed analysis of each theme is carried out; 6) Finally, the themes are written up with quotes from the data collected. The analysis is linked to existing theories.

Evaluation:

A thematic analysis can be used for a wide range of research questions. Rich, detailed data can be obtained, which can lead to a deeper insight into people's experiences, opinions and representations. However, thematic analyses are open to interpretation and hence subjective. They can be hard to replicate and so they have problems with reliability.

Longitudinal Studies

Description:

Longitudinal studies involve studying the same person or group of people over a long period of time. For example, researchers might look at the impact of childcare on children's cognitive, social and emotional development over a 10 year period.

Evaluation:

An advantage of longitudinal studies is that they allow researchers to follow the development and progress of an individual or group of individuals over time. There are also less likely to be participant variables as the same people are used and their progress can be tracked. However, longitudinal studies can be expensive. Furthermore, erosion of the sample (participants dropping out of the study) may cause bias.

Cross-sectional Studies

Description:

Cross-sectional studies involve gathering data at one moment in time from different groups of people so that one group is compared with another group on the same characteristics, behaviour or task i.e. a cross-sectional study might compare anorexic patients of different ages at the same time.

Evaluation:

Cross-sectional designs tend to be cheaper, quicker and more practical than longitudinal designs as participants are tested at one moment in time. However, as different participants are used in the conditions, participant variables can affect results.

Meta-analyses

Description:

Meta-analyses look at the findings of a number of different studies and draw conclusions. For example, a meta-analysis might investigate whether the media influences aggressive behaviour by analysing the results of 50 studies.

Evaluation:

Meta-analyses can be carried out quickly at little cost. They are useful when there is a lot of research on a specific topic such as the effect of the media on aggressive behaviour and conclusions need to be drawn. However, not all studies are equally reliable and valid and some studies may be included in a meta-analysis that distort results.

You need to be able to define quantitative and qualitative and give general strengths and weaknesses of both (including issues of reliability and validity.

Quantitative data is numerical data. Quantitative research e.g. laboratory experiments tend to use large samples of people or animals so that results can be generalised to the wider population. Statistical tests can be done on quantitative data to see how far the results are likely to be due to chance. If a quantitative research is repeated, often the same data will be found. This shows that quantitative data is reliable. However, the careful operationalising of variables in quantitative research means that real life events and interactions are not being measured (lack of validity).

Qualitative data is descriptive and often takes into account people's views and opinions. It can be gathered in natural situations so it is valid. However, qualitative data is harder to replicate and can lack reliability.

You need to know which research methods produce quantitative data and to be able to describe them.

Experiments, questionnaires with closed questions and structured interviews are good sources of quantitative data.
Questionnaires with closed questions consist of a list of pre-set questions that a participant answers usually involving yes/no or applying a scale.

Experiments are controlled studies often carries out in controlled conditions. An IV is manipulated and then a DV measured as a result. Objectivity is aimed for, hence the controls.

Structured interviews have set questions and there is an interviewer who asks questions.

You need to know which research methods produce qualitative data.

Case studies, unstructured interviews, clinical interviews and questionnaires with open questions produce qualitative data.

Case studies aim for an in-depth study of one individual or group. They gather information from many sources using more than one means of gathering data.

Unstructured interviews may begin with an aim and an idea of what questions are to be answered. They do not have set questions. The interviewer can explore areas that come up.

Clinical interviews involve an analyst listening to a client and using techniques such as free association and dream analysis. The aim is to uncover unconscious thoughts.

Questionnaires with open questions have preset questions but participants are able to express their views and opinions freely. There is no scale.

You need to be able to compare research methods.

If you are asked to compare research methods, you should consider the following:

Does the research method collect quantitative or qualitative data? If the research method collects quantitative data then it can be statistically analysed and is more objective. If the research method collects qualitative data it is usually more detailed and richer. However, the data is likely to be subjective.

Does the research method use primary or secondary data?

Does the research method give reliable data? Are studies using this research method easy to repeat?

Does the research method give valid data? Do studies using this research method collect rich, detailed in-depth data? Are studies using this research method carried out in participants' natural environment?

Does the research method require more than one researcher to carry out the study? For example, observations require more than one observer to establish inter-observer reliability.

How do the research methods gather data? Is any counting involved? Is any description involved?

Exam tip: When comparing, do not just describe each research method in turn. Instead, describe how the research methods are similar or different.

Exemplar exam question: A researcher wants to investigate how students feel about the way universities recruit applicants. The researcher decided to conduct a survey.

a) Explain how the researcher might design and carry out the survey. (6 marks)
Student answer:

The researcher could carry out a structured questionnaire with closed questions and a Likert scale to find out about students' opinions on the application procedure for university. Once the researcher has come up with their questions, they could test their questions on a few participants to see whether they make sense in a pilot study. They can then use any feedback from participants to adjust their questions. The questionnaire could then be set up on a website such as Survey Monkey so that participants can complete it in online in their own time. The researcher could then approach schools and ask them whether they would pass on the website address for their online questionnaire to students applying for university. The schools could be told that they will be given a copy of the research findings, which they may find useful. However, participants would need to know that their anonymity would be protected; otherwise they may be worried about being honest. Once a certain time period has elapsed such as 2 months the questionnaire could be closed.

Commentary:

This student has applied their understanding of questionnaires to the scenario well. However, they could have discussed how they decided on which questions to ask. It would have been necessary to conduct some preliminary research to decide what concerns students have about the university application process. There should also have been some discussion about sample size; a few hundred responses are required for the sample to be representative. Another point that could have been covered is how the data would be analysed. Quantitative data from a structured questionnaire using a Likert scale can be analysed statistically.

b) The researcher recruits her sample by sending leaflets round to school sixth forms asking students to take part. Explain the strengths and weaknesses of recruiting a sample in this way. (4 marks)

Student answer:

The sample was a volunteer sample. Participants who have volunteered for a study are less likely to drop out as they have agreed to take part in the study. However, they are also unlikely to be representative of the wider population as only certain people will volunteer to take part. Volunteers are often more helpful than the wider population and this can lead to demand characteristics.

Commentary:

This student could have expanded their point about why volunteers are unrepresentative of the wider population. Volunteers often have more time, are more willing to please and are more helpful than the wider population. An advantage of volunteer samples is that it can be quick and cheap to recruit volunteers as the researchers do not have to be careful about how they select participants unlike a quota sample.